China and Russia

China and Russia

The New Rapprochement

Alexander Lukin

polity

Copyright © Alexander Lukin 2018

The right of Alexander Lukin to be identified as Author of this Work has been asserted in accordance with the UK Copyright, Designs and Patents Act 1988.

First published in 2018 by Polity Press

Polity Press
65 Bridge Street
Cambridge CB2 1UR, UK

Polity Press
101 Station Landing
Suite 300
Medford, MA 02155, USA

All rights reserved. Except for the quotation of short passages for the purpose of criticism and review, no part of this publication may be reproduced, stored in a retrieval system or transmitted, in any form or by any means, electronic, mechanical, photocopying, recording or otherwise, without the prior permission of the publisher.

ISBN-13: 978-1-5095-2170-8
ISBN-13: 978-1-5095-2171-5(pb)

A catalogue record for this book is available from the British Library.

Typeset in 10.5/12 Sabon by Servis Filmsetting Limited, Stockport, Cheshire
Printed and bound in Great Britain by CPI Group(UK) Ltd, Croydon

The publisher has used its best endeavours to ensure that the URLs for external websites referred to in this book are correct and active at the time of going to press. However, the publisher has no responsibility for the websites and can make no guarantee that a site will remain live or that the content is or will remain appropriate.

Every effort has been made to trace all copyright holders, but if any have been inadvertently overlooked the publisher will be pleased to include any necessary credits in any subsequent reprint or edition.

For further information on Polity, visit our website: politybooks.com

CONTENTS

About the Author vi
Preface viii
Acknowledgments xvii

1 Russia, China, and the Changing International System 1
2 Russia in the Eyes of China 34
3 Russia's Pivot to Asia or Just China? Russian Views of Relations with China 67
4 From Normalization to Strategic Partnership 96
5 The Strategic Partnership Matures: Multidimensional Cooperation 128

  Conclusion: Beyond Strategic Partnership? Managing Relations in an Insecure World 172

Notes 194
Index 217

ABOUT THE AUTHOR

Alexander Lukin is a Russian political scientist and international relations expert. He currently works as the Head of Department of International Relations at National Research University Higher School of Economics in Moscow. He received his first degree from Moscow State Institute of International Relations in 1984, a DPhil in Politics from Oxford University in 1997, a doctorate in history from the Diplomatic Academy in Moscow in 2007, and a degree in theology from St. Tikhon's Orthodox University in 2013. He has worked at the Soviet Foreign Ministry, Soviet Embassy to the People's Republic of China, and the Institute of Oriental Studies of the Soviet Academy of Sciences. From 1990 to 1993, he served as an elected deputy of the Moscow City Soviet (Council), where he chaired the Subcommittee for Interregional Relations. His books include *The Political Culture of the Russian Democrats* (2000), *The Bear Watches the Dragon: Russia's Perceptions of China and the Evolution of Russian-Chinese Relations since the Eighteenth Century* (2003), and *Pivot to Asia: Russia's Foreign Policy Enters the 21st Century* (2016), and he has published numerous articles and policy papers on Russian and Chinese politics. He edited and contributed to the major Russian work on Russian-Chinese relations, *Russia and China: Four Hundred Years of Interaction* (Moscow, 2013), and is an Honorary Researcher of Heilongjiang Provincial Academy of Social Sciences. He was a visiting fellow at the Belfer Center for Science and International Affairs at Harvard University from 1997 to 1998. From 2000 to 2001, he worked as a research fellow at the Center for Northeast Asia Policy Studies at the Brookings Institution. Alexander Lukin has also worked as the Director of the Center for East Asian and Shanghai Cooperation Organization Studies at Moscow State

ABOUT THE AUTHOR

Institute of International Relations, as Chair Professor at Zhejiang University in Hangzhou, China, and as Distinguished Professor at Northwest University, Xian, China. He serves on the editorial boards of *Asian Politics and Policy*, *International Problems* (Belgrade), and *The ASAN Forum* (Seoul). In 2009 he was awarded a medal for Outstanding Contribution to the Development of Sino-Russian Relations, by China's leader Hu Jintao, and in 2012 a medal on the occasion of the tenth anniversary of the Shanghai Cooperation Organization for his contribution to its formation and development.

PREFACE

This book is an attempt to acquaint the English-speaking audience with the realities of relations between Russia and China as Russian and Chinese observers understand them. It argues that the current Russian-Chinese rapprochement is the natural outcome of developments in international relations in the late twentieth and early twenty-first centuries. Following the collapse of the Soviet Union, the major non-Western states began working together to create a counterweight to the preponderant influence of the West and its desire to build a unipolar world. The Russian-Chinese rapprochement stems from the fact that the leadership and elite of both countries share similar views on the geopolitical situation in the world, the main trends and dangers that exist, and the favorable prospects for those relations to develop and find expression in the emergence of a multipolar world.

There is no lack of English-language literature on Russian-Chinese relations after the collapse of the Soviet Union. An interested reader can find a lot of valuable material for various periods in their development in several informative academic works, such as the studies by Elizabeth Wishnick, Jeanne Wilson, Natasha Kuhrt, Gilbert Rozman, and Marcin Kaczmarski, among others. However, there are some general traits that differentiate these works from Russian or Chinese studies.[1]

Several approaches to Russian-Chinese rapprochement can be found in the English-language literature on the subject. Most obviously, there is a lot more skepticism about various aspects of Russian-Chinese strategic partnership. Some observers claim that this rapprochement is fragile, even ephemeral. They point to various problems that arise between the two countries and suggest that, while outwardly in agreement, Moscow and Beijing actually pursue different interests and distrust each other.

Bobo Lo's idea of an "axis of convenience" is the most striking here. It suggests that "Their partnership is an axis of convenience, driven by a pragmatic appreciation of the benefits of cooperation rather than a deeper like-mindedness," while "strategic trust remains elusive." At the same time, Bobo Lo states:

> Moscow worries about China's growing assertiveness in East Asia, the displacement of Russian influence from Central Asia, and the emergence of a China-centered or G-2 world in which Russia would play a subordinate role. It is also anxious about the growing asymmetry of the bilateral relationship, and the extent to which Russia now depends on China, both within Asia and in the international system more generally.

In addition, "Moscow and Beijing diverge fundamentally over how an eventual 'new world order' might look. Whereas Putin envisages a tripolar order based on the interaction between the United States, China, and Russia, the Chinese see the Americans as their only true global counterpart."[2] According to a more recent study by John Watts, Sofia Ledberg, and Kjell Engelbrekt, the Russian-Chinese "still frayed defence and security relationship ... remains a relationship based on convenience and only partially converging interests in the critical areas of military technology and defence posture, ultimately reflecting a long-standing strategic rivalry that will not be easily overcome."[3]

Lo mitigates his approach somewhat in later work, probably bowing to the obvious fact that Russia and China have stepped up their cooperation. He writes, "the two sides agree on much, not least the undesirability of a 'hegemonistic' United States," and mentions that bilateral relations have deepened considerably. In describing the history of those relations, he offers a detailed description of "how Beijing and Moscow have moved their relationship from one of cold confrontation in the 1980s to today's 'comprehensive strategic partnership of coordination.'" He concludes, however, that the condition of those relations "remains essentially what it has been for much of the past two decades," calling them a "partnership of convenience" and essentially asymmetric.[4] On the whole, this creates an impression of internal inconsistency, of someone who is reluctant to abandon his hypothesis in the face of a growing body of contradictory evidence.

Some "asymmetry" supporters acknowledge the reality of rapprochement and the fact that the leaders of both countries sincerely desire it. However, they argue that the growing economic imbalance in those relations is a sign of Russia's dependence on China.[5] Marcin Kaczmarski provides a typical example of this approach with his book *Russia–China Relations in the Post-Crisis International Order* (2015), in which he refers to the fall of Russia and the rise of China as the main features of their bilateral relations.

Finally, supporters of a third approach argue that the rapprochement is based on an understanding of common interests, common identity, shared views on the international situation, and similar foreign policy thinking.

This study offers a different approach than the one taken by the "skeptics," whose arguments are (often) out of sync with Chinese and Russian sources. In fact, according to the official Russian position, "International relations are in the process of transition, the essence of which is the creation of a polycentric system of international relations." This is how the Foreign Policy Concept adopted in 2013 describes it.[6] President Putin has never spoken in favor of a tripolar world nor expressed any expectation that one would emerge. China also envisages a multipolar world in the future. As Chinese leader Xi Jinping said when he addressed the United Nations General Assembly on September 28, 2015, "The movement toward a multi-polar world, and the rise of emerging markets and developing countries have become an irresistible trend of history."[7] That general position is enshrined in numerous bilateral documents, including the Russian-Chinese Joint Declaration on a Multipolar World adopted in 1997. Bobo Lo offers no evidence to back up his claim that Putin "envisages a tripolar order."

The supporters of asymmetry generally draw better-grounded conclusions, but even many of those are doubtful. First, in speaking of China's overwhelming might, they refer primarily to the Chinese economy, which has indeed significantly surpassed the Russian economy. However, Russia continues to outstrip China in terms of military might and global political influence (not least because Beijing is in no hurry to translate its economic might into costly foreign policy and military actions). Thus, it is premature to speak of China's overall superiority or of any broad asymmetry.

It is difficult to predict how the future will unfold for either country. History provides examples of rapidly developing countries – such as Japan – that were predicted to become the world's leading economy,[8] but instead fell into periods of prolonged stagnation. There are also cases of countries, such as China, that found the strength to break out of economic stagnation to achieve long-term growth. Of course, the simplest approach is extrapolate from current trends, but such predictions are often flawed.

However, even in the event that the current tendency persists and the overall power of China significantly surpasses that of Russia, it will not necessarily mean that Russia should be worried. All China threat theories are based on a West-centric assumption that China (just like Russia) is politically so different from peace-loving democratic Western countries that it strives for domination and aggression by its very nature. Meanwhile, one rarely hears that the much weaker Canada should be wary of the United States, or Belgium of France. The reason is that these countries share basic values and a worldview; they see each other as valuable partners and do not need to fear each other. It is true that in these pairs the strongest state is generally more influential, but that does not mean that the other should be wary of it. This book attempts to show that Russia and China are consistently moving toward a similar closeness (although their common vision differs significantly from that of the US and its allies). And if and when this goal is reached, the last mutual fears will be allayed.

The downside of the English-language material on Russian-Chinese relations stems from several problems common to many authors. First, many works do not draw on enough Russian and Chinese sources, particularly those available only in their native languages – and a number of works cite no such sources whatsoever.[9] Other works, while citing a variety of English-language sources, tend to include either exclusively Russian-language or exclusively Chinese-language sources – most often the former.[10] In some cases, that creates an impression of one-sidedness and makes it difficult to understand the motives of the other side. For example, the failure to draw on Chinese analytical literature referring to the importance of relations with Russia might have led Kaczmarski to see asymmetry in their relations and to conclude that a supposedly weakened Russia was more interested in those ties than an increasingly powerful China. In addition, the lack of awareness demonstrated by the English-language literature of the motivations of the two sides at times reduces it to a source of only secondary importance for Russian and Chinese researchers, who have often long since discussed and resolved the very issues in question.

Second, such explanations often miss the mark due to the widespread desire of international relations specialists to pigeonhole Russian-Chinese rapprochement and bilateral relations as a whole according to a particular international relations theory.[11]

Third, when writing about Russian and Chinese motives and actions, such authors often fail to discriminate between the official and dominant views that both reflect and determine countries' foreign policies, and the unofficial and even marginal opinions that have little influence on official policy. Thus, some authors often seek to validate their views by citing individual Chinese experts whose opinions they claim represent the official position of the country and its leaders.[12] After all, when they write "China" or "the Chinese," the reader naturally understands that to mean the official, or at least widely accepted position of the country. For example, in support of the suggestion that the Chinese are seeking bipolarity, Lo cites the opinion of Tsinghua University scholar Yan Xuetong, an expert whose views in no way reflect the official Chinese position. To the contrary, Yan Xuetong is known for advocating a Chinese-Russian alliance – the necessity for which both Russian and Chinese officials consistently reject.

In fact, some Russian researchers do express concern about Beijing's growing might and the possibility of Russia becoming dependent on China. However, they generally represent radical pro-Western or extremely nationalistic groups – neither of which reflects the general opinion of the expert community, much less the official Russian position enshrined in numerous documents. As for Lo's contention that China views Russia as a country in decline which cannot, therefore, serve as an equal partner, some individual Chinese experts do indeed hold this opinion and we will examine it later in this book. At the same time, some Chinese experts advocate the opposite position – arguing, for example, that China should establish a formal anti-Western alliance with Russia. However, neither reflects the official position, which is that China advocates forming an equal partnership with Russia.

Fourth, many authors – and particularly those in the press – clearly let political objectives color their interpretation of the results of analyses. In this area, it is often difficult to distinguish between strictly scientific research aimed at objective analysis, and "policy papers" written to pressure politicians into taking particular actions. This sometimes leads to a very serious bias.

Those who argue that Russia should orient itself toward the West, including commentators in the West, claim that Russian-Chinese rapprochement could turn Russia into a "satellite" or "raw materials appendage" of a more powerful and aggressive China.[13] However, when Moscow had a similar relationship to the far more aggressive West, they said that Russia was "entering the world economy" and joining the "civilized world." At the same time, when the West and China take almost identical actions in Russia, Western analysts interpret them differently. For example, when Western investors purchase large portions of state-controlled Russian mining companies and deposits, those analysts refer to it as profitable investments and successful privatization, but when Chinese corporations do the same thing, they portray it as an attempt to gain possession of strategic Russian reserves and as economic expansionism.

By contrast, those who advocate confrontation with the West write that Russia must inevitably form an alliance with China to put it in a stronger position to pursue an independent course.[14] This approach gives inadequate attention to China itself, thereby avoiding possible diversion from their main goal of creating a simplified bipolar world. In fact, both approaches are informed more by ideological preferences than by meaningful analyses of the actual situation.

There are, however, some commentators, who, while criticizing both Russia's and China's regimes, call for one country to be used against the other. Some claim that "the West can find more common ground with China, which benefits from stability, than with Russia, which benefits from disruption."[15]

A different group of Western analysts calls for aligning with Russia in opposition to China, the country they feel poses the greater long-term danger.[16] These analysts often try to prove that China, and not the West, poses the greater threat to Russia. They claim that the West's actions, including the expansion of its military infrastructure to Russia's borders and its anti-Russian sanctions, not only pose no threat to Russia, but actually benefit it. At the same time, they allege that China is hatching plans for world domination, the seizure of Russian territories, demographic expansion, and to force its northern neighbor into economic submission.[17]

Bobo Lo, for example, describes his political goals very clearly. He criticizes "voices suggesting that the West should ease up on Putin, claiming that sanctions ... have driven Russia into China's arms," as well as those who argue "that China, not Russia, is the main threat."[18] The logical recommendation based on these thoughts would be the continuation of a course of simultaneously confronting Russia and China that is anathema to the approach of the traditional "realists" – Richard Nixon, Henry Kissinger, and even Zbigniew Brzezinski – that attempted to tear China away from the Soviet Union as part of the "triangle" and use one against the other.

Thus, although the arguments Bobo Lo puts forward seem sound, in reality they differ little from the baseless claims made by Constantine Menges who, without citing a single official document or source, stated that China has some sort of "stealthy strategy toward global dominance" that includes plans to use Russia and its Far Eastern regions as a tool.[19] He suggests countering that strategy by supporting "democratic" (meaning pro-US) forces in both countries – a tactic that would undoubtedly drive Moscow and Beijing even closer together.

The views of those analysts who hold that Russian-Chinese rapprochement is based on the similarity of their views of the outside world, or what Gilbert Rozman refers to as their "parallel identities," is much more grounded in reality.[20] It is not by accident that most of them are well read in both Russian and Chinese language sources. Unlike Bobo Lo, no one can accuse Rozman of not being familiar with official documents or of not knowing which views reflect the official position and which are marginal. He has devoted his entire career to studying the positions that the East Asian ruling elites take toward the outside world and neighboring countries. According to Rozman,

> China's rhetoric in support of Putin's actions in Ukraine and Russia's rhetoric endorsing Xi's thinking about East Asia is not a coincidence. Rather, it is a feature of a new, post–Cold War geopolitical order. As long as the current political elites in China and Russia hold on to power, there is no reason to expect a major shift in either country's national identity or in the Sino-Russian relationship. Countries hoping to create a divide between the two – including Japan under Prime Minister Shinzo Abe – are bound to be disappointed.[21]

Jacob Stokes expresses a similar opinion: "A shared political vision for world order provides the foundation for Chinese-Russian cooperation. It is defined primarily by the desire to see an end to US primacy, to be replaced by multipolarity."[22]

Despite these authors' occasional ill-founded assessment, this conclusion is sound. Their problem lies elsewhere. In arguing that Russian-Chinese rapprochement threatens the world order they refer not to the relationship that exists in reality, but to the one that, in their opinion, should take shape following "the end of history" – a world order in which the US and its allies dominate and the values and views of their ruling elite hold sway. The new level of cooperation between Russia and China really does threaten that order. Or, more exactly, the attempt by the West to build such a world order contributed to the current Russian-Chinese rapprochement, which in turn made it impossible for the "end of history" scenario to play out as anticipated.

This, however, does not mean that China and Russia will necessarily clash with the US, as Michael Levin predicted about a decade ago.[23] What's more, not only does Russian-Chinese rapprochement in no way threaten the multipolar world order that is actually emerging, it actually serves as one of its major pillars.

In any case, a number of US and European authors consider the foundation of Russian-Chinese rapprochement to be the increasing similarity of their approaches to the outside world. John Garver argues that the formation of a strategic partnership with the new Russia Federation "was a major element of Beijing's response to the 'extremely unbalanced' international system that emerged after the Cold War."[24] Interpreting it as a result of the two countries' dissatisfaction with that system, he even calls their coming together a "Far Eastern Rapallo" and supports his analysis with texts of numerous bilateral documents. Elizabeth Wishnick maintains that "because of normative affinities, this has always been a partnership of consequence, rather than a tactical arrangement. Sharing norms does not imply holding identical positions on all issues; rather, Russia and China share a common perception of Western pressure on their domestic choices and constraint on their freedom of manoeuvre globally."[25]

Such conclusions much more accurately reflect the reality of Russian-Chinese rapprochement, but their authors are not at the center of political debate and have no significant impact on US and European foreign policy. Moreover, their research often fails to take a systematic or consistent approach to ascertaining the causes of Russian-Chinese rapprochement.

This book is an attempt to fill some gaps in English-language studies of Russian-Chinese rapprochement. The author did not aim at defining Russian-Chinese relations from the point of view of an International Relations theory, but concentrated more on explaining the realities on the ground by changing perceptions of the bilateral relationship and international relations in general of the leaders and elites in the two countries. The study looks at the process by moving from the general to the particular. Examining the general, global changes in the international system – that is, its gradual evolution from a bipolar to a multipolar model – the author observes that these changes have led to significant changes in the way Russia and China view the outside world and to relations between their political elites. It was these changes – driven by attempts by the United States and the European Union to preserve the unipolar order that emerged briefly after the collapse of the Soviet Union – that contributed to a growing rapprochement between Moscow and Beijing. Having gained its own logic and momentum, that movement has had a significant impact on the global order and has led to the creation of a system of cooperation in the non-Western world. This is seen in the creation and rising influence of such organizations and groups as the BRICS (Brazil,

Russia, India, China, and South Africa), the Shanghai Cooperation Organization, and the Association of Southeast Asian Nations, and in the emergence of a new non-Western community: Greater Eurasia. This process, in turn, is increasingly driving the international system toward a multipolar (polycentric) world.

The aims of this book have determined its structure. The first chapter examines the evolution of Russian and Chinese foreign policy concepts in the late twentieth and early twenty-first centuries as a factor in their development as independent centers of world politics. The second and third chapters show the evolution of the approaches taken by their respective political elites, both toward each other and in bilateral relations with others – demonstrating at the same time the gradual convergence of their views of the world and their growing understanding of the need for rapprochement. The book gives particular attention to indicating which views and approaches in each country belong to the mainstream and define foreign policy, and which are of only marginal significance. The fourth chapter presents official bilateral documents and describes expanding spheres of Russian-Chinese cooperation on the world stage in order to illustrate the growing convergence of their approaches. The fifth and final chapter discusses the impact of Russian-Chinese rapprochement on the world system and prospects for its development.

Realizing that many analysts who write about Russian-Chinese relations take an ideology-based approach, this author strives for maximum objectivity. Of course, it is difficult to achieve absolute objectivity in the social sciences because every researcher holds certain convictions that influence his or her findings.

Writing over a century ago, Max Weber complained that the development of social sciences "was not, however, accompanied by a formulation of the logical distinction between 'empirical knowledge,' i.e., knowledge of what 'is,' and 'normative knowledge,' i.e., knowledge of what 'should be.'"[26] Things have not changed much since that time.

Nonetheless, taking a cue from Weber and claiming that this study achieves a degree of scientific precision, the author takes pains to point out where he attempts to describe "what is" with respect to Russia and other countries, and where, by contrast, he makes a personal call for what "should be." Although the latter has a place in any discussion of policy, it has no place at all in objective academic inquiry. With this as our guide, we hereby attempt to present this study of Russian-Chinese rapprochement.

ACKNOWLEDGMENTS

The research for this book was supported by a grant from the Faculty of World Economy and International Affairs of the Higher School of Economics, Moscow.

This book is derived, in part, from two articles: Alexander Lukin, "Russia in a Post-Bipolar World," *Survival*, 58(1) (2016): 91–112, and Alexander Lukin, "Russia's Pivot to Asia: Myth or Reality?" *Strategic Analysis*, 40(6) (2016): 573–89.

1

RUSSIA, CHINA, AND THE CHANGING INTERNATIONAL SYSTEM

Although the Russian-Chinese rapprochement that began in the late twentieth century has a particular value and internal logic of its own, it is also an integral part of a larger trend in world politics. And while changes in the world order exert a significant, if not decisive influence on that rapprochement, the very fact of two major states developing closer ties affects the international situation as well. It is therefore impossible to understand Russian-Chinese rapprochement without first analyzing the main trends in the development of the international system in the late twentieth and early twenty-first centuries, as well as the evolution of the Russian and Chinese approaches to the outside world as a whole.

At the turn of the twenty-first century, the world entered a new period of development. The customary bipolar system of the Soviet Union and the United States that prevailed after World War II had collapsed following the self-destruction of one of its poles. One can long argue why this happened, but it is clear that the Soviet communist project was unable to compete and failed. In fact, Soviet ideology had cornered itself. Born of the Western secular Enlightenment tradition, it inherited its idea of technological progress and the satisfaction of people's material needs. But Soviet ideology vowed that faster progress would be achieved not by enhancing self-rule and respect for individual rights and private property, but by concentrating resources in the hands of the state, nationalizing property, and ensuring its fair distribution. This project proved economically unviable. Also, the Soviet Union pursued a policy that was based on the ideological goal of spreading its system to as many countries as possible, and eventually to the whole world. This wasted considerable, albeit not limitless, resources and exacerbated economic problems.

The world's first ever bipolar system of global confrontation between the two centers of power had had its positive and negative sides. The control exercised by the two centers over large parts of the world and the rules of the game they set in international relations provoked occasional conflicts on neutral territories, and virtually any local outbreak in the Third World turned into a standoff between the two main centers, with each supporting one of the conflicting sides. In addition, people living in countries and territories controlled by the Soviet center enjoyed very little freedom and had to struggle with the social abnormality of totalitarian regimes.

But those conflicts could hardly compare with the horrors of world wars. There were international rules after all, written and unwritten, and both the Soviet Union and the West showed their ability to find consensus on them (the Helsinki Accords, nuclear nonproliferation agreements, and documents reducing and banning weapons of mass destruction are the most vivid examples of that).

The West

The collapse of the Soviet center of power, which had overestimated its strength caused not by war but by outside pressure and internal problems, was followed by the triumph of the West.[1] Having sought global control, Soviet leaders lost much of what they could otherwise have achieved.

The situation in the early 1990s was marked by the strong, if not decisive, influence of the United States and its allies on international developments. Their victory in the confrontation with the Soviet camp had made the Western political and economic model more popular. Some of the former Soviet associates sought to join the West; others, including Russia itself, had elected leaders who sincerely showed their appreciation for the West. The United States and its allies were also unparalleled in terms of military capabilities.

However, the breakup of the Soviet camp did not affect other key tendencies in global development processes. Such non-Western centers of power as China, India, Brazil, and others continued to rise and become stronger. They tried to solve their own problems and protect their interests, at least near their borders. Being interested in cooperation with the West, they did not seek confrontation with it, as they had no means to do so, but at the same time they did not share many of the West's goals, to different extents and for different reasons, and were actually quite worried about some of them.

The former Soviet empire was a blend of different attitudes. While some of the Eastern European countries (excluding Serbia, which had not been part of the Soviet empire) had unconditionally agreed to join the Western system as its junior partners, the new Russian authorities hoped for equal cooperation based on a common understanding of global development goals. Central Asian republics feared a drive for Western-style democratization: some of them gravitated toward Russia, others tried to find a balance between Russia and the West, while still others chose autarchy.

In that situation, the United States and its allies could have pursued a balanced policy of keeping, wherever possible, much of their influence through improved relations with major global players. For example, Russia could have been integrated into the Western system to a large extent either by admitting it to the North Atlantic Treaty Organization (NATO), as George H. W. Bush's Secretary of State James Baker repeatedly suggested,[2] or by adopting a flexible policy combining real assistance (a new Marshall Plan) with due respect for Moscow's interests and concerns. This could have produced a close partnership with Moscow without any formal alliance with it, in much the same way as had been done with Mexico or Egypt under Sadat and Mubarak.

This was a realistic scenario, but it required some concessions and compromises, which, however, were not required to achieve the ideological goals pursued more and more vigorously by Western politicians. Intellectuals in the United States and Europe had long been leaning toward the ideology of "democratism," a one-sided mixture of political liberalism, the concept of "fundamental human rights," Enlightenment secularism, and colonial theories of Western supremacy. As a result, as had often happened in history before, the West tried to impose upon the world its own model as a universal solution.

The underlying principles of foreign policy based on the ideology of "democratism" are quite simple. Western political ideologists who set trends in foreign policy believe that the best way to integrate "backward" nations into the world of "freedom and democracy" is to submit them to political influence through economic and political alliances. For this to happen, they need leaders who understand that this will benefit their countries (that is, Western-leaning ones) and who will therefore work toward this end. Even if these forces fall short of "democratic" standards, it will not be a big issue. Once they submit economically and politically, they will be pushed up to the required level with Western prodding.

The course chosen by the West after the Soviet Union's breakup was based on this ideology rather than realism. Infatuated with victory, its leaders saw no reason to show any regard for the interests of other countries: the whole world would soon be at their feet anyway as all nations could not wait to melt into the West on the basis of its "universal" values, the only correct ones. This idea was expressly stated by Francis Fukuyama in his *The End of History and the Last Man*.[3] But the largest part of the world rejected, not without good reason, most of these "universal" values as an ideological smokescreen for the West's attempts to impose its hegemony. Many of those values also were at variance with the traditional cultures and religions prevalent in other major civilizations.

The West had overestimated its abilities both politically and culturally. The world was more complex and its values more diverse than Western leaders had realized, being intoxicated by their success but restricted by their ideology. The attractiveness and objective possibilities of the West were dwindling due to the economic and political rise of non-Western centers of power and due to demographic processes. Western capitals, and especially Washington, continued to act as if "history had come to an end," using pressure, and often force, to project their own vision of the world and even of internal life on other countries and whole regions that did not want to Westernize. This policy produced chaos in Iraq, Egypt, Syria, and Ukraine.

Some Western observers have eventually noticed this tendency, in hindsight. American foreign policy analyst Richard N. Haass wrote in his "The Unraveling" that the US actions have exacerbated global disorder:

> The post–Cold War order was premised on US primacy, which was a function of not just US power but also US influence, reflecting a willingness on the part of others to accept the United States' lead. This influence has suffered from what is generally perceived as a series of failures or errors, including lax economic regulation that contributed to the financial crisis, overly aggressive national security policies that trampled international norms, and domestic administrative incompetence and political dysfunction.[4]

Haass further says:

> Order has unraveled, in short, thanks to a confluence of three trends. Power in the world has diffused across a greater number and range of actors. Respect for the American economic and political model has diminished. And specific US policy choices, especially in the Middle East, have raised doubts about American judgment and the reliability of the United States' threats and promises. The net result is that while

the United States' absolute strength remains considerable, American influence has diminished.[5]

While Haass explores foreign policy flaws, Henry Kissinger points to the growing degree of ideologization in American policies as one of the reasons for their failures, but uses a different term: "The celebration of universal principles needs to be paired with recognition of the reality of other regions' histories, cultures and views of their security."[6]

Europe, too, has recently, and belatedly, been criticizing the policy based on the "end-of-history" ideology. An essay published by the European Council on Foreign Relations says that the way of life adopted by the European Union (EU) as a universal model for the whole world to use in the future was actually an exception for that world:

> The new European order was different from all previous post-war settlements ... The remaking of Europe took the shape of extending Western institutions, most of them created for a bipolar world. The unification of Germany became the model for the unification of Europe ... Europeans were aware of the distinctive nature of their order but they were also convinced of its universal nature. From the World Trade Organization to the Kyoto Protocol, and from the International Criminal Court to the Responsibility to Protect, European norms seemed to be in the ascendant. Europeans were convinced that economic interdependence and converging lifestyles would be the dominant source of security in the world of tomorrow. Intoxicated by its own innovations, the EU became increasingly disconnected from other powers – and saw only where others fell short of European standards rather than try to understand their different perspectives. This applied to the EU's neighbors, other great powers such as China, and even to allies such as the United States. And the claim of the European project to be, at one and the same time, exceptional and universal made it impossible for Europeans to accept any alternative integration projects in their continent.[7]

In general, the United States and Europe, as well as faraway Australia and New Zealand, and to a lesser extent Japan, should be viewed as one center of power cemented together by the common totalitarian ideology of "democratism," that is, the desire to impose their model upon the rest of the world. In the foreseeable future, the policy of this center of power, which remains the strongest in the present-day world, will be defined by the gap between growing ideological ambitions and dwindling relative capabilities. Faced with challenges that are both external (the rising influence of non-Western centers of power) and internal (the changing demographic and political situation), the West is objectively losing its influence in the world.

The popularity of the Western model and ideology was based mainly on the assumption, quite common among many non-Western nations, especially after World War II, that the Western political model could secure the highest level of economic well-being. Freedom is attractive, of course, for a part of the population in not-so-rich and autocratic states, but *along* with economic well-being, not instead of it. The majority of countries have always sought to adopt the Western model as the one that guarantees a more prosperous life. The rapid economic rise of China at the end of the twentieth and the beginning of the twenty-first centuries, and the economic and political failure of many countries where the United States and Europe had tried to impose their model of development (Russia in the 1990s, Iraq, Libya, etc.) led many to question the universal effectiveness of the Western slogans of "democratization," "market economy," and "free trade." The Western policy of diktat and constant bombing showed that the ideology of "democratism" was often used to cover up for attempts to establish political dominance. This understanding seriously undermined the West's "soft power" and at the same time added popularity to other models, primarily the "Beijing Consensus," as an alternative to the Washington one.

Mainstream Western foreign policy thinkers have failed to understand that the expansion of the West's model has reached cultural and civilizational limits. The Western system was straightforward to spread in Eastern Europe, where countries tired of Soviet control sought to join Western alliances for political and cultural reasons. The system was established or restored there relatively easily (although not everywhere). But this model is culturally much more alien to North Africa and Eurasia. Islam and Orthodox Christianity, which are gaining popularity in the post-Soviet space, reject Western "democratism," with its increasingly vague social roles of men and women, euthanasia, surrogate motherhood, same-sex marriages, and the like, not only for political but also for moral reasons. And they oppose it so strongly that they are ready to fight against this onslaught of sin. The conflict in the Ukraine, where a cultural and civilizational dividing line has cut the country into two, just as growing anti-Western movements have split up the Islamic world, was largely caused by these factors.

The West will gradually change. What will the United States be like in twenty or thirty years from now, if a considerable part of its population becomes Spanish speaking? In Britain, cities have growing

Muslim populations. In France, polls indicate that Muslims make up about 8–10 percent of the population.[8] What will its policy be like if their number reaches 30 or 40 percent? Will growing migration evoke a reaction from right-wing traditionalists? Fears of growing migration have already played a major role in Britain's vote to leave the EU and Donald Trump's election in the US. Western countries can respond to the migration crisis by shutting down their borders or taking other radical steps, but this will signify serious backtracking on many postulates of "democratism" and significant changes in foreign policy.

The first signs of change are already evident. The referendum victory by "Brexit" supporters and the election of Donald Trump to the US presidency were the result of the frustration that large segments of the population feel toward the policies and ideologies of the elites. Those elites amass great wealth from globalization by using cheap migrant labor and opening markets in developing countries under the banner of "free trade." At the same time, they ignore the negative consequences that their actions have had on ordinary citizens: the loss of jobs, a growing gap between the richest and poorest segments of the population and between the richest and poorest regions, the breakdown of families, the erosion of traditional values, and so on. In fact, the ideology of "democratism," "free markets," and "free trade" has essentially turned into an ideological justification for a course that enables major multinational companies that are largely controlled from the US and Europe to earn enormous profits, and that imposes the social and political value system of the Western elites on the rest of the world. At the heart of that ideology lies what Singaporean diplomat Bilahary Kausikan has aptly termed the "myth of universality: i.e. the postulates of [U.S. and European-led and approved] universal values, universal human rights, a united international community, international law, etc."[9]

In the meantime, while US and European elites have been talking about growing universality, new centers of power have been forming in such diverse states as China, Russia, India, Brazil, and others. Also, religious revivals are occurring not only in the former Soviet republics, but in the Muslim world and among both Christians and Muslims in Africa. And everywhere, in spite of all their differences, this integrative process is most often based on values differing from those preached by modern Western society. China speaks of collective Confucianism, the role of Hinduism is on the rise in India, traditional Christians in Africa firmly reject questionable moral innovations sanctioned by mother churches in Europe, and the Muslim world generally views modern Western society as the center of sin and depravity. Even moderate Muslim leaders do not accept Western civilization in its entirety, but try to create something of their own using its achievements. Former Malaysian deputy prime minister, current opposition leader and well-known theorist of Islamic civil society Anwar Ibrahim made this interesting statement on the subject:

> The Civil Society we envisage is one based on Moral Principles ... the Asian vision of civil society departs in a fundamental respect ... from the social philosophy of the Enlightenment ... that religion and civil society are intrinsically incompatible.... Religion has been a source of great strength to Asian society and will continue to be a bulwark against moral and social decay.[10]

At the same time the West is losing its moral leadership; its military dominance, though still in force, has weakened significantly; and the appeal of its material prowess is diminishing as other effective economic models emerge, most particularly China's. Events have repeatedly shown the error of the idea that Westernization is both a universal goal and an inevitable outcome once the authoritarian regimes resisting it are removed. The most recent examples are the anti-authoritarian revolutions in Arab countries that brought to power forces even more anti-Western than the governments they overthrew. It turns out that Europe is surrounded not by hostile rulers hindering Westernization, but by entire populations who consider Western society alien and undesirable. And it is their leaders who, as Alexander Pushkin once said of the Russian government, are often "the only Europeans" in their country.[11]

The international system is changing, moving toward greater diversity. However, in the foreseeable future, while "democratism" adapts to the new realities, the West can hardly be a source of peace and stability. On the contrary, its policy will continue to produce global conflicts that will most often erupt in territories that border on other non-Western centers of power with their own values. The main source of these conflicts will be attempts to impose the ideology of "democratism" on a population which is not willing to accept it.

Russia

The crisis in Ukraine in 2014 has placed Russia and the world before a new reality. The paradigm of international relations that developed after the collapse of the Soviet Union, and that defined the rules of the game for Russia and its key partners during the Yeltsin period and the early years of Vladimir Putin's presidency, is now undergoing a change. That period can be called the "post-Soviet consensus." What are its main features? Ever since the collapse of the Soviet Union, Russia has been considered, in principle, a partner of the West. And although it is not as close a partner as the member states of Western economic and political alliances, Russia was thought to share the West's basic foreign and domestic policy goals. The disagreements that arose over such questions as Yugoslavia, Iraq, Iran, and others were attributed to Russia's size and the short time it had spent under the West's influence. In any event, those differences were resolved fairly quickly. Russia's national peculiarities and its short experience with democracy were seen as the reason for the country's distinctive approach to domestic policy – something that Moscow leaders themselves mentioned.

The crisis in Ukraine and Russia's reaction to it have fundamentally changed this consensus. Russia refused to play by the rules. To understand this reaction one should analyze the difference between the Russian and Western approaches to the international situation.

The victory in the Cold War, as perceived by the West – achieved not through war, but as a result of communism's internal collapse – led to a euphoria that was best expressed by Francis Fukuyama, whose famous theory of the "end of history" proclaimed the ultimate success and universal recognition of Western values and the Western "progressive" social order. The West combined this euphoria with relative economic weakness (compared to the post–World War II period) in its approach to the Eastern European states and former Soviet republics that had been liberated from communism. Two options were theoretically possible at that point: either make a serious attempt to assimilate Russia into the Western system, or wrest piece after piece from this center of the inimical world in the belief that Russia had no real prospects anyway and that the future belonged to the West.

European and US advocates of the first approach made the argument to politicians that an anti-Russian course could lead to increased hostility from Moscow and that the reward would only be several smaller states that would end up becoming part of Europe anyway. Prominent US foreign policy theoretician George Kennan and several well-known senators and journalists were among those who lent their voices to this warning. However, their admonition went unheeded. The administrations of former US presidents Bill Clinton and George W. Bush took the second path by expanding NATO while trying to convince Russia that the foreign forces nearing its borders did not pose a threat to its security. European Union leaders did the same thing by pushing that organization ever closer to Russia's borders. No consideration was given even to those pro-Western Russian liberals who argued that such policies fueled the growth of anti-Western sentiment in Russia and strengthened the position of those who supported authoritarianism. The thinking in Western capitals was that the people of all countries intrinsically aspire to form Western-style unions and alliances, that they believe in the same values the West promotes, and that if the leaders of this or that country hinder this naturally progressive movement, a wave of popular protest would eventually sweep those rulers away. What's more, the price tag for fully bringing Russia into the Western sphere was higher than those countries were willing to pay.

Today it is difficult to say whether a different approach to the postcommunist states would have produced a more positive result for the West. However, it is obvious that the course taken by Clinton and Bush significantly strengthened the authority of those forces in Moscow that believe Russia should not join Western alliances, but instead become an independent center of power – the center of Eurasian integration in the framework of a multipolar world. Whether those policies played a decisive role in that trend is unimportant: what is clear is that objective as well as subjective factors stand behind Russia's current ambitions.

Russia had a different view of the world's post–Cold War development. The "post-Soviet consensus" was based on an understanding with the West that both sides would move toward closer cooperation, remain responsive to each other's interests, and agree to make mutually acceptable compromises. In the Kremlin's view, however, only Russia fulfilled those conditions. While not entirely abandoning the idea of national interests, Moscow showed that it was ready to partially sacrifice them in order to cooperate with and become part of the "civilized world." However, despite an abundance of encouraging words, the "civilized world" continued thinking in Cold War terms and sincerely believed it had emerged from that confrontation the victor. Forgetting all of its promises, such as the pledge not to expand NATO eastward, the West set out to achieve all that Soviet resistance had prevented it from accomplishing during the Cold War. This included expanding its sphere of influence to an ever greater number of countries and territories and moving its military installations ever closer to Russia's borders – in some cases onto the territory of Russia's traditional allies.

There are differing explanations for this approach. The current Russian leadership believes that the West is pursuing the purely geopolitical foreign policy objective of bringing an ever greater number of countries and territories into its orbit in an attempt to become the dominating force in a "unipolar world," and that its values of democracy and human rights are only an ideological cover. That is seen as the reason for Western "double standards." Thus, Europe only half-heartedly chastises the regimes in Estonia and Latvia for their failure to grant civil rights to a significant portion of their Russian-speaking populations. That is also why the West is unable to see the presence of radical nationalists in Ukraine, and instead views them as people working on behalf of "progress." The West has no difficulty in justifying the past actions of those groups or in closing its eyes to certain crimes – as it did with nationalists in Kosovo, the Croatian army in Serbian Krajina, and so on. A good example is the behavior of European Union foreign policy chief Catherine Ashton, who condemned Right Sector militants for attempting to seize Ukraine's Verkhovna Rada (parliament) building after the anti-Russian opposition had come to power, but who effectively supported them in the same action earlier, when Ukraine's parliamentary majority consisted of "bad guys" who had not fully aligned themselves with the EU. At the same time, European officials take great pains to stigmatize the crimes committed by those whom they consider "regressive" forces.

It was not Russia, but the West that destroyed the idea of creating a new system of global politics based on international law when that opportunity arose following the collapse of the Soviet Union. It was not Russia, but the West that, believing in the "end of history," used its temporary omnipotence to create a world in which powerful states could seize anything that was there for the taking, destroy any borders and violate any treaties for the sake of a "good cause." It was not Russia, but the West that deliberately destroyed the postwar legal system based on the sovereignty of states and advocated the theories of "humanitarian intervention," "the responsibility to protect," and so on. It was not Russia, but the West that pressured the International Court of Justice into ruling that Kosovo's unilateral declaration of independence did not violate international law. Russia repeatedly warned that the precedents set by the bombing of Serbia, the secession of Kosovo, and the military actions in Iraq and Libya would undermine the system of international law – including the principle of the inviolability of borders in Europe enshrined in the Helsinki Accords. Were it not for the United Nations (UN) Security Council, any powerful state could decide for itself what constitutes a "good cause" and which piece of territory it could grab for itself.

As a result, Russia sees the West's position on Crimea – in which it cites the principles of territorial integrity and the inviolability of borders – as nothing more than a case of extreme hypocrisy.

As long as its Western influence had only spread to the small countries of Eastern Europe, everything went well. But it ran into problems with Russia. Moscow refused to fully integrate into the Western system and insisted on maintaining its own approaches, at least on several issues it considered of particular importance. This was not because Russian leaders were innately anti-Western: to the contrary, Boris Yeltsin and Vladimir Putin began their terms in office with concessions aimed at winning reciprocal responses from their Western partners. However, they received only empty promises in return, and circumstances forced them to take a tougher stance.

What were those circumstances? Numerous opinion polls show that most Russians do not consider Western society ideal. Russia differs in this way from Eastern Europe – and even there the West has some problems. Poland and Hungary, where conservative Catholicism is strong, find many modern European moral standards unacceptable, while Bulgaria and Romania must contend with rampant corruption and weak democratic institutions. Just the same, those countries are not overly large and the West can swallow them up gradually, gaining their cooperation with welfare and security guarantees. Russia is far too large and cannot Westernize without the support of the majority of the Russian people. However, most Russians do not want the country to Westernize and have little interest in such leading issues of Western society as human rights, equality for women, gay marriage, etc. To the contrary – many Russians find those questions irritating. The Russian Orthodox and Muslim faiths, both of which are resurgent in Russia, believe not only that Western society is not perfect, but that it is the very center of sin. Accordingly, they speak of the need to follow their own path. Moscow views the West's persistent attempts to impose alien values, wrest away neighbors with whom Russia shares close cultural ties, and position troops ever closer to Russia's borders as a policy of encirclement and gradual asphyxiation.

Of course, Russia does have a Westernized minority, especially in large cities, but its numbers are small. As a result, the principle of Western democracy in which the majority either sets the national agenda or else actively influences it, coupled with the West's hostile foreign policy, means that any Russian leader who appeals to the country's traditional and conservative majority will enjoy the greatest popularity. The West cannot see beyond its own ideology to understand this situation. In fact, research has shown that all ideologies tend to discount or deny the existence of facts that do not fit within its framework.

Today, the Western expansion is tearing apart countries close to Russia. It has already led to territorial splits in Moldova and Georgia, and Ukraine is splintering before our eyes. The distinguishing feature of these countries is that cultural boundaries pass directly through their respective territories, and their leaders can only maintain unity by accommodating both the interests of residents living in regions attracted to Europe, as well as those in regions wanting to maintain their traditional ties with Russia. The West's lopsided support for pro-Western nationalists in former Soviet republics has led to severe internal conflicts and the oppression of Russian-speaking populations – a problem to which Russia could not remain indifferent. And when it came to "brotherly" Ukraine and the threat of NATO forces appearing in Crimea – a region for which Russia has special feelings and most of whose residents consider themselves Russian – a reinvigorated Russia decided it had nowhere left to retreat. Russia annexed Crimea in response to the aspirations of a majority of its residents and to NATO's obvious attempt to move too close to Russia's borders and push Russia's fleet out of the Black Sea.

Moscow's abrupt reaction clearly caught the West by surprise. In late March 2014, NATO's Supreme Allied Commander Europe, General Philip Breedlove, said with surprise that Russia is acting "much more like an adversary than a partner." But given the fact that NATO has acted that way ever since its founding and did not change its approach to Russia even after the end of the Cold War, Moscow's actions should hardly have come as a surprise. In fact, it was only a matter of time before Russia changed its policy.

What might result from that change? Of course, one can hope that cooler heads will prevail in the West and that it will seriously consider Russia's proposals for ensuring the rights of pro-Russian populations in the former Soviet republics. However, for Western ideologists, accepting Russia's proposals would mean admitting that someone other than the West has the right to determine what constitutes social progress and what is good and what is bad for other societies and states. It is unlikely that the ideology of "democratism" will tolerate that. For now, the West prefers to support pro-Western radicals throughout the former Soviet republics, thereby triggering new conflicts. Under these circumstances, Russia must seriously consider refocusing its foreign policy to the south and east. The advantage of that approach is that it could help Russia develop its own Asian regions. The disadvantage is that it could make Russia dependent on strong Asian partners, primarily China. However, the West's hostility and lack of understanding leave Russia with no alternative.

In fact, Russian concerns and dissatisfaction with Western policy began as far back as the 1990s. For example, the Russian Federation's National Security Concept drafted in 1997 and revised in 2000 listed the following security threats:

> – the striving of particular states and intergovernmental associations to belittle the role of existing mechanisms for ensuring international security, above all the United Nations and the OSCE;
> – the danger of a weakening of Russia's political, economic and military influence in the world;
> – the strengthening of military-political blocs and alliances, above all NATO's eastward expansion;
> – possible appearance of foreign military bases and large troop contingents in direct proximity to Russia's borders;
> – proliferation of weapons of mass destruction and their delivery vehicles;
> – a weakening of the integration processes in the Commonwealth of Independent States;
> – outbreak and escalation of conflicts near the state border of the Russian Federation and the external borders of the member states of the Commonwealth of Independent States;
> – territorial claims against Russia.[12]

In February 2007, in his remarks to the Munich security conference, President Putin maintained that "the unipolar model is not only unacceptable but also impossible in today's world," criticized "unilateral and frequently illegitimate actions" that "have caused new human tragedies and created new centres of tension," and deplored NATO expansion despite Western promises.[13]

Similar themes can be found in the Russia's Foreign Policy Concept adopted in February 2013, a year before the Ukrainian crisis. It argued that "arbitrary and politically motivated interpretation of fundamental international legal norms and principles" posed a danger to international peace, law and order. It also stressed that "Russia maintains a negative attitude towards NATO's expansion and to the approaching of NATO military infrastructure to Russia's borders in general as to actions that violate the principle of equal security and lead to the emergence of new dividing lines in Europe."[14]

Of course, this and similar criticisms referred to unilateral actions by the US and NATO in Yugoslavia, Iraq, and Libya, and served as a warning that Moscow viewed NATO's expansion to its borders as a threat to Russia's security. However, the West ignored all of these warnings and labeled Russian leaders as reactionaries and enemies of progress. Under such circumstances, it was only a matter of time before a serious confrontation broke out.

The year 2014 was pivotal for Russia's foreign policy. The crisis in Ukraine expedited its refusal to follow the West and led to confrontation with it. This essentially marked a dramatic turn in the foreign policy Moscow had pursued since 1991. Although the period between 1991 and 2014 saw both close cooperation and disagreements with the West, Moscow always made strategic concessions in the end. Today such concessions are highly unlikely, and only tactical arrangements can be possible since Russia has lost faith in the United States and Europe as political and economic partners and has realized that it cannot establish friendly relations with them without its complete political submission. So Moscow has begun an actual – not only verbal (as was the case before the Ukrainian crisis) – political and economic pivot toward the non-Western world.

When the Western expansion came to its closest partner, Ukraine, Russia had to react to show that further advancement would cost the West dearly. Although it has not been able to take the strongest actions due to limited resources and economic dependence, Russia is doing and will be doing its best to stop the expansion of the West's power toward its border. The new Russia has rejected Soviet and any other totalitarian ideology. It is not trying to force its political model upon other countries. Moreover, despite authoritarian reality, this model has been proclaimed as conforming to Western standards, with certain characteristics of its own due to cultural traditions. In Ukraine, as anywhere else, Russia is fighting not for the right to impose a model of the perfect society, but for purely geopolitical goals and mere survival. Its leadership simply wants to avoid Russia being encircled and put under the political control of the United States and its allies, and it wants its neighbors to remain friendly, or at least neutral.

The United States and the West in general view the conflict with Russia as local, albeit extremely dangerous in that Moscow's actions undermine the West's global development project designed to gradually engage all countries on its own terms as subordinated "pupils" diligently trying to live up to Western standards. It is local because Russia is not the most dangerous challenge on the way, although it is the most trenchant one for the time being. In fact, the West is much more worried about the prospects of seeing a multipolar world emerging in the future. It has no idea how to Westernize vast China, and things are not going quite smoothly with India, Brazil, and many other centers of power.

China

Chinese foreign policy has passed through several stages in its history. In the 1950s it was largely defined by a strategic and ideological alliance with the Soviet Union and its struggle against world imperialism. Moscow granted Beijing a certain degree of autonomy in Asia and Africa, and considered China the leader in the fraternity of "Third World" socialist states. When China broke with the Soviet Union, and especially during its "Cultural Revolution," Beijing pursued a course of revolutionary dogmatism and attempted to foment change across the Asian continent by supporting a host of radical anti-Western movements. In the 1970s, after China and the US established closer ties based on mutual anti-Soviet sentiment, Mao Zedong put forward his "Three Worlds Theory" in which China was the self-proclaimed leader of all developing "Third World" countries. Within the framework of that theory Beijing soon decided that one member of the "First World" – the "social imperialist Soviet Union" – posed the greatest danger, and that the need to resist that threat justified cooperating with the other member – the United States. The idea of creating a united front against the Soviet Union persisted until the end of the 1970s, at which point the need to devote serious attention to domestic reforms forced Beijing to normalize relations with Moscow and gradually abandon the idea. From the very beginning of the reform process, the Deng Xiaoping leadership decided that the country's foreign policy course must also undergo fundamental changes. At the 12th Congress of the Communist Party of China (CPC or CCP) held in September 1982, Chinese leaders formulated an "independent foreign policy" concept that essentially rejected the idea of forming alliances with any of the "superpowers," cast the Soviet Union and the United States as either partners or opponents, and most importantly, subjugated all foreign policy goals to the greater goal of achieving the country's economic development. This concept defines Beijing's official foreign policy course.[15]

In fact, China has striven since the early 1980s to spur economic development by establishing good working relations with all countries, but especially with those that can provide it with the most investment and new technologies. As part of this policy, Beijing devotes particular attention to resolving territorial and other disputes with neighboring states by every means possible, including compromise, in order to boost trade and economic cooperation, both generally and in border areas. Although Beijing has spelled out fundamental interests on which it will not compromise – such as claims that Taiwan and Tibet, and earlier, Hong Kong and Macao are part of China, as well as other issues of territorial integrity – China takes a modest approach on other issues. In order to avoid wasting valuable resources, Beijing does not intervene in international conflicts that do not concern it directly and typically only states its point of view on the question.

The situation has changed somewhat in recent years, however. The very logic of focusing on development compels Beijing to take a more active role in world politics. First, China's successful economic development in recent decades has strengthened the country so considerably that it is now difficult to imagine reaching a solution to many of the world's economic and political problems without Beijing's participation. Second, China's economic development model based on rapid growth and exports has led to a shortage of raw materials, among other resources, and the need to seek new markets for its goods – and both lie beyond the country's borders. Finally, China's domestic problems with the environment, surplus labor, and other issues have begun to directly affect other countries, especially its neighbors.

In an attempt to offer a theoretical justification for its expanding role on the world stage and dispel fears that a more powerful China poses risks to the world, the country's leading ideologues put forward the theory in 2003 of a "peaceful rise." It essentially argues that a stronger China is not a problem for the rest of the world, that the country is focused exclusively on growth, and that such growth actually helps its neighbors develop as well. It states that cultural interactions between states, though not the main instrument of peace, can also promote mutual understanding.

Formulated and promoted by the vice dean of the Central Party School (CPS), Zheng Bijian (who served as deputy director of the CPC Department of Propaganda back in the 1990s), the concept of a "peaceful rise" was adopted at the highest levels of the Chinese government. Despite the good intentions of its authors, the idea of China's "rise" – although a peaceful one – caused mixed reactions and even fear in various quarters. As a result, Chinese leaders abandoned it as an official concept and returned, first, to the idea of "peaceful development" that Deng Xiaoping had originally put forward, and later to what is now the official concept of creating a "harmonious world."

Chinese leader Hu Jintao officially proposed creating a "harmonious world of lasting peace and common prosperity" at the sixtieth anniversary celebration of the United Nations in September 2005 in New York. And in a speech at Yale University in April 2006, he said that social harmony had always been important to China and that the country had begun efforts to build a harmonious society. At the same time, he said that Chinese society "is inclusive and is eager to draw on the strength of other civilizations to pursue peace and development through cooperation, and play its part in building a harmonious world of enduring peace and common prosperity."[16]

In effect, this is the same program of independent foreign policy applied to new circumstances. Its purpose is to reassure the world regarding China's development goals, and show that China plays a constructive role in the world and that its growing strength is actually beneficial for everyone else as well. Beijing's peace offensive and its skillful use of "soft power" did produce some results.

In the long term, a rising China will be a much bigger challenge to the Western ideology of global dominance than Russia, which still remains quite weak. China, the second largest economy and the most densely populated country in the world, poses a threat not because of its military power, which still falls short of American and even Russian capabilities, but because communist China succeeded where the Soviet Union had failed – it built an effective and attractive economy that is not based on the Western political model. And this is much more dangerous for the West as it makes people and governments in many countries doubt its fundamental postulate that an economy can be effective and generate prosperity only if a country accepts the ideology of "democratism." Moreover, the Chinese economy has become so interdependent with the American and European economies that it would be very hard to deal with Beijing in the way Russia was dealt with. The West depends on China economically just as much as China depends on the West. And if there is an open confrontation, the united West may eventually rein in China, but the costs will be too high for the world economy to bear.

A rapidly developing China has lately been pursuing a more vigorous foreign policy. Under Xi Jinping, Beijing pushed forward with ambitious plans to launch the Silk Road Economic Belt and Maritime Silk Road projects. While their economic aspects remain vague, their political meaning is quite clear: China offers its own development concepts, alternative to Western ones, at least for some of the Asian regions (the former project targets mainly Central Asia, the Near East and partly Russia; the latter one, Southeast and South Asia and

Oceania). They should create a common framework for the economic, and possibly political, future of these regions. What Beijing offers to these countries is basically a concept of codevelopment supported by substantial material resources. Its message reads: join the Silk Road space, not the area of "democratism." The fact that despite Washington's objections, some of its allies have already joined the Asian Infrastructure Investment Bank proposed by Beijing is a clear indication that Chinese projects are quite appealing.

Another sign of China's enhanced role in foreign affairs is the frequent calls for revising the concept of Tao Guang Yang Hui (韬光养晦; Hide Brightness, Nourish Obscurity) put forward by Deng Xiaoping in the early 1990s as a beacon in charting the country's modest and cautious foreign policy course during the period of reform and openness.[17] Although during Xi's rule strategic planning continues to be restricted by the country's "key interests," the area of these key interests keeps expanding. While under Deng Xiaoping, it focused only on the issue of Taiwan and control over Tibet and Xinjiang autonomous regions, today it has been broadened to include the protection of China's positions in territorial disputes with Japan over the Diaoyu (Senkaku) Islands and in the conflict in the South China Sea. Some Chinese experts also insist that the list of key interests should include the need to secure a worthy place for China in the world in general.

It is widely believed in China that the main obstacle on this path is the United States. The majority of Chinese analysts insist that as a world power that is losing influence but struggling to keep it, America is trying to contain China as its main competitor. The United States, with the assistance of its allies and friendly states, is trying to encircle China militarily and strategically, antagonize its neighbors, and blow the "Chinese threat" out of proportion. Military analyst Dai Xü says in his book on "The C-Shape Encirclement" that China has been encircled almost completely except in Russia and Central Asia.[18] There are some experts in China who suggest taking decisive action to break through this encirclement, for example, by building naval bases abroad or tasking the army with protecting Chinese entrepreneurs' investments in other countries.

In recent years China has witnessed the domestic publication of articles and books that openly urge Beijing to use any means necessary, including the armed forces, to promote its economic interests. These interests not only include, but depend on the ability of Beijing to control natural resources. In a 2009 bestseller, "Unhappy China," the authors are vocal in asserting that the Chinese are better than anyone else in the world at controlling and utilizing natural resources.

Since China currently has a scarcity of natural resources, the authors suggest that Beijing needs to usurp the world's resources and to utilize them for the good of humankind. The Chinese army, in the opinion of the authors, must be highly active in helping China obtain natural resources outside of its borders.[19] One of the book's authors, Wang Xiaodong, had written earlier that the main problem facing China is the lack of "living space."[20] Official Chinese representatives and experts have usually stated that the ideas propagated by the authors of "Unhappy China" are merely the private opinions of citizens; however, when engaged in more open dialogue they admit that these views are also held by influential factions within the military and security agencies.

This open secret was aired in 2010 through the publication of several books and articles by official military analysts who held similar views. In a highly popular book, "The China Dream," published in 2010, Senior Colonel Liu Mingfu, a professor at the National Defense University of the People's Liberation Army (PLA), wrote that China must strive to have the most powerful military in the world. If it did not achieve this dream, then the efforts of the United States (through an inevitable struggle, and perhaps a war) would relegate China to the sidelines of the international arena.[21] In the preface to one publication, General Liu Yuan – political commissar of the Academy of Military Science and son of the former Chinese leader Liu Shaoqi – also called for abandoning restraint and proclaimed that war was inseparable from the history of civilization and culture.[22]

In his book, Dai Xü provides similar arguments. According to him, the American strategy is to surround China by an iron ring of allied states – Japan, Vietnam, India, and the American troops in Afghanistan. In Dai Xü's eyes, China's recent history is a series of battles with one conqueror after another: Great Britain in the nineteenth century, first Japan and then the Union of Soviet Socialist Republics (USSR) in the twentieth, and now the United States in the twenty-first. "I believe that China cannot escape the calamity of war, and this calamity may come in the not-too-distant future, at most in 10 to 20 years," writes Dai Xü. "If the United States can light a fire in China's backyard, we can also light a fire in their backyard."[23] Dai recommends strengthening the military, particularly the navy and air force.

Such statements cause suspicion abroad because they contradict the theoretical doctrine as well as the practice of the Chinese military establishment. After the failure of the Chinese "bloody lesson" in Vietnam in 1979, the Chinese army has not been active abroad except in a peacekeeping capacity under the auspices of the UN, and in military exercises under the framework of the Shanghai Cooperation Organization (SCO). It was always believed that the main goal of the PLA was Taiwan. According to experts, the modernization of the Chinese military and its purchases of arms were both geared toward annexation of Taiwan.

China's diplomacy was also designed to assure the world that China's intentions were exclusively peaceful in nature and that Beijing's external policies were structured to facilitate internal development. Beijing avoided issuing statements about its external interests and did not get involved in international conflicts other than to issue statements that formulated Beijing's position on the topic at hand (mostly, the Chinese basically called for finding the solution through peaceful dialogue). Officially, Beijing's foreign policy dictum has not changed, but today it is obvious that there are many critics of this strategy inside China – including a large number of the military brass. Ostensibly, these critics do not challenge the formal policy, but in practice their ideas are in direct contradiction to the credo established in the late 1970s by Deng Xiaoping.

Nationalist sentiments grow stronger when territorial disputes heat up. Thus, the confrontation with Japan over the disputed islands seems to have prompted Chinese military analysts to ratchet up their rhetoric. In numerous speeches, Rear Admiral Luo Yuan, deputy chief of International Military Studies at the Academy of Military Science, has proposed launching a guerrilla sea war against Japan by using hundreds of fishing vessels, turning the most disputed island that is currently under Japanese control into a naval training ground, or withdrawing from the postwar treaty with Japan and seizing the disputed island by force. "A nation without the martial spirit has no future," he declared in late October 2012 at a conference in Shenzhen.[24] Commenting on the possibility of a naval battle with the Philippines during confrontation over the Scarborough Shoal (Huangyan Islet) in 2012, Luo Yuan was reported as saying: "We have repeatedly exercised forbearance – and our patience has run its course. There is no more need to take caution." He also suggested that if Manila could not rein in its "nationalist warmongers," "let's do the job for them."[25]

At the same time, Chinese leaders continue to adopt a moderate tone in their official statements. Official Chinese representatives usually comment on such opinions by saying that they do not reflect the official position, and that, in a free country, everyone can speak as they please. Chinese leaders publicly declare allegiance to the foreign policy of Deng Xiaoping concerning modesty and the need to ensure peaceful conditions for internal development. There are signs that they are trying to hold back the overly zealous advocates of revitalization: sometimes they have to use the excuse that they were misunderstood, while their most outspoken comments are quickly removed from internet sites. However, their supporters are clearly beginning to have influence. Public criticism is growing (primarily on the internet) that the Foreign Ministry and diplomats are too "soft" and do too little to defend Chinese interests. To some extent, the Foreign Ministry serves as a convenient scapegoat because it is simply inadmissible to ever criticize the higher authorities, even on the internet.

Disagreements Come to the Surface

The fact that serious battles were being waged within Chinese society and government as to how China should proceed with its foreign policy first became clear from discussions with Chinese experts. Some experts deny that Chinese foreign policy has become more forward and aggressive, and claim that China must merely become more steadfast in stating its positions on certain issues. In regard to the aforementioned books, proponents of this line claim that these publications had no serious impact or influence on the Chinese public and were barely even noticed. As for increasing China's influence on the world stage (and even controlling the world's natural resources), these thinkers explain that the majority of Chinese don't seriously think like this and that the ideas expressed in books such as "The China Dream" should not be seen as calls for Chinese hegemony. They continue to give assurances that China's rapid development does not make wars inevitable and that China will continue using methods of peaceful growth. According to them, the modern world is different from the past when the growth of one country sparked unrest and suspicion leading to wars. Today, they assert, global development is based on mutual cooperation – such as that between Russia and China.

Experts who toe this line point to China's participation in combating the global financial crisis as an example of Beijing's cooperative, noncombative attitude. For instance, China has incrementally increased its contribution to the International Monetary Fund. At a November 2010 meeting in Shanghai with a group of Russian academics, a leading Chinese military theorist and former deputy chief of the PLA's General Staff, General Xiong Guankai, expressed his open disagreement with the authors of the books noted earlier published by Chinese military experts. According to General Xiong, the belief that China must become a global leader in all aspects, including the military sphere, is shared neither by the Chinese government nor by the majority of military experts. Rather, most Chinese experts are focused on China's development and not on making China the international leader. Xiong Guankai agreed with the opinion voiced by the Chinese foreign minister Yang Jiechi that China must become merely one of the poles in a multipolar world. Xiong Guankai used a variety of examples to illustrate his assertion that most Chinese leaders did not share the nationalist point of view.

There exists another point of view, however. On this issue it is interesting to hear the opinions of researchers from the Central Party School who first presented the concept of a "peaceful rise" back in November of 2003. During a November 2010 meeting between the author of this book and the vice chairman of the China Reform Forum, a body formed by the CPS to deal with foreign scholars, Ding Kuisong, the Chinese expert, stated that the People's Republic of China (PRC) continued to develop according to the designs first established in the "peaceful rise" theory. During the conversation, he made two remarks which deserve particular attention. In his opinion, there are no differences between the doctrine of "harmonious world" and that of "peaceful rise." The only reason why "peaceful rise" is no longer the party doctrine is due to poor terminology. According to Ding, the term "rise" is a "Western" concept and the Chinese, wanting to clarify that this rise was not a threat, automatically added the word "peaceful" to the notion. Ding Kuisong added, in rather critical terms, that the phrase "peaceful rise" caused havoc among "those egghead scholars at the Academy of Social Sciences," and thus had to be scrapped and replaced with "peaceful development" and then "harmonious world" – the creation of which is now the ultimate foreign policy goal of the country.

What one can gather from these discussions is that there is an ongoing heated debate on the question of how to best utilize China's increasing power in foreign relations. It seems that there are at least two factions in the debate. The first faction can be called "moderate" – people who are proponents of continuing Deng Xiaoping's "modest" foreign policy that focuses exclusively on providing China with the materials and investment necessary for internal development. In their opinion, a disputatious and aggressive foreign policy can repel foreign countries and reflect negatively on China's economic interests and continued internal development. They are countered by the "radicals" who believe that China's national interests have grown beyond the borders of the PRC and that these interests must be defended through aggressive diplomacy and, in some cases, armed intervention.

Over time, the dispute began to surface in print, and initially in foreign publications. In an interview with the *Wall Street Journal* in the fall of 2010, Chu Shulong, a professor at Tsinghua University and a renowned expert on the US, said, "The Chinese military is too powerful in decision-making, especially on foreign policy." He complained that the Central Military Commission had only one civilian, Central Committee General Secretary Hu Jintao, who "is so busy, he can't take care of the military, so the military makes its own decisions without the involvement of civilian leaders."[26] Such a suggestion that the army is inadequately supervised by CPC authorities and that it has its own agenda is an unusually strong accusation for an official in China, where the army has been considered an instrument of the party ever since the country's founding.

In an interview published in the Japanese *Asahi Shimbun* newspaper in October 2012, leading Chinese international relations expert Wang Jisi noted that official policy in China runs counter to public opinion. On one hand, he said, "The leadership in China is very prudent and very sober-minded" in stating that China is still a developing country that still lags far behind the power of the US – and is not even in second place; that Beijing does not adopt the "Group of Two" concept that would link it with the US; and that China has no intention of getting into a global confrontation with Washington. On the other hand,

> One popular view is that China has already surpassed Japan as number two, and should not be afraid to challenge America. According to this view, China should behave more like the United States in the world – ready to use military force or economic weapons to coerce other countries to accept China's righteous demands. They argue that Beijing is now "too soft" in its relations with the United States, Japan, or the Philippines. They have nostalgic feelings about the Mao era when China was, allegedly, more defiant to the outside world.[27]

In a move that was uncharacteristic of Chinese custom, the disagreements between the two groups were made public in the spring of 2016 by Wu Jianmin, Chinese foreign policy theorist and practitioner, former Chinese ambassador to France. Speaking on March 30, 2016 at the China Foreign Affairs university he formerly headed, Wu Jianmin openly criticized Hu Xijin, the *Huanqiu Shibao* (*Global Times*) political tabloid editor-in-chief and former war correspondent in Yugoslavia and Iraq. Although the tabloid publishes a range of opinions, it is known to favor authors who call for a more assertive policy, sometimes in a rather sensational way. Wu Jianmin accused Hu Xijin of using excessively sharp words in his articles and claimed that Hu could not see the big picture and the general trend of world events despite being a learned man.[28]

Wu Jianmin stated that the essence of the new era, unlike previous ones, is a general trend toward peace and expressed regret that many in China, out of inertia, continue thinking and speaking of wars and revolutions and asking, "If we can't beat America, can't we at least strike the Philippines?" He referred to the foreign trips undertaken by Deng Xiaoping that, in his opinion, played a role in formulating reforms and the openness to the outside world, and proposed maintaining this course.[29]

In response, Hu wrote an article on his micro blog on April 7 saying that Wu represented an outdated mode of diplomatic thinking according to which the media should only report the achievements of diplomacy without commenting on or criticizing it in any way. He even appealed to democratic ideals, saying it was undemocratic to demand a prohibition against the publication of opinion contrary to that of the Foreign Ministry, and that in other countries the media is more hawkish than the official diplomatic line.[30] This discussion sparked active debate on the Chinese internet between those holding sharply opposing views.

Despite the fact that hawkish proposals are quite popular among some segments of the elite – especially the military and security communities – they do not represent the official position. They can, however, influence that position in some situations. The official Chinese position is much milder. The attitude of Chinese mainstream analysts toward the idea of "global governance" is quite indicative in this respect. While it considers current global governance theory and practice a Western scheme designed to protect US and European dominance around the world, Beijing does not want it to be undermined or scrapped, but overhauled so that China and other non-Western states can get proper representation and a voice in it.[31]

The correctness of this interpretation was recently confirmed at the highest level. Speaking in September 2016 at a study session for members of the Political Bureau of the CPC Central Committee which was devoted to global governance, Xi Jinping said: "We must actively participate in global governance, we will take more international responsibilities, and in so doing we will try our best but not overreach ourselves."[32]

However, Xi's vision of the system of global governance which China should work for seems very different from that supported by the US and its allies. Xi called reform of the existing system of global governance "the trend of our times" because the international balance of power has shifted and the international order needs to become more reasonable and just to protect the common interests of China and other developing countries. He stressed that China should increase its voice in international affairs, and that the core of the international order should be the principles of the United Nations Charter. He also explained that China has been engaged in the process of setting rules for new areas such as the oceans, the polar regions, cyberspace, outer space, nuclear security, anticorruption, and climate change. In stressing that China needs to play a bigger role in making rules for these areas, including the internet, the polar regions, deep sea and outer space, he said that it will extend greater support to cooperation mechanisms and projects on educational exchange, dialogue among civilizations, and ecological conservation. The Chinese leader also called for strengthening the role of the Chinese Belt and Road Initiative, as well as cooperation within such non-Western institutions as the Shanghai Cooperation Organization, the Conference on Interaction and Confidence Building Measures in Asia (CICA) and the East Asia Summit.[33]

Overall, the official position is more in keeping with the views of the Foreign Ministry and the arguments of the "doves," although official foreign policy statements give reason to believe that the arguments of the "hawks" have not fallen on deaf ears either. The "hawkish" public mood has already led Chinese officials to push the country's "core interests" more actively. While claiming that its foreign policy is fundamentally different from that of all other great powers since it never creates military bases abroad or uses unilateral economic sanctions against other countries to achieve political aims, in 2017 Beijing opened its first navel base in Djibouti (calling it a "support facility"). It also used economic sanctions in 2010 against Japan (protesting against the detention of a Chinese fishing trawler captain), in 2016 against Mongolia (trying to prevent the Dalai Lama's visits to that country) and against South Korea (in an attempt to stop the deployment of the THAAD system).

Speaking at the Central Conference on Work Relating to Foreign Affairs in Beijing in November 2014, Xi Jinping again emphasized that China

> should recognize that the growing trend toward a multi-polar world will not change. While being fully aware that the global economic adjust-

ment will not be smooth sailing, we need to recognize that economic globalization will not stop. While being fully alert to the grave nature of international tensions and struggle, we need to recognize that peace and development, the underlying trend of our times, will remain unchanged. While being keenly aware of the protracted nature of contest over the international order, we need to recognize that the direction of reform of the international system will remain unchanged. While fully recognizing the uncertainty in China's neighboring environment, we should realize that the general trend of prosperity and stability in the Asia-Pacific region will not change.

Xi also said that China should "work hard to form a network of high interdependence and mutual benefit through extensive and mutually beneficial business and technological cooperation." While saying that China "should make more friends while abiding by the principle of non-alignment and build a global network of partnerships," he also underscored that "We should firmly uphold China's territorial sovereignty, maritime rights and interests and national unity, and properly handle territorial and island disputes."[34]

So China is generally not interested in confrontation with anyone or in revolutionary changes in the existing world system. But it is determined to press for its evolution in a way that would benefit the country.

In this respect, China's response to the idea of the "Group of Two" put forward by Zbigniew Brzezinski in 2009 is quite interesting. Brzezinski's proposal was fully in line with the ideology of American dominance. He basically offered the role of a junior ally to China that was supposed to solve American problems where Washington could not do so on its own.[35] But Beijing politely turned down such a flattering offer that fundamentally ran counter to its foreign policy principles, which bar interference in the internal affairs of other countries and regions. Instead it made a counter-offer and invited the United States to build "a new type of relationship between major powers." The idea was that China would become not the US's agent in the world but its equal partner and would share its responsibility for some of the global problems that should be addressed on the basis of mutual advantages and compromises. But the United States is unlikely to agree to that.

On the whole, China, just like Russia, has left the idea of global communist totalitarianism far behind and no longer seeks to impose its model of development upon others. Instead, it is trying to occupy a place in the world that would match its new power and historical role, surrounded by peaceful and friendly states. But its economic interests go far beyond its territory. These aspirations, supported by economic success, significant financial resources, and the Chinese model of modernization without democracy, which is becoming increasingly popular with authoritarian leaders in developing countries, are a real challenge to the Western ideology of "democratism," according to which China, and actually the whole world, should Westernize and sooner or later submit to Western influence.

Many in the West consider the Chinese experience to fit into the theory of modernization, which holds that China is basically treading in the footsteps of Japan and the Asian Tigers, and economic modernization should be followed by democratization, as in South Korea and Taiwan. But Chinese experts reply to this by saying that China is so different in size from these countries that it cannot be compared with any of them. China is a separate civilization, and it will develop in its own way, using traditional Chinese recipes, not Western ones. Numerous publications that have appeared lately in China also conclude that traditional Chinese concepts of world order are much more useful than Western approaches.[36]

Time will tell whether China goes its own way or follows the path of other countries, in other words, whether it is going to turn into a big Taiwan (a developed democratized Chinese society) or a big Singapore (an economically and politically effective authoritarian society). But it is doubtful that even a democratized China would look up to the United States or anyone else in its policy and give up its own interests. At present, anti-American and anti-Japanese sentiment is much stronger in Chinese society than in the country's leadership.

Some US experts, like David Shambaugh, have been speaking of an imminent collapse of Communist Party rule in China.[37] Although this is most likely wishful thinking, at least for the foreseeable future, the Chinese system of power may face serious complications or even a crisis in the more distant future due to economic problems. But as the experience of the Soviet Union and Russia shows, even a hypothetical collapse of Communism and a drawn-out crisis can hardly lead to the Westernization of such a large country as China and its submission to Western interests.

At any rate, if the current tendencies persist, tensions between China and the West will inevitably increase in the long run, but not because of moral values, as in the case of Russia or Eurasian countries. Western moral novelties are much more acceptable for the pragmatic Chinese culture, which rejects monotheistic religion with its unknowable God whose commandments cannot be questioned. But Chinese culture is very different from Western culture in terms of social goals and cannot understand the West's eagerness to put the individual and the individual's rights above the public good and social justice. Nor can Chinese people accept the ideal of the minimal state that takes no care of its citizens. The highest value here is not the rights of the individual and minorities, but a well-organized society that can guarantee the well-being of the majority. It is these differences that will add to the geopolitical divergences, making them ever deeper. However, the existing economic interdependence will help to curb tensions and keep them from evolving into direct confrontation.

Whichever foreign policy line China ultimately adopts in the future, it will be a more active approach than the present one. Most likely, Beijing will simply maintain and gradually intensify its current policy course. Several factors will contribute to this intensification: the growth of China's power and influence, the interests of its outward-expanding economy, and the pressure of public opinion that holds that China is now ready to begin acting like a superpower. There are no influential forces in China demanding that leaders integrate the country into the global system on unchallenged Western terms: there are only those who call for caution so as not to undermine economic development. It is therefore inevitable that China will move toward stepped-up activity and greater independence. Of course, activity on the international stage can take different forms at different times – from greater participation in international peacekeeping operations alongside other countries, including Western states, to the decisive use of force to resolve territorial disputes. Naturally, the consequences of such actions will also vary. However, political, cultural, and ideological differences between China and Western "democratism" will deepen with time, and an increasingly powerful China will have ever less desire to compromise. That will eventually make China an alternative to the West as a major center of global influence.

Other Centers of Power and Their Associations

Apart from the aforementioned countries, India, Brazil, and several other states are turning into powerful non-Western centers. Being the biggest democracy in the world, India does not blindly follow the West. Like China, it pursues an independent foreign policy and tries to maintain constructive relations with all major global actors. In 2004, Indian prime minister Manmohan Singh described his country's foreign policy as "cooperative pluralism." Later he explained that the "idea of unity in diversity" and the philosophical tradition that inspired it "remain our great inheritance that we would like the entire world to embrace. The notion of cooperative pluralism and respect for diversity that is the basis of our democracy must also be the basis of global governance in the twenty-first century."[38] According to Indian experts, India has a unique experience. Having existed for centuries as a multicultural and multiconfessional country, it has preserved its civilizational unity based on respect for other people's views and traditions. This unique experience laid the foundation for Indian democracy, and the country wants to share it with the rest of the world to make it as pluralistic as its own society is. Based on these views, India refuses to put pressure on other countries and never joins any military actions initiated by the West or the world community in general. At the same time, India is one of the main suppliers of troops for the UN peacekeeping forces, whose mission is to maintain peace, not punish anyone.

Clearly, this ideal is at variance with the Western ideology of "democratism." While sharing its respect for democracy, it rejects the idea of imposing "progressive" ideals and models by force and punishment for deviating from them. And although India follows the West morally, it still remains firmly adhered to traditions. The leader of the Hindu nationalist Bharatiya Janata Party, Narendra Modi, and his government, which came to power in 2014, have further amplified the feeling of India's mission in the world and traditionalist tendencies inside the country. In 2015 Modi stressed that "diversity is the pride of India."[39] So India is likely to become less oriented to the West and pay more attention to other centers of power, even though economic interests and the closeness of their political systems will continue to sustain its cooperation with the West.

India is trying to improve relations with China because of economic imperatives, but serious problems in bilateral relations remain and the two countries are still locked in a territorial dispute. But more importantly, the world is witnessing the emergence of geopolitical disagreements between the two rising non-Western centers of power, whose interests clash in several island states that previously were within India's sphere of influence but are now a target of Beijing's economic expansion: the Maldives, the Seychelles, Mauritius, and Sri Lanka.

In 2015, Brazil was the world's ninth largest economy, with its gross domestic product exceeding that of Canada or Russia. Politically, it is a typical Latin American country with strong left-wing tendencies that have always existed in this part of the world in response to US attempts at domination. Two of the country's recent presidents, Lula da Silva and Dilma Rousseff, have been representatives of left-wing forces, and this has been the main reason for growing disagreements with the United States. Brazil's foreign policy in many ways has counteracted the American one.

Brazil's foreign policy concepts stress autonomy, which implies autonomy from other major powers, most importantly from the US. The earlier concepts of "autonomy through distance," "autonomy through participation" of the administration of Fernando Henrique Cardoso (1995–2002), and "autonomy through diversity" of Lula da Silva (2003–2010) and Dilma Rousseff (2011–16) differ only in the level of engagement with international institutions and the role of cooperation with non-Western emerging powers such as India, China, and Russia. According to a leading Brazilian foreign policy expert and diplomat, Gelson Fonseca, "Autonomy ... does not mean 'distance' from controversial international issues in order to protect the country against undesirable alignments ... Autonomy means participation, means the wish to influence the open agenda with values that express traditional [Brazilian] diplomacy."[40] The autonomy strategy is unlikely to change even if the new president, Michel Temer, returns to the "participation" approach.

Consolidation of Non-Western Centers

The collapse of the Soviet Union in the early 1990s caused a fundamental change to the long-standing system of international relations that was based on the confrontation between two centers of power. Although back in the Soviet era some researchers noted a trend toward a multipolar world as the leading states in each region grew in power, the Soviet Union's sudden departure from the scene left something of a vacuum. Although many states, even outside the Western world, disliked the Soviet Union and criticized it, its absence left many states, especially larger ones, wary of a certain threat. That threat stemmed, first, from the instability in the international situation resulting from the end of a bipolar system that had guaranteed a certain order, and second, from the possibility that the one remaining center of power – now freed from any external checks and balances – might encroach on the interests of others.

Thus, when the United States celebrated its victory in the Cold War and Francis Fukuyama declared the "end of history," China, India, Brazil and many other countries of Asia, Africa, and South America viewed that development with some uneasiness. Had the US shown restraint, subsequent events might have unfolded somewhat differently, but under Bill Clinton, and to a greater extent George

W. Bush, Washington set out to secure that victory and achieve world dominance for the United States. Europe either could not or would not pursue an independent course and, as always, kept in line with Washington's policy.

Under such circumstances, the disgruntled states have begun building bridges between themselves. That cooperation was not initially directed against the West because all of the participants in that process are largely tied to the Western system and value their collaboration with it. However, they looked for ways to coordinate their positions on those aspects of the new Western-dominated world that did not suit them. That desire led to the creation or strengthening of institutions and groups in which Western states did not participate: Association of Southeast Asian Nations (ASEAN) and various formats of associated cooperative endeavors, the Shanghai Cooperation Organization, Community of Latin American and Caribbean States (CELAC), and of course, the BRICS (Brazil, Russia, India, China, and South Africa).

Post-Bipolar System

Russia's refusal to follow the Western course is only the first poignant sign of confrontation between the West's united world project and the emerging multipolar world. So, at this point, the post-bipolar world can be described as interim and in transition from the global dominance of the West after the end of the Cold War to a multipolar world which is still forming (and no one knows if it can become a reality). In a multipolar world the influence of the Western center of power will diminish, while that of the other centers (China, India, Brazil, etc.) will grow. New centers of power will try to create zones of influence around their borders by snatching influence there from the West. This policy will be fiercely resisted by the West (as is now the case with Russia and China). Weaker non-Western centers of power will try to coordinate their actions against the most powerful center, but this does not mean they will aspire to create an anti-Western alliance. If the zones of influence of non-Western centers of power collide, conflicts may erupt between them (for example, China and India seem to be poised to start fighting for spheres of influence). The West (especially the United States) may use this struggle in its own interests. Because of its complexity, a real multipolar world with several more or less equal centers of power may not be so inevitable.

Medium or regional centers of power with their own goals and regional policy views, such as Vietnam, South Africa, Nigeria,

Venezuela, and the like, will play an important role in this new system. They can form temporary alliances with larger centers of power in order to achieve some local goals (as Vietnam is doing now, trying to use the United States in its territorial conflict with China). But the post-bipolar world will not fall apart completely into big and small centers of power. It will still face the same or ever more acute global problems that can only be solved jointly: a shortage of resources, overpopulation, pollution, nonproliferation of weapons of mass destruction, and others. Terrorism, primarily that brewed by Islamic extremism, poses a deadly global threat to humankind as a whole. Islamism is a second totalitarian ideology which cannot be traced to any one state but which nevertheless is quite attractive and wields some sort of "soft power" amplified by a radical reaction to the "immorality" and "sinfulness" of the modern world. This is one of the reasons why young Muslims living in Western countries, where they can clearly see the discrepancy between their beliefs and Western civilization, often become radical Islamists.

The resolution of these problems will require a mechanism for interaction, which can be created if the main centers of power come to a consensus on the limited area where their views converge and "agree to disagree" on all other issues, while avoiding sharp confrontation. This will essentially revive the notion of "peaceful coexistence" that was part of the bipolar world. Its meaning was stated during Nikita Khrushchev's rule: while not sharing global development goals or social system ideals, we refuse to wage wars against each other and will try to come to agreement where agreement is possible. Existing global governance institutions such as the UN and its Security Council would be the best choice for the working bodies of this mechanism, as they simply have no alternative. But this does not mean that this system should not change. On the contrary, it should be gradually reformed by mutual consent in order to ensure more adequate representation for the growing centers of power. The only alternative to this would be an unpredictable world with no rules, where all fight against all.

The development of Russian-Chinese cooperation should be considered in the overall context of the formation of a multipolar world. The following chapters of this book look at the changing Russian and Chinese approaches to the global situation as the trend toward multipolarity intensifies, as well as the way those policies add momentum to that trend.

2

RUSSIA IN THE EYES OF CHINA

The Fate of the "Elder Brother"

From the time the People's Republic of China was founded in 1949, its relations with the Soviet Union/Russia have passed through several stages, changing from an alliance to a period of confrontation, and culminating in today's "strategic partnership and cooperation." What began as a friendship between two communist giants (1949 to the end of the 1950s) shifted to a period of polemics and confrontation (the early 1960s to the end of the 1970s), normalization (the end of the 1970s to 1989), the establishment of relations with modern Russia (the 1990s), and finally, the formation of a strategic partnership (from the early twenty-first century to the present). Each of these stages had its own particular causes and characteristics. And over that period, the Chinese authorities and members of the expert community naturally changed their views concerning the Soviet Union, and later, Russia.

In the 1950s the Soviet Union was a natural ally for the newly founded People's Republic of China. First, Stalin's Soviet Union armed the Chinese communists and provided significant assistance in both their defeat of the Kuomintang army and their rise to power. Second, during the first decade, the Chinese and Soviet communists were united by their ideology to form a common view of the historical process and the future world. Third, the United States and its Western allies left Beijing no other choice. If any senior Chinese officials remained who hoped to maintain at least partial ties with the "capitalist world," that became impossible after the outbreak of the Korean War and the persecution of "procommunist elements" in the US. The Chinese leadership understood it. In his memoirs, Chinese diplomat Liu Xiao recalled the instructions he received from Mao Zedong and Zhou Enlai before leaving for Moscow to take up his post as China's first communist ambassador to Russia. "The Soviet Union plays an important role in the world revolutionary process and occupies an important position in international relations," Mao emphasized. "It is important for us to develop Chinese-Soviet relations and strengthen Chinese-Soviet friendship; China needs to build; we need the comprehensive assistance of the Soviet Union."[1] Zhou Enlai spoke in a similar vein.[2]

Chinese authors writing in the 1950s about bilateral relations deferred to their Soviet colleagues by recognizing the Soviet Union as the leader of the international communist movement and China as its "younger brother." They described China as a student receiving assistance, but also as the first communist state in Asia that was responsible for spreading communism and the struggle against imperialism on that continent.[3] This is understandable because it was the party platform and contradicting it was impossible at that time. Mao Zedong, the "Great Leader" himself, repeatedly spoke of the great friendship with the Soviet Union. In March 1953 he wrote in an article in the *People's Daily* marking Stalin's death: "The Communist Party of the Soviet Union is a party nurtured personally by Lenin and Stalin; it is the most advanced, the most experienced, and the most theoretically cultivated party in the world. This party has been our model in the past, is our model at present, and will still be our model in the future."[4] In a speech in 1957, and referring to the Soviet-Chinese treaty of 1950, he said:

> China has received brotherly assistance towards its socialist construction in many fields from the Soviet Union . . . Soon after it was founded, the People's Republic of China concluded a Treaty of Friendship, Alliance and Mutual Assistance with the Soviet Union. This is a great alliance of two great socialist countries. We share the same destiny and the same life-spring with the Soviet Union and the entire socialist camp. . . . We regard it as the sacred international obligation of all socialist countries to strengthen the solidarity of the socialist countries headed by the Soviet Union.[5]

During the later rupture between Moscow and Beijing, both sides leveled numerous accusations against each other with regard to this earlier period in their relations. The initiative also came from Mao, who was now accusing Moscow of all kinds of sins. Along with Chinese scholars, he voiced complaints regarding the 1950 treaty and its accompanying documents. Mao Zedong argued that Stalin had imposed "two bitter fruits" on China: agreements on joint companies, and an additional agreement on the prohibition of foreign capital in Manchuria and Xinjiang. Mao likened these agreements to the practice of imperialist powers that had imposed unequal treaties on China in the past.[6]

To understand the reason for their disagreements during those years, it is necessary to delve into the theory of communism, on the one hand, and to understand the peculiarities of Chinese communist thinking, on the other. According to the theories of Karl Marx, classical communism is the final social and historical formation, a society characterized by an abundance of goods that adheres to the principle of "from each according to his ability, to each according to his needs." Such a society must come about as a result of social revolution in a developed capitalist society which already has an abundance of goods, but where the bourgeoisie prevents their equitable distribution – thus preventing that society from observing the principle of "from each according to his ability, to each according to his needs." Once the proletariat overthrows that government and takes power, it implements equitable distribution, or what is known as communism. Moreover, that should happen throughout the world, and not only in one country. However, in the Soviet Union, and later in China, the communists came to power in backward societies, and their ruling authority did not spread throughout the world. This led to the formation of so-called "rightist" and "leftist" communist groups. The "rightists" argued that, under such circumstances, some sort of transitional period was needed during which some elements of capitalism – such as a market economy and private ownership – would be permitted, so that capitalism would eventually develop to the necessary level under the aegis of communist leaders. The "leftists" maintained that the complete and immediate socialization of the entire economy would liberate the working class from oppression and that the resulting widespread enthusiasm would lead to economic growth. They also insisted that preserving selected elements of capitalist exploitation was a betrayal of communist ideals.

In the Soviet Union, Stalin used the "rightist" ideology to crush the "leftists," then went on to destroy the "rightists" because he was not prepared to allow either private initiative or the enthusiasm of the masses. He introduced a concept of socialism as the first step of communism, but characterized by a fully socialized economy that did not yet have an abundance of goods. But because Stalin viewed China as a less developed society than the Soviet Union, he recommended that the Chinese communists, after coming to power, start on a "rightist" course by preserving elements of private ownership, labor unions which would even have a right to go on strike, representation of society's "nonproletarian" strata in government bodies, and so on.

That immediately led to disagreements within the Chinese Communist Party. One group of leaders (Liu Shaoqi, Deng Xiaoping, and others) – the "rightists" in this context – proposed a transitional period in line with Stalin's recommendations. The "leftists," led by Mao Zedong and Gao Gang, advocated immediate socialization of the economy. The political victory of the "leftist" communists in China led them into an ideological conflict with the bureaucratic "centrists" in the Soviet Union. The "leftists" in China believed that the rapid and full socialization of production, the introduction of the direct distribution of goods, the elimination of money, and other such measures would lead to a huge wave of enthusiasm from the masses that would enable China swiftly to surpass highly developed capitalist societies. They were even skeptical of the communist bureaucracy and considered it an obstacle to development and the initiative of the people. This gave rise to Mao Zedong's idea of a periodic "Cultural Revolution" whereby he would demolish government bodies every ten years. The guarantee that this was the right path lay in bypassing the bureaucracy and merging the initiative of the masses directly with unbounded leader worship. Traditional education was rejected in the belief that communism could only be created by new masses who were unspoiled by the old culture and who possessed a wholly transformed awareness. In foreign policy, "leftist" Chinese leaders considered war against world imperialism not only useful, but even necessary for communism to become victorious on a world scale.

Soviet communists, by contrast, considered bureaucracy the very basis of their authority and were strongly averse to all unorganized initiatives. At the same time, they followed a far more cautious course, supported traditional education and culture and, after Nikita Khrushchev came to power, spoke out against an excessive cult of personality and in favor of "peaceful coexistence" with the capitalist world.

Chinese authors accused the Soviet Union of egoism, providing inadequate assistance during the Civil War between the communists and the Kuomintang, and even trying to divide China into two parts. They claimed that it attempted to install individuals sympathetic to Moscow and the Communist International in the Chinese leadership, failed to reject imperialism by refusing to withdraw its troops from Chinese soil, forced Beijing to make economic concessions, refused to supply China with nuclear and other weapons, and so on. With regard to the situation at that time, they accused the Soviet Union of abandoning communist principles, refusing to recognize that the war with imperialism was an inevitable tool in communism's historic victory on a world scale, rejecting the idea that a true communist economy should emerge at once, and so on.

Until recently, China has publicly declared that the 1950 Treaty of Friendship was "unequal" and that Moscow had tried to impose certain undesirable conditions on Beijing. Unlike in the period of disagreement between China and the Soviet Union, however, Beijing acknowledges the positive role the treaty has played and its necessity at that time. For example, former Chinese ambassador to Russia and renowned Chinese expert on Russia Li Fenglin expressed this opinion during the year marking the sixtieth anniversary of the treaty. In his view, "The Chinese-Soviet alliance was crucial for the consolidation of power in the new China and for the country's economic importance. However, if one speaks in terms of a ward, as China was, Chinese-Soviet relations were unequal, and the Chinese-Soviet treaty was also unequal."[7]

In the 1950s, the "leftist" authorities in China had not consolidated their hold on power, the "rightists" enjoyed considerable influence, and the Chinese leadership accepted the leading role of the Soviet Union. By the end of the decade, however, polemics gradually overtook that friendship. Chinese communists criticized the Soviet Union for bureaucratization and hindering the building of communism – that is, for "revisionism" with regard to the true Marxist doctrine. The Chinese viewed Moscow's rejection of leader worship not simply as a threat to Mao Zedong's authority, but also as a sign of bureaucratic degeneracy. Beijing also accused Moscow of pursuing a foreign policy of "social imperialism" that served the interests of its own bureaucracy, and not those of world communism. For Beijing, this meant that the Soviet Union had rejected the positive role of the war against imperialism.[8]

Only in that context is it possible to understand the attitude of Chinese authors toward the Soviet Union at that time. They faulted the Soviet Union for both its domestic and foreign policies. Regarding the former, they disliked the Soviet Union's bureaucratization, lack of faith in the people's initiative, and underestimation of the role of the leader (as seen in criticisms of Stalin). They faulted Moscow's foreign policy for colluding with imperialism at the expense of China, rejecting the concept of the need for world war, and reviving the imperialism of the tsarist period. Beijing leveled the particular charges that, in the

1950s and earlier, Stalin pursued imperialist motives under the guise of friendship by failing to fully support the Chinese communists during the Civil War, cooperating with the Kuomintang, dictatorially anointing the Soviet Union as China's "big brother," attempting to hold onto Soviet military bases in Dalian and Port Arthur on Chinese territory, obtaining concessions such as the Chinese Eastern Railway and several joint projects in Xinjiang, refusing to transfer nuclear weapons to China, failing to support the "liberation" of Taiwan, and so on. China also blamed the Soviet leadership for its unwillingness to admit that tsarist Russia had pursued an exclusively imperialist policy toward Beijing by attempting to seize Chinese territory, and that the Russian-Chinese treaties of the nineteenth century that determined, among other things, the border between the two countries were "unequal."[9]

Explaining the Sino-Soviet split, a group of official Chinese historians headed by Hu Sheng, president of the Academy of Social Sciences, wrote in the early 1990s:

> Conflicts and disagreements between China and the Soviet Union had two aspects. One was ideological. Acute differences arose between the two parties concerning their positions on the international situation, the strategy and tactics of the world communist movement, and their respective foreign and domestic policies. The other aspect concerned the leadership of the Communist Party of the Soviet Union that attempted to dictate its will, demanding that the CCP carry out its instructions. It tried to control China and to tie it both militarily and diplomatically to its strategy of "Soviet-American cooperation aimed at world domination."[10]

After China launched political reforms and its relations with the Soviet Union and Russia gradually improved, Beijing acknowledged that many of its earlier allegations had been unfair. For example, in an important book on China–Russia relations published in 2009, Chen Kaike of the Institute of Modern History of the Chinese Academy of Social Sciences took a more positive approach, praising the role of the Russian Orthodox Mission in China (which at that time behaved as a de facto diplomatic mission) in developing Russia's policy towards China during the Taiping Rebellion (1850–64).[11] Zhang Li of the Center for the History of the Northeast at Dalian University took a more balanced and equitable view of Russia's policy towards China during the Boxer Rebellion (1898–1901).[12] And Wang Xiaoju of the Institute of World History of the Chinese Academy of Social Sciences wrote positively about the role played by the Russian diaspora in the development of Northeast China.[13]

Towards Strategic Partnership

The normalization of relations between the two countries began long before today's problems in relations between Russia and the West. Normalization, reaching back to the serious crisis that accompanied armed clashes on the border at the end of the 1960s, began as early as the final years of Leonid Brezhnev's time in office. After the largely unsuccessful military campaign by China in Vietnam and strong international reaction to Soviet intervention in Afghanistan in 1979, it became clear to the leaders of both countries that the continuous sharp confrontation was harming both their internal positions and their international prestige. From the start of perestroika and the deepening of China's reforms, Moscow and Beijing increasingly refrained from ideological arguments and more and more actively discussed concrete questions of a bilateral partnership. Choosing an independent foreign policy, Beijing shifted away from forming a united front against the Soviet Union and stopped seeing Moscow as its main enemy. For Gorbachev, normalization of relations with China became one of his main foreign policy objectives, which was supported inside the country by both reformers, who saw Chinese reforms as an example to be imitated, and conservatives, who were pleased with the successes of a communist neighbor.

The collapse of the communist regime in the Soviet Union was deeply disappointing for Chinese communists. Because it was a politically sensitive issue, there are few direct references to those apprehensions in Chinese literature. However, in an article published in *Renmin Ribao* on December 16, 1991, Chinese foreign minister Qian Qichen stressed that "the internal political situation in the Soviet Union has become extremely worrying."[14] According to Evgeny Bazhanov, Chinese leaders and experts saw several potential sources of trouble. First, they viewed the collapse of the Soviet Union as a major blow to the international communist movement. Second, Beijing worried about its potential impact on the security situation in Eurasia and the world in general. Third, Beijing saw a danger in the prospect of a rapprochement between Russia and the West that could change the global balance of power. Fourth, it believed that the collapse of Marxism in the Soviet Union could negatively influence the ideological situation in China.[15]

The Chinese authorities treated the new Russian state with some caution, and for understandable reasons. Of course, Chinese leaders had criticized various aspects of the Soviet Union's domestic and foreign policies, but they could not have imagined that the world's first and most powerful communist state and its allies would not only fail to correct their shortcomings, but would entirely cease to exist. Beijing also could not fail to take note of the fact that Moscow had begun to emphasize the fundamental role of human rights in foreign policy and had declared the importance of its international commitments in this regard.

Geopolitical considerations also played a role. Liu Dexi and Sun Yan, researchers at the CPC's Central Party School and Beijing University, characterized the impact that the collapse of the Soviet Union had on the international situation and China:

> With regard to the international situation, China felt that the collapse of the Soviet Union and Russia's accession to the Western camp meant the end of the bipolar model, thereby turning the United States into the sole world power and enabling it to begin addressing international problems from that position. The peoples of the world will face the major challenge of combating hegemonic actions and power politics. The collapse of the second world nuclear power raises the issue of nuclear arms control ... Radical changes in Eastern Europe and the breakup of the Soviet Union dealt a severe blow to the cause of world socialism and the international communist movement, and led to their serious diminution. That unquestionably created an unfavorable situation for socialist China – where the authorities belong to the Communist Party – and forced on it the necessity of stern reflection.

Among other dangers, the authors noted the possibility of instability near China's borders due to conflicts between the newly independent states.[16] In addition, the collapse of the Soviet Union came at a difficult time when Beijing was experiencing worsening relations with the West over its suppression of antigovernment protests in 1989.

Despite feeling a natural ideological distrust of the new Russian authorities, the Chinese communists were pragmatic when faced with the reality of the situation. They decided to strengthen socialism in China through economic development, and for that they needed to have good relations with all countries, particularly neighbors. Seeing in Russia a potential economic, trade, and to some extent political partner, Beijing decided to pursue the same course toward Moscow as it had toward other nonsocialist countries since the beginning of reforms – namely, to do business with the government in power, despite ideological differences, and to derive the greatest possible benefit from the situation. After putting down antigovernment protests in 1989, Beijing became especially wary of "public disorder" and worried that the worst possible scenario for China would be for Russia to completely collapse and fall into chaos.

As a result, Chinese authorities at the highest level decided to develop relations with Moscow. As early as March 1990, Deng Xiaoping said: "Whatever changes have occurred in the Soviet Union, we should calmly develop relations with it, including political relations, based on the five principles of peaceful coexistence, and without engaging in ideological polemics."[17] "Based on this statement," Qian Qichen, foreign minister at the time, would later write, "Chinese diplomacy developed a course for relations with Russia in the political, economic, and other fields, and also with other Commonwealth of Independent States countries on the basis of equality, mutual benefit, and non-interference in each others' internal affairs, disregarding their various ideologies and social systems."[18]

Speaking at a meeting of the Standing Committee of the National People's Congress on December 25, 1991, Qian Qichen explained:

> The collapse of the Soviet Union signaled the end of the US-Soviet confrontation, the Cold War between the East and West, and the bipolar structure of the world community that has existed for almost half a century since World War II. The Chinese people have relations of traditional friendship with the peoples of the former Soviet republics. The Chinese government, supporting the principle of non-interference in the internal affairs of other countries, respects the choice of the peoples of other states and will continue to develop friendly and cooperative relations with these republics.[19]

China required several years to develop the optimal policy toward Russia. According to Viktor Larin, Beijing based its approach "on a realistic assessment of the situation and on involving Russia's political, economic, and social potential toward helping with China's economic development." He also explained that China's active approach toward its northern neighbor was "to some extent also connected with leaders' fears of the possible establishment of 'ties between Russia and NATO.'"[20] Chinese author Xi Laiwang described the principles of China's relations with Moscow as "three don'ts" and "three dos": "do not enter into an alliance, do not oppose each other, do not take action against a third party," and at the same time, do "be good neighbors, good partners, and good friends."[21]

The decision to fully develop relations with the new Russia in a pragmatic manner was linked to internal developments in China. Those in the Beijing leadership who, following the events of 1989, had advocated a more traditional and ideological approach to the outside world, and who opposed many aspects of the country's market-based economic reforms, again lost their influence at the 14th Congress of the CPC in October 1992. That Congress confirmed the course set by Deng Xiaoping for accelerating economic growth and deepening market reforms, a policy requiring that China have normal relations with the outside world and develop mutually beneficial cooperation with neighboring states, of which Russia was the largest.

By the first half of the 1990s, Chinese leaders had already begun making anti-unipolar references in their approach to Russia. Beijing began to realize that Russia – whose relations with the West were gradually growing more complicated – could become a partner in the struggle against the dictates of the dominant power center led by the US. China was careful, however, to voice that idea without referring directly to the United States. Still, its relations with Russia were based on principles that were clearly meant as an alternative to the unipolar world that Washington was bent on achieving. Chinese leader Jiang Zemin clearly formulated these principles during a visit to Russia in September 1994. He outlined his vision for bilateral relations in his keynote address at the Moscow State Institute of International Relations (MGIMO University) on September 3. Saying that theirs was a "new type" of relationship, Jiang Zemin listed the following six principles necessary to their further development: (1) strengthen mutual understanding and trust; resolve all problems in the spirit of enduring friendship and good-neighborliness; (2) show mutual respect for the development path chosen by each side and steadily develop normal relations between the two countries; (3) do not change the basic policy of developing friendship and cooperation between the two countries, regardless of how the international situation develops; (4) make full use of favorable conditions in the two countries, actively develop mutually beneficial and complementary economic relations, promote common prosperity; (5) strengthen law and order, develop personal contacts in a healthy and orderly way, turn the Chinese-Russian border into a bridge of peace, friendship, and prosperity; (6) enhance mutual consultation and cooperation, expand joint constructive, active work for worldwide peace, stability, and development.[22]

China also increasingly valued relations with its northern neighbor. In late 1996, Chinese leader Jiang Zemin presented new principles necessary for relations with Russia: "good neighbors, equality and trust, mutual benefit and cooperation, common development."[23] Two years later, in an interview with the newspaper *Rossiiskaya Gazeta*, he again referred to Russian-Chinese relations as "international relations of a new type" based on five principles of peaceful coexistence, generally accepted norms of international law, and the conscious choice of the leaders of the two countries based on "the aggregate positive and negative experiences the two countries have accumulated throughout the history of their relations." He noted that these relations are "not those of alliance, are not confrontational, and are not aimed against any third country."[24]

China welcomed the shift in Russian foreign policy away from the ideological and toward the pragmatic, and saw it as resulting from Moscow's disappointment with the policies of the West. A leading Chinese expert on Russia, Li Jingjie, wrote,

> The collapse of the Soviet Union led to the end of the ideological confrontation between the US and Russia. In order to prevent the Communist authorities from coming to power again, the United States fully supported Russian "democrats" in conducting radical reforms. Russian "democrats" held numerous illusions about the US-led West. For the sake of early entry into the "big family of the world of Western civilization" and the creation of a "great Euro-Atlantic community stretching from Vancouver to Vladivostok," they sought Western aid for Russia along the lines of a "Marshall Plan," pursued a one-sided foreign policy oriented exclusively to the West ... As can be seen, Russia found no place at all for China in its foreign policy. However, serious consequences resulted from Russia following in the US wake in international affairs and carrying out radical domestic reforms according to the scenario of international financial organizations and US experts. The disdainful attitude of the US toward Russia's interests, as well as its pervasive "imperial behavior" as the self-proclaimed "sole superpower" caused dissatisfaction among the Russian authorities. The Russian leadership began to realize that a policy of one-sided orientation toward the West was unacceptable and that only a balance between the East and the West would meet Russia's national interests ... President Yeltsin's visit to China in December 1992 took place against such a backdrop. The establishment and development of good-neighborly and friendly relations between Russian and China met those needs well. The strengthening of good-neighborly, friendly relations between such great powers as China and Russia undoubtedly helped China overcome the isolation it experienced as a result of the anti-China policy of the US.[25]

Overall, Russian-Chinese relations developed incrementally in the 1990s. Their growing trade and economic cooperation provided an important stimulus to strengthening bilateral relations and gradually became a significant factor in the economic life of both countries. China obtained a range of products from Russia that it could not procure elsewhere, either at all (e.g. weapons, due to Western sanctions), or in sufficient quantities, and developed its northeast region through cross-border trade. Beijing appreciated Moscow's decision to assume the debts that the Soviet Union had incurred toward China. With Russian manufacturing in decline and the economy in recession, trade with China ensured the survival of Russia's military-industrial complex and several heavy industries. It also helped solve the labor shortage and the need to supply the inhabitants of eastern Russia. That was important, despite the various problems associated with the delivery of low-quality goods, smuggling, and an increase in Chinese migration.

Changes in the Chinese Approach to Russia under Putin

As the new Russian president, Vladimir Putin restored order to the system of governance, and this had a positive impact on Russian-Chinese relations. China has always valued order, especially after the "Cultural Revolution." Moreover, in the 1990s Beijing had serious concerns about the unpredictability of its northern neighbor. China always had some worries regarding Boris Yeltsin because of the instability of his policies and even his personal behavior.[26] A strong opinion developed in China that under the new Russian leader it was possible to build fresh and deeper relations with Russia. In addition, developments in the international situation and concerns about increased US foreign policy activity required that China step up its search for highly trustworthy foreign policy partners. In that context, an important step was the signing of the Treaty of Good-Neighborliness and Friendly Cooperation with Russia in 2001.

Speaking at the fifth anniversary commemoration of the signing of that treaty, China's ambassador to Moscow, Liu Guchang, explained its necessity and significance.

> In the spring of 2000, in the context of preparations for Vladimir Putin's first visit to China as Russian president, China conducted a comprehensive assessment of Sino-Russian relations in the 1990s. We found that for almost ten years, from the moment the smooth transition was made from Sino-Soviet to Sino-Russian relations in 1991, China and Russia, as two major powers, grew continually closer and the ties between them rapidly developed ... At the same time, we felt that since China and Russia are two major neighboring countries, the level of development of our relationship was still very far from its enormous potential and the expectations of our peoples, and that significant potential for their development existed. Although the settlement of a number of border

issues between the two countries represented serious progress, negotiations in the remaining areas advanced with great difficulty; bilateral cooperation in specific areas was slow, the annual volume of trade hovered around $5 billion–$7 billion; and the public's mood concerning the development of bilateral relations left much to be desired. The idea of a so-called "Chinese threat" still held currency in Russia; in China, prejudice and concern often sounded regarding the prospects of Russia's course. Discussions between the two sides on a number of sensitive issues were not truly candid. The Chinese side carefully studied the situation and concluded that the root of the problem was a lack of mutual trust. We had an idea: to reach agreement on and sign a legal document that would reflect the goals and principles of the more than one dozen documents both sides had adopted in the 1990s, and that would put them in legal form. That would eliminate suspicion, strengthen mutual trust and provide guidelines for the development of relations between the two countries.[27]

Evaluating the international significance of the agreement, Liu Guchang said, "The Treaty gives the UN a central place with regard to international peace and development, opposes unilateral actions that bypass the UN, and demonstrates that the international community is striving relentlessly toward multi-polarity and the democratization of international relations." He also stressed that, in five years' time, the concept and principles of the treaty would "remain relevant benchmarks for the healthy development of modern international relations.[28]

And although Moscow took steps to improve relations with Washington after the terrorist attack on the US in 2001, China took a more cautious position. Whereas China had no disagreements with Russia, it had serious concerns about the US, including the belief that Washington was using its fight against terrorism as a pretext for remaining too long in Afghanistan and Central Asia – drawing close to China's borders in the process. Although at the official level, Beijing spoke a great deal about the need to work together to fight terrorism, unofficial Chinese observers leveled rather sharp criticisms at the US for causing a large number of casualties among the civilian population of Afghanistan and undervaluing the role of the UN. Many in Beijing viewed the deployment of international coalition forces in Central Asian states as a manifestation of "hegemony," with a desire to encircle China and to move closer to the troubled areas of Xinjiang and Tibet.

The reason for this approach is that, although in China there are different views concerning US policies, many considered the threat from the US to be as great as that from Islamist terrorism. Beijing worried that Washington's desire for international cooperation would evaporate as soon as its mission in Afghanistan was completed, and that the US troops it left behind would not stabilize the situation in neighboring Muslim regions – which Beijing would not oppose – but would threaten Chinese interests.

Because of these fears, China took an ambiguous view of Russia's sharp policy shift toward unconditional support of the US and the West after September 11, 2001, seeing in that move a possible bias in favor of the West. Many in China thought that Russia received nothing in return for its unconditional support of the US in its anti-terror operations. They were seriously concerned that Moscow would return to the unilateral concessions of its pro-Western policy of the early 1990s, or that Russia could even join the "hegemonic" US course. Were that to happen, China would inevitably stand alone against the US – a situation Beijing definitely did not want.[29]

As a result, from the Chinese point of view, there was a threat that Russia and the US could reach a deal on missile defense and the expansion of NATO without regard for Beijing's interests. By the way, some circles in Russian society had the same doubts about Moscow's new course. Beijing would have liked to see Moscow take a more active position by pressuring Washington to formally abandon its plans for a new missile defense system or else pursue only a limited deployment, to halt the expansion of NATO, and to sign formal strategic arms reduction agreements. Moreover, Moscow could have coordinated its position actively with China on all these issues, especially because the two countries shared almost identical positions on each.

Chinese experts most likely concluded that Russia changed its policies not out of a desire to maintain a balance between the US and China, but out of necessity in reaction to Washington's course. Thus, according to a senior analyst of the official Xinhua press agency, Wan Chencai, after the events of September 11, 2001,

> [Russia] lost a great deal and gained very little by entering into a "strategic partnership" with the United States. The US did not reckon with the fact that Russia opposed the war in Iraq – a conflict that further constricted Russia's strategic space. Therefore, although Russia maintained its "strategic partnership relationship" with the US after the war, it did not want to become a "junior partner" to Washington. Russia should strengthen its relations with China, not only to improve its position in dealings with the United States, but also because of internal factors.[30]

However, concerns that Russia would make a new pivot to the West quickly evaporated. The new Chinese leader, Hu Jintao, chose Russia for his first visit abroad, and spoke at the MGIMO on May 28, 2003. In clear language, he laid out the reasons why Beijing values its relations with Moscow. Expressing satisfaction with Vladimir Putin's political course, Hu Jintao stated that the Chinese people are glad that "in recent years Russia has firmly defended state sovereignty and territorial integrity, and maintains social and political stability and relatively rapid economic growth." Referring to the international arena, he said that Russia "actively advocates a multipolar world and the democratization of international relations. Its place in the world is steadily rising." The Chinese leader also hastened to dispel Russian fears about the intentions of the new Chinese leadership by declaring that Beijing would continue the previous course of bilateral relations "in carrying out comprehensive strategic cooperation in such fields as politics, the economy, science and technology, the humanitarian sphere, international affairs, and so on . . ."[31]

On March 20, 2003, the United States launched military operations in Iraq to overthrow the regime of Saddam Hussein. During the preparatory stage, the US tried unsuccessfully to give legitimacy to those operations by obtaining the approval of the UN Security Council. That, in turn, prompted Russia and China to adopt a united position of withholding support for the US, which at that time was not supported even by some close allies – France and Germany. This time, Beijing took a favorable view of Moscow's position, which was far more balanced and consistent than its approach to the crisis in Yugoslavia and, later, its unconditional support of the methods the US employed in fighting terrorism.

The Chinese leader visited Russia twice in 2005, and his participation in the sixtieth anniversary commemoration of victory in the Great Patriotic War on May 8–9 was very symbolic. During that visit, Hu Jintao invited Soviet veterans to a reception at the Chinese embassy in Moscow, where he personally paid tribute to the assistance the Soviet Union extended to China during the war years. This recognition was important because, during the schism between the two countries, China customarily blamed the Soviet Union for providing too little assistance, and for sending most of that aid to the Kuomintang rather than to the communists, thereby inhibiting the CPC. The Chinese leader said:

> In that brutal war, the Chinese and Soviet people fought shoulder to shoulder and cemented their wartime friendship. At the crucial moment,

the Soviet Army extended invaluable assistance to the Chinese people in ending the anti-Japanese war. Many of the veterans here in the Embassy today took part in the fighting in northeast China. I take this opportunity to express my heartfelt gratitude. The Chinese people will be eternally grateful to the Russian people for this assistance.[32]

By the second half of the first decade of the twenty-first century, an impression had formed in China that relations with Russia were developing steadily. Beijing saw that the two countries shared common views on most international issues, and both envisaged a future world based on multipolarity. The Chinese foreign minister explained this unity in an interview on June 24, 2007 with the magazine *Russia-China: 21st Century*. "China and Russia hold common positions on such major issues as working to establish a multipolar world, and establishing a just and rational international order," he said. "They have close contact and cooperation on Iraq, the nuclear problem in Iran, and North Korea. That has played and does play an important role in facilitating a successful resolution of these problems and in promoting peace and stability in the region and the world." The Chinese foreign minister also stressed that, in order to jointly cope with challenges and ensure international and regional security, the two countries had abandoned the stereotypical thinking of the Cold War era and outdated models of interstate relations according to which states must be either allied or in confrontation.[33] According to Yang Jiechi, the new type of interstate relations – involving no formal alliance and nonconfrontational, not directed against any third countries, and aligned with the purposes and principles of the UN Charter and other universally recognized norms of international law – set a "good example for the international community of how to develop interstate relations."[34]

The specific phrasing used in this and similar official statements is important. Thus, the reference to the Russian-Chinese desire for a multipolar world and the establishment of a just and rational international order was, of course, intended to convey that the current unipolar world toward which Beijing contends Washington and its allies are striving is both unjust and irrational. The mention of bilateral cooperation on Iraq, the Iranian nuclear problem, and North Korea implies that Beijing opposes US policy in those regions – as well as that of Japan and South Korea with regard to North Korea.

It also tacitly criticizes those unnamed opponents (clearly, the US and its allies) for not having rejected stereotypical Cold War thinking and of using their old alliances to continue their policy of confrontation with others that are not a part of their group – primarily China and Russia. And finally, it is clear that Russian-Chinese relations are important for China not only for their own sake, but also as a model for the type of relations Beijing would like to build with other major powers such as the US and Japan. However, those powers typically shun such a model in favor of a more confrontational course that challenges China to alter its approach to foreign and domestic policy.

Leading Chinese experts who are at liberty to speak more freely confirm these conclusions. Thus, Li Jingjie, the former director of the Institute of Russia, Eastern Europe and Central Asia of the Chinese Academy of Social Sciences, wrote in 2006 that it is characteristic of their bilateral relations that Beijing and Moscow respect the free choice of their respective populations.

> The leaders of the two countries have repeatedly stated that the people of every country have the right to make an independent choice as to the social system, ways, and models of development in accordance with national characteristics. This position taken by China and Russia differs from that of the 1960s and 1970s, when China and the Soviet Union competed to take the most "orthodox course" in Marxism while accusing each other of "revisionism" and "dogmatism"; it also differs from the position of the US, that exports "democracy" by interfering in the internal affairs of other countries under the pretext of "humanitarian aid."[35]

At the same time, the Chinese believed that several factors hindered them from achieving the development goals to which they aspired. Among those factors, according to many in China, was the lack of understanding in Russia as to the true goals of Chinese foreign policy. Government officials as well as members of the expert community made statements to this effect. The China Association for the Study of the History of Sino-Russian Relations held a seminar in Beijing in late 2005 devoted to Cultural Factors in Sino-Russian Strategic Cooperation. Participants discussed both the achievements and problems in Sino-Russian cultural cooperation. One problem mentioned was the "unfortunate tendency" among those in China to equate today's Russia with the Soviet Union. According to Guan Guihai, deputy dean of Peking University School of International Studies,

> Many people in China, even those who are well-educated, continue to perceive Russia through such cultural symbols as songs like "Moscow Nights," "Katyusha," and so on, and few are familiar with modern Russian culture. There is also a trend in China to categorize Russia as a Western state because it rejected socialism and the Communist Party

leadership. Consequently, they believe that China and Russia "follow different paths."

Regarding the situation in Russia, he points to the widespread notion of a "Chinese threat" that, although not a dominant concept, nevertheless exerts a negative impact on mutual trust and strategic partnership.[36]

Responding to a journalist's question in 2007, the Chinese ambassador to Russia, Liu Guchang, said that despite the rapid development of bilateral relations and a deepening understanding of China among the general population, Russians remained "not very highly" informed about China. He divided those with little knowledge of China into three groups: those who have heard something about China's development, but remain unfamiliar with the real situation and have only a poor understanding of modern Chinese life; those who hold no opinion of or interest in China and have no idea of modern China; and the few who, under the influence of biased Western media, have formed a prejudiced attitude toward China and its foreign and domestic policies. At the same time, Liu Guchang argues that the Chinese do not know enough about Russia.[37]

Listing the problems and challenges in Chinese-Russian relations, Li Jingjie wrote in 2006 that there is, to some extent, a perception in Russian society of a "Chinese threat." He noted that part of the Russian population has misgivings about China's rapid growth and worries that China's rise will shift the balance of power away from Russia, disturb the geopolitical balance in East Asia, and turn Russia into a junior partner. Some also worry that China's growing influence in Central Asia could impinge on Russian interests there, that economic cooperation between Russia and China is insufficiently developed, and that the youth of both countries know very little about each other.[38]

At the same time, according to Li Jingjie, Russian concerns about the "Chinese threat" stem from differences in the two civilizations, the fact that the two countries have several diverging interests, and that China is on the rise while Russia, "after the collapse of the Soviet Union, has been in a long phase of strategic contraction." The situation "depends on China, that must prove by its actions that its development not only poses no threat to Russia, but presents it with a historic opportunity." For their part, Russians must "overcome their psychological hang-ups and reconcile themselves to the fact that the neighboring state is developing and growing stronger."[39]

Some Chinese authors have even expressed concerns that the very existence of Russian fears of a "Chinese threat" and misgivings about Chinese policy could eventually lead Russia to return to a "pro-Western bias."[40]

The Current Chinese View of Relations with Russia

Today, according to the Chinese view, relations with Russia are developing smoothly and form an important part of Beijing's foreign policy. There are important reasons for this approach. The change of government in Kiev in the Ukraine in 2014, supported by the United States, provoked a civil war and responses by Russia, which led to a sharp confrontation with the West. This situation was interpreted in Beijing as not unique. On the one hand, the response is always alarm at any attempt to undermine the territorial integrity of an existing state, since China has in mind its own separatists. This precisely explains its support for the territorial integrity of Ukraine. On the other hand, its leaders, recalling the chaos of the "Cultural Revolution" and the disturbances of 1989, always prefer stability to any disorder. China lays the blame for undermining stability on the United States and the European Union, considering that they were attempting to expand their spheres of influence at Russia's expense. It sees Russian moves as responses. Characteristic is this Xinhua commentary: "For the rest of the world, once again, people see another great country torn apart because of a clumsy and selfish West that boasts too many lofty ideals but always comes up short of practical solutions."[41]

Although Russian countermeasures are considered in Beijing to be extreme and not fully conducive to stability, on the whole, the Russian position is met with understanding and even approval. Thus, according to the Xinhua commentary, "Russia may no longer be interested in competing for global preeminence with the West, but when it comes to cleaning a mess the West created in the country's backyard, Russian leaders once again proved their credibility and shrewdness in planning and executing effective counter moves."[42] By "mess" or "disorder," Beijing usually means a situation created by Western-sponsored actions aimed at undermining stable (often authoritarian) regimes all over the world, which in its opinion can effectively secure the country's economic development and growing cooperation with China. This term was used to describe the Tiananmen Square crisis in 1989, "color revolutions" in Arab states, etc. For China, countering this tendency even far from its borders is a means of protecting itself since it understands that the same tactics can be used by the West in China. From this point of view, China would only welcome Russia's growing will to counter Western expansionism.

Feng Shaolei, one of China's leading Russia experts, notes with regard to Ukraine that Beijing is guided by its own interests, but bases its position on the principle of ensuring the stability of the global post–Cold War community. He unequivocally states that China has consistently stood for territorial integrity and the sovereignty of independent states, and that, taking into account the unusually complex "historical intertwining" in the region, it advocates an active dialogue on the issue of territorial jurisdiction and exclusively political methods of conflict resolution. At the same time, as Feng Shaolei observes,

> China opposes the substitution of sanctions for political dialogue and the shifting of responsibility from one to the other when the true picture is not known, and also does not accept the killing of civilians. China has clearly stated its readiness to lend a helping hand to Russia during a time when it is undergoing economic difficulties. China resolutely opposes any policy of isolating Russia.[43]

From a geopolitical point of view, Chinese leaders – who view world politics as an arena of battles for spheres of influence, even if this is sometimes concealed by various ideological slogans – cannot approve in general of the blow delivered to Russia by Western expansion by use of force. Yet, paradoxically, China benefits from the fact that Russia's resolute countermeasures delay the West's expansion in China's direction, and in this case it was not China caught in confrontation, while its economic cooperation with the West has not suffered. As for ordinary Chinese citizens, judging by commentaries filling the Chinese internet, many not only approve of the actions of Vladimir Putin, they regard his decisiveness as an example to their own leadership, which, in their opinion, displays unnecessary softness toward Japan, the United States, Vietnam, and other states wishing to harm China. Although Russia and China would have continued to draw closer even without the Ukrainian crisis, the cooling of relations between Russia and the West accelerates this process.

The current official Chinese vision of Russia and Russian policy was stated very clearly in an article that Fu Ying, former Chinese deputy foreign minister and current chair of the Foreign Affairs Committee of the National People's Congress, published in *Foreign Affairs* in early 2016.[44] Both the status of the author and the place of publication are quite remarkable. Because Fu Ying was not directly involved with Russia as a diplomat and could hardly be familiar with the details of the two countries' bilateral cooperation, the article was probably to some extent a collective effort by the Chinese diplomatic corps. The choice of an influential US journal clearly demonstrates that the article was intended for a Western audience (although a translation was also published in the Chinese newspaper *Guangming Ribao*[45]). The author apparently felt it necessary to explain to China's Western partners its motives and reservations concerning rapprochement with Russia, and also to emphasize that – as is evident from the article's subtitle – "Beijing and Moscow are close, but not allies." Because that is actually the official position China and Russia take on the issue, there was certainly no need to explain it to anyone in either of those countries.

More interesting is the author's conclusion: "The Chinese-Russian relationship is a stable strategic partnership and by no means a marriage of convenience: it is complex, sturdy, and deeply rooted. Changes in international relations since the end of the Cold War have only brought the two countries closer together."[46] Fu Ying also states that, although some Western analysts and politicians supposed and possibly hoped that the conflicts in Syria and Ukraine would create tensions or even a schism between Beijing and Moscow, such expectations were clearly unjustified.

At the same time, Fu Ying says that China and Russia will not enter into a legally binding alliance or form an anti-Western bloc, and also notes some differences between them. In particular, she thinks, Russia's policy continues to focus mainly on Europe, while China focuses on Asia; Russian diplomacy has more experience on the global level and "tends to favor strong, active, and often surprising diplomatic maneuvers," whereas Chinese diplomacy, to the contrary, is reactive and cautious. The author also notes that not everyone in Russia has managed to adapt to the changing balance of forces between the two countries, giving rise to the theory of a "Chinese threat" and concerns over growing Chinese influence in Russia's "near abroad." And despite the resolution of the border issue, "Chinese commentators sometimes make critical references to the nearly 600,000 square miles of Chinese territory that tsarist Russia annexed in the late nineteenth century."[47] However, as Fu Ying notes, those differences have not led to a cooling of bilateral relations. To the contrary, she argues that they continue to grow stronger, primarily because of the evolving geopolitical situation in the world.

Most mainstream Chinese experts view Russian-Chinese relations similarly to Fu Ying. Thus, when speaking of the prospects for developing trilateral cooperation in the international arena between Russia, China, and the US, Feng Shaolei states that the objective basis for such cooperation is even stronger now – even after the Ukrainian crisis. There is a need for trilateral cooperation to combat international terrorism, in regions such as Central Asia and the Asia-Pacific, and on a number of other issues. He points to President Vladimir Putin's non-confrontational statements regarding US policy and efforts to continue cooperation despite disagreements, and even feels that China could act as a mediator between Russia and the US on a number of issues, just as Russia played a similar role in the past. However, he also argues that a number of factors hinder trilateral cooperation. The first, in his opinion, is the ideologized Western approach to the concept of "democracy." Second is the European interpretation of the concept of a "nation-state" – one that cannot serve as the basis of all current international processes because China and Russia face complex questions of territorial integrity or border disputes, in contrast to the US which long ago became an "island of security" and has yet to face such geopolitical border challenges. Additionally, Feng Shaolei argues, the "postmodern" phase of national development in Europe is also quite remote from the political problems that China and Russia face. Third, there is a lack of mutual understanding and consideration for the other side's position, as happened during the Ukrainian crisis. In effect, the Chinese expert is pointing out that the United States and Europe on the one hand, and China and Russia on the other, understand the foundations of the modern world and international relations differently.

In general, Chinese academics speak favorably of Russia's "pivot to Asia," while discouraging excessive hopes that China could solve all of Russia's problems. Thus, according to a leading Chinese expert on Russia and Central Asia, Zhao Huasheng, following the crisis in Ukraine, "The West applied sanctions against Russia and Russia sped up its 'pivot to Asia.' Under such circumstances, Russia pressed emphatically for quick results, hoping for the delivery of large quantities of Chinese capital." Zhao Huasheng notes that when Russian markets did not receive the expected volume of Chinese capital, Russian experts saw political reasons behind it, arguing that China feared a negative reaction from the West. But, according to Zhao, China had no such concern; to the contrary, China increased its investment in Russia and economic support in general following the Ukrainian crisis. But he points to several reasons for this impression in Russia: first, large projects take time to reach fruition; second, political support alone cannot guarantee investment because "it is unrealistic to hope that China would blindly invest large amounts without thinking of profit"; and third, there is still a problem of the different approaches to business and business culture that exist in Russia and China.[48] Zhao Huasheng pointed out that, although Russia's "pivot to Asia" policy did stimulate cooperation with China, it also aims to increase cooperation with other Asian countries such as Japan, India, Vietnam, and the two Koreas.[49]

The Shanghai Cooperation Organization and Central Asia

There is a great deal of discussion in China concerning cooperation in Central Asia and the role of the Shanghai Cooperation Organization. According to Zhao Huasheng, the desire of Central Asian states to avoid becoming victims of a confrontation in the region between the major powers is itself a solid basis for Russian-Chinese cooperation there. "This factor largely prevents relations between China, Russia, and the US in Central Asia from becoming a destructive confrontation," he concludes.[50]

Dong Xiaoyang, deputy director of the Institute of Russia, Eastern Europe and Central Asia of the Chinese Academy of Social Sciences, aptly described China's geopolitical interests in developing relations with Russia within the framework of the SCO. He said that both countries feel the need to harmonize their policies on the world stage because they will soon find it difficult to resolve problems of conflicting interests and disagreements with the United States and other Western countries. This is because the US and the West would like to see a "weak Russia," and so far, that stance has not changed. Dong Xiaoyang also sees no change in the situation whereby Russia and the US simultaneously act as diplomatic partners and rivals. "The US and the West strengthen and extend their influence into Russia's traditional zone of influence," he writes. "One means for countering this policy is the expansion of Russian-Chinese cooperation within the framework of the SCO."[51]

Skepticism about the work of the SCO also exists in China, but it is mainly due to concerns that the body is too slow in formalizing economic cooperation.[52] Questions on the Chinese side arise mainly because of Russia's lack of interest in strengthening multilateral economic cooperation within the SCO framework.

China is primarily interested in Central Asia not for economic reasons or out of a desire to control it, but for the strategic purpose of eliminating the threats it produces that could lead to instability or terrorism in China itself. According to Li Fenglin,

China attaches great importance to the SCO and regards it as one of the strategic pillars of the country's development. China's interests are the following: the creation of favorable conditions for developing the country, providing the northwest region with a peaceful, secure, and strategic external environment that includes the fight against the "three evils" [terrorism, separatism, extremism], and ensuring the openness of the region; establishing and maintaining eternal friendship and good neighborly relations with the SCO member states, cooperation in all fields – political, economic, security, humanitarian, regional integration, minimizing the negative effects of globalization, achieving the harmonious development and general prosperity of all SCO member states; and increasing the political influence of China so that, together with SCO member states, it can introduce a new global political and economic order.[53]

Many of these issues are related to security rather than the economy.

In his voluminous work *Chinese Diplomacy in Central Asia*, Zhao Huasheng describes Beijing's hierarchical system of interests in the region: first, the fight against terrorism and the pursuit of energy sector interests; second, the economy and SCO; and third, geopolitical interests and border security.[54] Naturally, Chinese scholars view the SCO as a means of achieving that country's interests. Zhao Huasheng explains that "although economic interests and the SCO are among China's most important strategic interests in Central Asia, on the scale of Chinese strategic interests, they rank lower than the fight against 'Eastern Turkestan' and energy resources: they are of secondary importance in the system of Chinese interests in Central Asia."[55]

This approach is a natural one and should not cause concern in Russia as long as the fundamental interests that both Russia and China have in Central Asia coincide. Most Chinese experts agree that Beijing is willing to take Russia's traditional interests in the region into account. Responding to Russian concerns about China's growing role in Central Asia, Li Fenglin said bluntly: "China has no intention of becoming a leader at either the regional or global levels. China understands Russia's desire to preserve its traditional influence in Central Asia." At the same time, China will not be passive simply because Russia has not been active enough. Li Fenglin rightly points out that China has no objection to the statement that "'Central Asia is like Russia's backyard.' That is true. We understand that, but you have to take care of your backyard, water the flowers, so that it does not become overgrown with weeds."[56]

Zhao Huasheng contends that Russian and Chinese strategic interests in Central Asia are close or coincide with regard to keeping existing borders safe, the fight against terrorism, maintaining regional stability, geopolitical interactions aimed primarily at limiting the military presence of the US and NATO in the region, and opposing the US policy of promoting "democratic reforms" that leads to "color revolutions."[57]

At the same time, many Chinese experts dislike the ineffective functioning of the SCO and therefore view it as only a supplementary tool for pursuing Beijing's strategic interests in Central Asia. That makes it necessary to conduct much of the actual cooperation between China and Russia in Central Asia outside the SCO framework.

Qiu Huafei also closely links China's policy in Central Asia with its desire to expand cooperation with Russia. In his view, Beijing's relations with Central Asia "aim to legitimize the Chinese position on major international issues, strengthen relations with Russia, and serve as a counterweight to US power and influence."[58]

The decision by Xi Jinping to propose the Silk Road Economic Belt (SREB) in 2013 meant, in particular, that China would give greater attention to economic cooperation with Russia and Central Asia as potential markets and transit areas. After the value of the ruble fell in 2014, Russia became more amenable to forming a free trade zone with China and agreed to start talks on the subject. China responded enthusiastically. In addition, Beijing has realized that Russian and Kazakh initiatives for Eurasian integration and the recently created Eurasian Economic Union (EAEU) do not run contrary to China's interests and could even be used to its advantage.

This became clear when Russian and Chinese leaders signed a joint statement of cooperation in May 2015 in Moscow on developing the EAEU and SREB. And although some Chinese experts initially expressed doubts regarding the potential of the EAEU, that attitude has since changed significantly. Recognizing Russia's traditional interests in the region, Feng Shaolei notes in this connection that the key issue is to establish spheres of linkage between the SREB and the region in which Russia traditionally plays an important role, and to search for opportunities to cooperate in ensuring the regional stability and economic complementarity that provide for the region's steady development. "That is the most important task for Russian-Chinese partnership and cooperative relations in the next several years."[59]

Accordingly, a group of Shanghai experts led by Li Xin published a report in March 2016 that looks at prospects for linking those two projects. It offers a "road map" of steps toward that goal. The first phase involves reaching agreement with the EAEU on unifying infrastructure, coordinating trade flows, and starting talks on the creation of a free trade area (FTA) between China and the EAEU. The second phase involves putting the FTA question on the agenda of the SCO with the goal of creating it within the framework of that organization in 2020–5. In the third phase, the SCO would expand upon the FTA to create a Continental Economic Partnership. The fourth phase calls for creating a Common Economic Space spanning all of Eurasia by approximately 2030.[60]

Korea

China supports Russia's moderate position on settling the nuclear issue on the Korean peninsula. That position firmly demands the denuclearization of the peninsula, but only by peaceful means, through negotiations – preferably in the six-party format. That position is based on concerns that the North Korean regime could collapse and result in a humanitarian catastrophe.

While China definitely does not want a nuclear state on its borders, it takes a more ambiguous stance toward the possible unification of the two Koreas. Beijing has never formally objected to the prospect of unification, but Chinese experts have often expressed fears that a united Korea would become an economic competitor to China and ally itself with the US and Japan, thereby strengthening all three. Moreover, for Chinese leaders, many of whom remember the Korean War, abandoning support for North Korea would be to cast it as a failed state and tantamount to abandoning many deeply rooted foreign policy ideals and philosophies. An entire generation of Chinese youth was raised with stories of the heroism of the Chinese "volunteers" who fought in the war against "US imperialism," and many formally joined the pioneer movement when they visited the monument to those who had fallen in that war. In addition, North Korea is one of the few remaining "socialist" states. Rejecting that heritage would be psychologically difficult. It would also be a "tough sell" to the Chinese people and would inevitably give rise to questions about the ultimate fate of communist regimes in general. Therefore, even while it is fully aware of the nature of the Pyongyang regime – openly referred to by many Chinese experts as "feudal" – and while it expresses dissatisfaction with the opportunistic course it pursues, Beijing continues to exercise extreme caution in applying pressure against the regime out of fear that it might collapse.

Alternative Views

There are other, nonofficial views in China's academia on relations with Russia. There are two trends here. One concerns the "Russia skeptics." These are experts who, paradoxically, are either pro-Western or simply specialize in the study of the US and the West and who argue that Russia is too weak and its economy too troubled to withstand a serious confrontation or even to emerge from its current stagnation. This category also includes nationalists who argue that Beijing should adopt a more aggressive foreign policy because China has now become so strong that it can behave as a superpower on a par with the United States. Both groups argue that China should hold talks either exclusively or primarily with the real authority in the world – the US – and that Russia deserves less attention from Beijing.

Others have expressed similar, if somewhat more muted criticisms of Russia, such as Xing Guangcheng, director of the Research Center for Chinese Borderland History and Geography at the Chinese Academy of Social Sciences, Feng Yujun, former director of the Institute of Russian Studies at the China Institute of Contemporary International Relations, former journalist of the Central Party School newspaper Xuexi Shibao Deng Yuwen, and others. Thus, according to Feng Yujun, Russia's confrontation with the US over Ukraine is unlikely to substantially diminish or affect its pivot to Asia. "US policymakers realize that Russia is at most a regional power, not a global one, and is, therefore, unable to pose a serious challenge to US hegemony," he writes.[61] Xing Guangcheng believes that "factors at both home and abroad will delay and limit any rise of Russia in line with the strategic goals set out by the Putin regime." In his view, "at present Russia is declining at a very fast speed, and it will be a long process with lots of difficulties for it to rise again."[62]

In the summer of 2016 the little-known scholar Han Kedi of the Institute of Russia, Eastern Europe and Central Asia published an article in the English version of the *Huanqiu Shibao* newspaper (*Global Times*) in which he leveled a variety of charges against Russia for having "superpower" aspirations reminiscent of the 1980s. Han accused the Russian authorities of overtly supporting the "China threat" theory, lacking delicacy in dealing with some of its China policies, and giving too little care to the interests of the Chinese and the big picture of the bilateral relationship. He also maintained that Russians are deeply Eurocentric and some of them believe that "with the US rebalance to the Asia-Pacific and treating China as its arch rival, Russia will have more strategic room." He maintained that "Russia's consistent accusation that US practices hegemony and intervention in other countries' internal affairs is right but blemished by ulterior motives." "What Russia condemns the US for is actually what Russia wants to do. Moscow wants to regain its superpower status, pursues hegemony and instigates its own color revolutions. Russia's plan is to denounce US-led rules and build Russia-led rules," he claimed. After summing up these and many other accusations, he concludes that Sino-Russian relations are important, but should not be exaggerated. The direction of the article is clearly seen from its last phrases, in which Han claims that China should keep in mind that "some supporters won't make much difference in face of outside pressure" and that "China's national security and sovereign integrity do not depend on diplomacy, but on good governance and its people's support."[63]

These accusations and allegations should be viewed in the overall context of the polemics of many *Global Times* writers who express an assertive point of view and of traditional Chinese diplomats who argue that China should continue to act cautiously and make no drastic moves in the outside world. Some of those who advocate activism argue that in the inevitable future struggle with the US, China can only gain a worthy place in the world system by relying exclusively on its own strength. It is clear that the primary intention is to compromise and discredit Russia, the largest and closest strategic partner.

Supporters of a more traditional cautious approach argue that international cooperation and strong partner relations are the best guarantees of domestic development and stability. Russia is not China's most important partner in the world system in this regard, but it does play an important and very positive role.

At the same time, some who advocate a more assertive foreign policy believe that China will need allies for its future struggle with the US and that Russia should be foremost among them. They further call for creating a formal Russian-Chinese alliance. Among them are such well-known foreign policy experts as Yan Xuetong, Zhang Wenmu, a professor at the Center for Strategic Research at the Beijing University of Aeronautics and Astronautics, and a number of military analysts.[64] Many of them are often called "left" in the internal Chinese context, meaning being anti-Western and supporting a traditional Communist-type foreign policy.

According to senior colonel Dai Xü, the US sees the Eurasian continent as the main battlefield on the chessboard of its hegemonic plan. China and Russia can resist American strategic ambition only by allying with each other, since their power is too weak to withstand the pressure from Washington. At the same time, Dai Xü points out that even if it is not economically advantageous, security is more important than the economy. He believes that China and Russia should abandon their policy of nonalignment and form an alliance to counter the US strategic offensive, thereby forcing the "American tiger-predator to eat grass."[65]

According to Zhang Wenmu, who also supports the idea of a Russian-Chinese alliance, the Russian response to the Western incursion into Ukraine was a lesson for China that it should act with similar resolve. He criticizes the Chinese experts who argue that the US is the global boss and that Beijing would only come out the loser in any confrontation with Washington. He believes that such an approach only encourages the US to act according to the principle: "Give him an inch and he takes a mile." Characteristically, Zhang quotes Mao Zedong in calling the US a "paper tiger." He advocates following Russia's example by creating a "security space" around China's borders and allying with Russia in the struggle against the US in order to preserve the "Yalta peace framework."[66]

Of course, Chinese citizens are not free to discuss international issues at will, and expressing certain opinions could easily land an individual in jail. At the same time, some of the opinions expressed do not reflect official government positions. China does permit debate within certain limits, the expression of many unofficial opinions, and even some criticisms. The ideas that have been mentioned that a partnership with Russia would be both useless and even harmful to China, and its opposite, that the two countries should form an alliance, represent such unofficial positions. Analysts who mistakenly believe those are official positions either lack knowledge of the real situation in the Chinese expert community and the mechanisms by which Beijing formulates foreign policy, or else deliberately distort the facts in order to influence their country's policy toward China or Russia.

Such interpretations are mistaken, whether or not they are intentional. Neither group of Chinese supporters of assertiveness expresses the official position, which is that China advocates an equal partnership with Russia. The article by Fu Ying already discussed clearly states the official position, and describes some of the real differences between the Russian and Chinese approaches.

In a written interview to the Russian media on the eve of his visit to Moscow in early July 2017, Xi Jinping formulated five main indications of the fact that the "China-Russia comprehensive strategic partnership of coordination is now stronger than ever": first, the high level of political and strategic trust; second, sound mechanisms for high-level exchanges and all-round cooperation; third, working hard to align their development strategies; fourth, solid public support for stronger relations; fifth, close strategic coordination in regional and international affairs. According to the Chinese leader,

> As major countries in the world, permanent members of the UN Security Council and emerging economies, China and Russia both stand for the basic norms governing international relations with the purposes and principles of the UN Charter as the cornerstone. We both support progress toward a multi-polar world and greater democracy in international relations. We both resolutely uphold the outcomes of World War II and international fairness and justice. Our two countries have close coordination and collaboration in the United Nations, G20, APEC and other multilateral institutions. We have jointly proposed and set up various multilateral mechanisms such as the Shanghai Cooperation Organization (SCO) and BRICS and worked hard for their development, which contribute to peace and stability in Central Asia and Northeast Asia, which are our common neighborhood. The fact is, our concerted efforts in international affairs are like an anchor for peace, security and stability in our region and the world amidst the turbulent and volatile international situation.[67]

Thus, China officially considers Russia an important partner for achieving its national interests in the world. Beijing feels that Russia can help China more easily resist the trend toward a unipolar world, despite the fact that Russia is not gaining in strength as quickly as it might and still faces a number of problems itself. Thus, Russia is an important and friendly strategic partner, while the US is the most important partner – but one that is more adversarial than friendly. Most Chinese experts share this view. Thus, according to Feng Shaolei, "Regardless of the criteria used for evaluating Russia's potential, whether political influence, economic potential, military might, diplomatic traditions, or geopolitical condition, it is far from what would be considered a 'regional power' [as US President Barack Obama characterized it]. Russia remains a world power, one that is going through a process of transformation."[68]

Most Chinese authors have long noted that the Russian-Chinese rapprochement is based not on short-term interests, but increasingly on a common understanding of global processes and a similar vision of the future world order. Thus, Xü Zhixin, a scholar at the Institute of Russia, Eastern Europe and Central Asia, speaks of the converging national interests of the two countries in a volume on

"Chinese-Russian Relations in the New Century." In particular, he notes that Russia plays an indispensable role in ensuring the security of China and is an important trade and economic partner as well. He also explains that China views its relations with Russia as part of its overall strategy on the world arena, as a major factor in its peaceful foreign policy course.[69] China Foreign Affairs University associate professor Gao Fei explains that a convergence of the two countries' political cultures has made this mutual understanding possible.[70]

Conclusions

Although China initially had misgivings about cooperating with Russia when it first emerged as an independent state in 1991, that position has since evolved to the current understanding of the need for close interaction. This was largely the result of China's growing influence in the region and the world, and the resultant change in its foreign policy approach, as well as what Beijing views as the generally hostile attitude taken by the US and West toward China.

The following paragraphs summarize the official Chinese approach to cooperation with Russia.

1. China regards Russia as an important geopolitical partner. China has almost no official allies (and even its only formal ally, North Korea, ignores China's position). The West, and especially the United States, takes an adversarial approach and tries in every possible way to contain the growth of Chinese influence. This could lead to a serious conflict in the future, but one that both sides should avoid at all costs.
2. Given this situation, Beijing must search among the major powers for partners that, while not necessarily in complete agreement with China, are generally supportive of Beijing's desire for a multipolar world, speak out against US domination of the global system, and can work with China as a counterweight to that influence. Russia is the most important of such states because it is a neighbor, has a friendly relationship with China, and acts decisively to prevent encroachment by the West.
3. Russia shares China's desire to preserve the existing system of international law with the leading role of the UN Security Council and, like China, is critical of Western attempts to undermine the role of that organization by circumventing the Security Council.
4. Although in its current condition, Russia plays a far smaller

role in Chinese politics than China plays in Russia's politics, all the same, for a number of reasons, China prefers that Russia be stable and strong – though perhaps not too powerful. Beijing sees a stable Russia that is capable of becoming an independent power center as serving as a counterweight of sorts in China's partner/rival relationship with the United States and Western Europe. Russia serves as one of the guarantors capable of ensuring China's "independent foreign policy."

5. Russia, like China, has a non-Western, or not fully Westernized political system. Its strong leader has complete control over the situation in the country, and this system is much more effective than that which existed under Yeltsin: Beijing knows exactly whom it is dealing with and what is under discussion, and unpredictable societal forces cannot influence international agreements once they have been made. Moreover, the Russian leadership is concerned about the same issues as the Chinese: internet security, Western attempts to influence the domestic situation using agents in civil society, "color revolutions," and so on. Moscow, like Beijing, opposes interference in its domestic affairs and political pressure from the West. Whereas Russia was excessively pro-Western in the early 1990s and some senior leaders would even now like to revive a pro-Western stance, Russia's confrontation with the West has become too severe for that to happen. There are some concerns regarding Russia's attempts to alter existing borders without observing the principle of the territorial integrity of states. This could create unwanted conflicts, destabilize Eastern Europe, and even serve as a bad example for some Chinese regions. The Chinese approach is more restrained: Beijing is willing to cooperate with everyone, including pro-Western regimes in the former Soviet republics, for the sake of the country's own economic interests, and because economic cooperation, rather than confrontation, leads to stability. At the same time, the fact that Russia stopped the West from advancing closer to China's borders is a positive outcome. In return, China has a certain obligation to support Russia both politically and economically, and to make some compromises that Moscow finds acceptable – without, of course, harming its own interests too much in the process. This is why in recent years Beijing has taken a purposeful and constructive approach to resolving border, migration, and bilateral trade issues.

6. Russia has traditional interests in Central Asia. Beijing must therefore coordinate its economic activity in the region with

Moscow – including within the framework of the SCO – in order to avoid upsetting Russia and provoking a counterresponse.
7. China can provide general support for Russia's commitment to Eurasian integration and reach an agreement with the EAEU, although it is difficult to say whether this would bring any significant economic payoff. In any case, the opportunity remains to develop bilateral cooperation with EAEU member states.
8. Russia shares China's position on such major regional issues as nuclear arms on the Korean peninsula, Iran's nuclear program, the conflicts in Iraq, Libya, Syria, and others.
9. Some people in Russia fear China's intentions. However, such concerns appear baseless because, from Beijing's point of view, China pursues a strictly peaceful foreign policy that presents no present or future threat to any other country. The Chinese leadership should consider such concerns, but more importantly, it should dissuade its advocates by example, by conducting a peaceful foreign policy and actively explaining its rationale to the Russian people. The stable situation on its border with Russia, and on the borders with its other neighbors, is of great significance for China's development – that is, for carrying out the goals set by the country's current leadership.
10. Russia constitutes an extremely important source of various commodities that China either cannot obtain from other countries (such as armaments), or else can purchase in only limited quantities elsewhere (such as oil, lumber and other raw materials). Russia can also be useful to China for a number of other economic projects, particularly within the framework of the SREB initiative.

3

RUSSIA'S PIVOT TO ASIA OR JUST CHINA? RUSSIAN VIEWS OF RELATIONS WITH CHINA

Russia's Pivot to Asia

Russia's rapprochement with China is part of Russia's strategy of a "pivot to Asia." It can only be understood if it is analyzed within the general context of Russian foreign policy in which relations with Asia have recently become a leading if not the most important part.

People have been debating for more than a century whether Russia is part of Europe or Asia. In Russia, opinions on the subject varied, depending on the period and people's political inclinations. Ancient Rus' assimilated Christianity from the Byzantine empire – the most advanced geopolitical center of world civilization at the time. Prior to the split within the Christian church, civilization was seen as a unified whole and the question of the division between Europe and Asia did not yet exist. From the time of Peter the Great – who "cut a window through to Europe" – and throughout the eighteenth century, Russia was officially considered a part of Europe. Catherine the Great even put it in writing in her *Nakaz* (Instruction) that stated: "Russia is a European power."[1] Of course, the empress was not referring to Russia's geographic location. By emphasizing Russia's connection to all European countries, she wanted to show the enlightened nature of her reign, that her country was part of the civilized world and that it was moving along the path of progress.

In the nineteenth century, the government of Nicholas I put forward a new official concept of Russia not as a European country, but as a special power based on the well-known trinity – "Orthodoxy, Autocracy, Nationality" – and free from the struggle between classes and landed estates. That theory was intended to provide ideological justification for the emperor's overriding policy goal: protecting the country from the spread of revolutionary influences from Europe and thereby preserving the immutability of the existing social system. Members of Russian society held differing views: pro-Western thinkers called for methodically building life according to the European model, while Slavophiles criticized the government for causing Russian identity to take on an increasingly formal, bureaucratic and statist nature that did not consider the native Russian – or more precisely, the Slavic tradition of self-rule.

That debate continued in Soviet times, although it took on a decidedly Marxist form. The theory of the so-called "Asiatic mode of production," which was banned by Stalin, meant that Russia was a part of Asia, while most official ideologues argued that the Soviet Union, although traveling along a common path of human development, had taken the lead and was showing the way for others. At the same time, Russian emigrants put forward the now popular theory of "Eurasianism" that saw Russian civilization as the successor of some "Turan" (non-Slavic) Eurasian nations: Turkic, Finno-Ugric, Mongolian and others. This theory was spawned by frustration over the "decay" of Europe and as an attempt to explain – and, at times justify – rule by the clearly "non-European" Bolshevik regime in Russia.

Following the collapse of the Soviet Union, cooperation with Asia was no longer a theoretical question, but a practical one. The growth of the Asian economies and the geopolitical importance of the Asia-Pacific region elicited a wave of expert recommendations during the final years of the Soviet Union that called for Moscow to devote greater attention to Asian states. They managed to exert a certain influence on leaders, convincing them to pursue a normalization of relations with China. But the highpoint of the pivot to Asia came with the now-famous speech that Mikhail Gorbachev delivered in Vladivostok in 1986 in which he offered the first detailed description of the situation in the Asia-Pacific region and introduced the task of forming a comprehensive security system there. That speech paved the way for subsequent steps for achieving that goal: the opening of the previously closed militarized city of Vladivostok to international cooperation, and the resolution of differences that had prevented the normalization of relations with China. However, Gorbachev was inconsistent in implementing many of the recommendations he listed in that speech, and he was further hampered by the tumultuous events in the country's political life.

The failure of the Soviet authorities to give proper attention to the development of their own eastern territories was a weak link in their Asia policy. As part of an ideology that called for the accelerated "recovery of fraternal republics," they allocated significant resources to the Central Asian republics, even as they failed to make the rapid development of Russia's Siberian and Far East regions an important strategic objective.

Unlike Pyotr Stolypin, Nicholas II's prime minister, who saw the need for the geopolitical development of Siberia and considered it crucial to the country's future, Soviet leaders took a more utilitarian view of the region. During Stalin's rule, his system of forced labor camps was the primary source of economic development in Siberia and the Far East. Later, Nikita Khrushchev decided to develop scientific centers there. In the 1970s and 1980s, the Soviet authorities established major military facilities in the region. Their presence and continued maintenance led not only to worsening relations with China, but also to the creation of new industries and social infrastructure in those territories. Even the construction of the famed Baykal–Amur railway was motivated primarily by a military objective: it offered an important backup to the Trans-Siberian railway that ran uncomfortably close to the Chinese border. Meanwhile, that border remained on "lockdown," thereby preventing the Soviet Union from actively integrating with the growing economies of the Asia-Pacific countries.

Following the collapse of the Soviet Union and the loss of a number of its western territories, Russia in a sense moved geographically closer to Asia. Today, although the majority of its population lives in the European part of the country, two-thirds of Russia's territory lies in Asia. However, opinion polls indicate that most Russians – even those living on the Pacific coast and near the Chinese border – feel that they are Europeans. Indeed, most Russians really are of European descent, but fate and historical circumstances have thrown them onto the Asian continent. But now having relocated, Russians must take stock of the situation – and not by promoting exotic theories about their Asian roots, but by recognizing that the future of the country depends largely on its approach to and relationship with its Asian neighbors.

Russians are not the first to have shed a purely European consciousness: Spaniards who wound up in South America in the nineteenth century had to accept that they were now part of life on that continent; and in the twentieth century, the white South African minority had to come to terms with being a part of the African continent with all its problems, while Australians and New Zealanders had to face the reality that their countries were far from Europe and that they would have to establish economic ties with the much closer Asian states.

The continued growth of the Asian economies and the shift of the global center of economic life to the Asia-Pacific region have made it an urgent practical necessity for Russia to develop relations with its Asian partners – and especially those in Central, East and South Asia.

The people of Central Asia, having long lived with Russia as part of the same country, have now become very close to the Russian people, and like Russians, are part of the same post-Soviet culture, with all of its pros and cons – even while they are also heirs to their own unique and ancient civilizations. The Central Asian states are either participants or potential participants in the Eurasian integration project that Russia is actively promoting. They are partners to Russia in various international organizations, foremost among them the Shanghai Cooperation Organization that also includes the region's largest economic force: China. Like Russia, those states are extremely concerned about the situation in Afghanistan, from which the main threat to regional security is emerging.

East Asia is a dynamically developing region and the focus of key economic and political interests of the international community, including Russia. The growth of China – Russia's main trade partner since 2010 – is both a great opportunity and a challenge. Russia is actively developing trade and economic cooperation with Japan and South Korea. The main problem facing Russia, especially its Asiatic territory, is the nuclear arms race on the Korean peninsula that threatens to erupt in nuclear disaster. Russia is also slowly stepping up its interaction with ASEAN member states.

Finally, South Asia is a vitally important region for Russia and the potential for cooperation remains far from fully realized. Russia's relations with India are extremely important because that country is rapidly developing, has a population of 1.25 billion, and more importantly, is a unique and independent center in world politics. It is a country that wants to finally determine its own path and not kowtow to other power centers – and particularly not to the United States or China, with their complex bilateral relations. Other countries in the region are also important for Russia's foreign policy objectives.

After several years of futile attempts to become part of the "civilized West" in the 1990s, the leaders of the new Russia have come to understand the vital importance of developing relations with their Asian neighbors and have begun gradually turning in that direction. What is the nature of that pivot? Its symbol is the old coat of arms adopted by the new state: a two-headed eagle that, according to Russian officials, now looks simultaneously toward both the West and the East.

That means that strengthening relations with Asia should not be considered an alternative to cooperating with the West – especially with Europe, with which the Russian people largely identify and share historical ties as well as political, trade, economic and cultural interests. In a more utilitarian sense, cooperation with the West – as it is broadly defined and where the most advanced technologies are found – remains a key condition for solving Russia's strategic modernization goals and achieving a breakthrough in domestic development. However, without increasing cooperation with Asia's rising economies, Russia will also fail to achieve that goal, along with another strategically important objective: developing the economy of the Siberian and Far Eastern territories.[2]

Thus, by pivoting to Asia, Moscow is not turning away from Europe, but giving Asia a level of attention commensurate with Russia's practical interests and the realities of the twenty-first century. More generally, the experience of the twentieth century showed the futility of Moscow's attempt to pursue an anti-Western course by allying with the Asian giants, and of its efforts to align itself exclusively with the West.

Russia is too big and its culture is too unique to completely merge with Confucian authoritarianism, or conversely, with the anti-religious liberalism of Europe. Thus, even from the cultural and civilizational perspective, it became clear that Russia should establish its own, independent place in the world. At this stage, Russia can best achieve this goal by developing relations with its Asian partners to at least the level of those it has maintained until now with Europe.

Russia's Views on China in the 1990s

The newly independent Russia inherited a good working relationship with China from the Soviet Union. However, despite the heavy influence of Gorbachev's "new thinking," Yeltsin's foreign policy views still included a forceful rejection of the Soviet legacy. Immediately after the collapse of the Soviet Union, Russian foreign policy primarily focused on relations with the West and a fascination with the "common European home," forgetting almost entirely about relations with the East. And, although Russian Foreign Ministry officials naturally acknowledged that China had some importance for Russia, they constantly emphasized the greater importance of the West and their desire that Russia become a full-fledged member of the Western community. As early as August 1991, at a rally in Moscow celebrating victory over the coup plotters, Russian foreign minister Andrey Kozyrev proclaimed Russia's new official position that the US and other Western democracies were the natural friends and allies of democratic Russia, just as they had been the natural enemies of the totalitarian Soviet Union.[3] Kozyrev described the practical policy inspired by that outlook as "the path from a cautious partnership to a friendly one, and eventually to allied relations with the civilized world and its structures, including NATO, the UN, and other organizations."[4]

According to Evgeny Bazhanov, "despite the significant impact of Gorbachev's legacy on the foreign policy of the new Russia, its leaders made a sharp break with the recent past." At an introductory meeting with the staff of the former Foreign Affairs Ministry of the Soviet Union, Gennady Burbulis, secretary of state in the first administration of Boris Yeltsin, and his colleague, foreign minister Andrey Kozyrev, explained the fundamental difference between the Gorbachev era and the challenges of the present. According to Burbulis, the previous authorities continued to divide the world into socialist and capitalist camps and still believed in the possibility of building a communist society – and such views tended to perpetuate the atmosphere of confrontation and rivalry. Kozyrev stressed that Moscow would continue on its course toward full-fledged partnership and integration with the West.[5]

This policy emerged from the ideology of the democratic perestroika movement that argued that Russia should strive to build a perfect society like that in the "democratic West,"[6] and from the domestic political situation in which the developed Western countries provided at least moral support to the Yeltsin administration in its struggle against domestic adversaries. That support was most evident during the putsch in August 1991, and later, during the events of October 1993. Moreover, the "democratic" leadership in Moscow believed it was impossible to build a modern Russian society without material assistance from, and closer economic ties to the developed Western countries. As Bazhanov described it,

> The democratic forces that came to power were eager to quickly build a free, law-based society and a prosperous market economy in Russia. They viewed the West as the main political and ideological ally in that grand enterprise. As Russian leaders pointed out, "Wealthy, developed, and civilized countries are vital for Russia's economic, spiritual, and

political rebirth." Kremlin leaders insisted that to turn away from the West would be to miss a unique opportunity to transform Russia.[7]

The Russian president repeatedly stated that Russia and the US had common interests and that they must maintain a stable partnership. Addressing a session of the UN Security Council on January 31, 1992, Boris Yeltsin announced, "Russia considers the United States and the West not as mere partners but rather as allies. It is a basic prerequisite for, I would say, a revolution in peaceful cooperation among civilized nations." The president explained that Moscow now shared the same basic foreign policy principles with the West. "Our principles are clear and simple: supremacy of democracy, human rights and freedoms, legal and moral standards," he said.[8]

The same day, Boris Yeltsin met in New York with Chinese premier Li Peng, who was also attending the UN Security Council meeting, and the two reaffirmed their desire to develop good neighborly relations based on the principles of peaceful coexistence.[9] The Russian president noted the dissimilarity between the social systems and ideologies of the two countries, but offered friendship despite these differences. He noted that "ideology differentiates us from China, but we are neighbors and we must cooperate."[10]

Beijing could not but be concerned about Moscow's constant emphasis on the fundamental role of human rights in foreign policy and its pronouncement that a country's international commitments in this area were of top priority. Speaking before the UN, Boris Yeltsin said,

> Our topmost priority is to ensure all human rights and freedoms in their entirety, including political and civil rights and decent socio-economic and environmental living standards. I believe that these questions are not an internal matter of states but rather their obligations under the UN Charter, the International Covenants and conventions. We want to see this approach become a universal norm. The Security Council is called upon to underscore the civilized world's collective responsibility for the protection of human rights and freedoms.[11]

However, very soon Moscow began gradually shifting its foreign policy focus. Speaking at a meeting of the Supreme Soviet on October 22, 1992, Andrey Kozyrev said, "Russia should not narrow the scope of partnership by choosing between the East and the West. The range of its interests is much broader, and it must consider the widest possible range of interactions."[12] There were several reasons for this shift. First, the Russian "democrats" who came to power became acquainted with the real Asia and learned that it was not as backward as they had imagined. Above all, they had considered China a backward state holding onto Soviet-style communism. Yeltsin played a significant role in this regard. Prior to his first visit to China in December 1992, he did not believe the Chinese economy had achieved any real success – something he characteristically admitted openly. "I thought that the reforms in China existed only on paper," he said. However, during the visit, he concluded that "the Chinese Communist Party differs significantly from their comrades in Russia" and even jokingly offered to send some of those Russians to China to study "how to implement reforms."[13]

The second reason was that Russian leaders understood that in China under Deng Xiaoping, the authorities' mechanism for making decisions, including those affecting foreign policy, had changed. Igor Rogachev, Russian ambassador to China, noted:

> Deng Xiaoping and his like-minded colleagues made a great contribution by institutionalizing China's domestic and foreign policy, making the political course much less subject to the whims of the supreme leader, and creating a working mechanism for identifying the true national interests and developing the political course based on them. Such a mechanism operates in Russian-Chinese relations also. The steady development of those relations no longer depends on the will of one or even several leaders, but expresses the common aspiration of large and influential groups that formulate and implement China's foreign policy.[14]

Not all Russian leaders initially favored closer ties with China. The "reformers" associated with acting prime minister Yegor Gaydar made no secret of the fact that they considered China a dangerous and worthless neighbor.[15] The new Russian leaders knew very little about their neighbor and Russian government ministers underestimated the level of development in China. For example, during his visit to China in 1992, the Russian minister for foreign economic relations, Petr Aven, seriously proposed supplying China with Russian home electronics – products that were unpopular even in Russia.[16] However, the Russian leadership soon had to change its approach, and this contributed significantly to the development of bilateral ties.

The Russian leadership moved toward closer cooperation with China under pressure from various forces that strongly opposed Moscow's previous China policy and its foreign policy as a whole. Representatives of the defense industry, which suffered substantial economic hardship under the economic policy implemented by Gaydar, expressed considerable interest in relations with China. One of the most important proofs of the influence wielded by the military-industrial complex over relations with China was the appointment of Arkady Volksky – a well-known defense lobbyist and active advocate of the Chinese economic reforms – to chair the Russian part of the Russian-Chinese Committee of Peace, Friendship and Development of the 21st Century. This formally nongovernmental agency created by Jiang Zemin and Boris Yeltsin during their meeting in Moscow in April 1997 was given the task to "actively involve broad segments of the general public and the business community in strengthening ties between Russia and China."[17]

Political forces in the Russian State Duma also tended to encourage the leadership to improve relations with China. For example, the Communist Party and its allies enjoyed considerable influence in the Duma in 1995–9, and the International Affairs Committee actively advocated stronger ties with China. Even in the Foreign Ministry, there were people who pressed for speedy development of relations with China. According to one participant in those events, Russian diplomat Igor Morgulov, "there were forces [in the Foreign Ministry] that constantly hounded the leadership." Among the most active was the Russian embassy in China led by Igor Rogachev.

> Yes, there was a "Kozyrevan" period when ministers looked at relations with the US and the West through rose-colored glasses. But they quickly sobered up in early 1994 and a more positive assessment of China emerged. That is, we quickly got onto the right path, and it is to the credit of our Chinese partners that they had the wisdom not to downgrade relations with us during that period. We overcame difficult times together, and our relations have been developing steadily since 1994. This is largely due to I. Rogachev, whom I would call the patriarch-ideologue of developing Russia's relations with China . . .[18]

Neither should the role played by the academic community in influencing Russia's policy on China be underestimated, although it was largely expressed indirectly by creating a certain public atmosphere through publications in the press, on television, etc. Still, the academic community also had a direct impact on China policy. This is particularly because a number of international affairs experts joined the ranks of the political elite by participating in free elections.

At the same time, the leaders of several border regions in the 1990s – primarily the Primorsky and Khabarovsk regions – constituted another influential group putting pressure on Moscow leaders, in this case favoring a more cautious stance toward China. They insisted on strict border controls and harsh measures against Chinese immigration, and exerted influence mainly through personal meetings with representatives of the federal government, the financing of media campaigns, and through the Federation Council. In 1994, they convinced leaders to repeal the visa-free regime for crossing the border and partly to change their approach to demarcating the Russian-Chinese border. Under Yelstin, regional leaders held so much influence that they could make some border-related decisions independently. For example, the governor of the Khabarovsk region, Viktor Ishaev, introduced a system of permits for Chinese vessels to sail on the Khabarovsk side of the Amur River, although no such permits were required by a bilateral agreement. On several occasions, the Primorsky and Khabarovsk authorities created their own rules for inviting Chinese tourists, and so on. The ruling authorities in several Siberian and Far Eastern regions attempted to boost their popularity among voters by exploiting and even encouraging anti-Chinese sentiment over Chinese immigration, claiming that China had secret plans for a "demographic expansion" into the Russian Far East. A book was even published in Vladivostok in 1996 with the telling title of "The Yellow Peril" in which articles from the nineteenth and early twentieth centuries appeared side by side with photos of modern-day Primorsky police arresting Chinese market merchants. Overall, the influence and active anti-immigration propaganda of the authorities in a number of Far Eastern regions often proved a hindrance to advancing Russian-Chinese cooperation and, coupled with Moscow's erratic behavior, created a real mess in border-related issues.

Such anti-Chinese sentiment found little support in Moscow, with only the occasional senior official in the capital taking up the idea of the "yellow peril." On the whole, Rogachev was correct in suggesting that "the Russian government's stated policy of developing an equitable and trust-based partnership with China aimed at strategic interaction in the twenty-first century" reflected what in Russian society was "a consensus that there was no alternative to having broad and good-neighborly cooperation with the great neighbor."[19]

As a result, around the mid-1990s, Russia took what might be called a position of "balance and equidistance" in its relations with China and other Asian power centers. Speaking at a meeting in the Kremlin in July 1995, President Boris Yeltsin formulated the new approach:

> China is a country of prime importance for us. It is our neighbor, with whom we share the longest border in the world and with whom we

are forever destined to live and work side by side. The future of Russia depends on how successfully we cooperate with China. Relations with China are extremely important for us in terms of global politics. We can lean on China's shoulder in relations with the West. Then the West would treat Russia with great respect.[20]

Russia changed its approach to human rights after the departure of foreign minister Andrey Kozyrev. Even though, after 1992, Russian officials did not publicly criticize China for human rights violations, while speaking at a conference in London in October 1995, Igor Rogachev mentioned that Russia and China had different approaches to that issue and stated that Moscow had raised those issues with the Chinese leadership. "Russia holds views that are in many ways different than those of China. However, we have a regular and useful dialogue on human rights issues," he said. "The list of issues under discussion is growing, as is the extent and depth of their treatment. We are trying to convince our Chinese partners of the need for a more tolerant and civilized attitude toward discussions at international forums of the human rights situation in various countries, including China, and to not attempt to block those discussions." Rogachev noted that China was making progress in upholding human rights and spoke against the use of punitive sanctions only where there was a clear desire for "real progress toward improving the situation." A few years later, he reported that Russian representatives opposed attempts by some states to "defame" China for its position on issues related to Tibet or Xinjiang, and that they had blocked any discussion of China's actions from the agenda of the UN Human Rights Committee.[21] Russian representatives on that committee, although initially siding with the West, began first abstaining from voting, and then voting against the Western position and supporting China. Beijing's support for Moscow over Chechnya and the general change in mood in Russia played a major role in this shift.

At the same time, Moscow, like Beijing, was opposed to forming an alliance, and Russia did not want to focus exclusively on China. In numerous articles and interviews, deputy foreign minister Georgy Karasin explained this approach by saying that the Russian double-headed eagle should look to both the West and the East.[22] In a lengthy article devoted to Russian-Chinese relations, Karasin's subordinates, Yevgeny Afanasyev, director of the First Asian Department, and department head Grigory Logvinov, explained in turn that "Russia has no alternative but to establish long-term friendly partnerships with the countries of the West and the East . . . Russia's foreign policies for the West and East do not contradict each other. They are in organic unity, appropriate to Russia's unique geographic position."[23]

According to Karasin, "the strategic partnership with China is an objective function of Russia's national interests, the needs of global development."[24] He noted that "Russia and China are two major powers, poles of the emerging multipolar world."[25] Elsewhere Karasin argued that China "is confidently becoming a global center of power" and that a strong and stable China met the security interests of Russia and was a useful economic partner.[26]

Moscow sought to address both strategic and economic objectives by developing cooperation with China. For this reason, it made every effort to expand trade and economic cooperation, finalize border negotiations, and to cooperate on international issues, in the UN and other international organizations.

A Multipolar World

The common ideal of a multipolar world played a significant role in the rapprochement between Russia and China. Russian leaders gave official recognition to the concept, a view that tacitly includes an aversion to global hegemony by the US, whose influence had increased considerably in the world since the collapse of the Soviet Union. According to Igor Rogachev, from a Russian perspective, the whole point of multipolarity is that it "should have no place for the dictates of one or of several states."[27] As Karasin wrote, the support of the two powers for the trend toward multipolarity "is particularly relevant now, when the international community still faces the inertia of the old way of thinking that characterized the Cold War, claims to exclusive leadership, and attempts to reduce the development of international relations to unipolarity."[28] Of course, these and similar statements were very clear allusions to the US inasmuch as no other state was capable of achieving "exclusive leadership."

In describing Russia's official position toward China during the Yeltsin era, it is necessary to make one important point regarding the political system of Yeltsin's Russia as a whole. Because the system of coordination was disrupted badly in Russia's foreign policy – and in most other areas of activity – the Foreign Ministry often pursued a course on China that was at odds with or even ignored the approach taken by regional authorities, not to mention by independent and private institutions. Even senior officials often made contradictory statements with regard to strategy. President Yeltsin himself sometimes made statements that could be interpreted as an attempt to form an alliance with China and switch to an openly anti-Western policy. Just recall this statement he made about US President Bill Clinton during a visit to China in December 1999:

> Clinton apparently forgot for a few seconds what Russia is. Russia has a full arsenal of nuclear weapons, but Clinton decided to flex his muscles. I want to tell Clinton: he should not forget what sort of world he is living in. There was no way and there is no way that he can dictate to people how they should live, pass their free time . . . We will dictate, and not he. . .[29]

Considering that Russia and China stated officially during that meeting that they were "a united force for ensuring the world's security and stability," the West was naturally shocked.[30] However, it soon became clear that it had only been an emotional outburst and did not signal a fundamental shift in Russian foreign policy.

Russian defense ministers Pavel Grachev and Igor Rodionov often made "extraordinary" statements. During a visit to China in the spring of 1995, for example, then defense minister Grachev proposed – clearly without having run it past the Foreign Ministry or consulting beforehand with the Chinese – creating a system for collective security in Northeast Asia with the participation of Russia, China, the US, Japan, and both Koreas. Beijing, which has a policy of never entering into multilateral security relations, issued a polite refusal.[31] Later that same year, Grachev made another remarkable statement, warning that China was using peaceful methods to conquer the Russian Far East.[32] His replacement, Igor Rodionov, frequently confounded Beijing, at one time listing China among the states "that strive to expand their zone of influence and reduce the political significance of the CIS countries in addressing key regional issues," and at another calling for a "long-term strategic partnership" with Beijing, or else announcing plans for military cooperation in the Far East with the US and Japan – even though China considered any increase in Japanese military capabilities a security threat.[33] In the area of practical cooperation, interested agencies and individual officials often set their own interests above those of state policy.

An example is the scandal of 1992 when Russia established unofficial relations with Taiwan, breaking with Moscow's official position. A close advisor to Yeltsin, Oleg Lobov, convinced the president to sign a decree establishing practically official representation of Russia in Taiwan as a means for obtaining credit from Taiwan, which among other things would cover the work of the representation. The order was retracted after a few days after protests from China, the Russian Ministry of Foreign Affairs, and other Russian government agencies.[34]

There were also unofficial views on Russian-Chinese relations. Pro-Western liberals and radical nationalists were for different reasons both apprehensive of China. While the former viewed it as an anti-Western communist regime hostile to the "civilized" democratic world, the latter saw it as one of many numerous enemies of Russia's unique civilization, too pro-Western with its market-oriented economic reforms. At the same time, moderate nationalists and supporters of the influential Communist Party of the Russian Federation called for an anti-Western alliance with Beijing.[35]

As with many other areas of Russian life, Moscow's policy toward China in the 1990s suffered from one major problem – instability. The reason is that Moscow – despite the fact that two-thirds of Russian territory lies in Asia and despite numerous declarations concerning the importance of the East – continued to regard the US and the West as the center of the world and the primary focus of its main interests and actions. That is why Moscow sometimes forgot about China in its eagerness to establish relations with the West, and why, if any disagreements with Western capitals did arise, it sought support in other parts of the world, including Beijing.

A leading Russian Asia expert, Gennady Chufrin, pointed out that "for Moscow, relations with China should be on a par with Russian-US relations, and perhaps more important by a number of parameters," and is no doubt correct in concluding:

> We still use China only as a means of scoring political "points" at home. One person tries to best an opponent by alluding to the "Chinese model" while another cites the "threat from the East" and still another tries to outdo his rivals with an eye-popping initiative and poses for a photo in military garb or formal diplomatic attire next to Jiang Zemin. As a result, the huge Chinese mainland remains on the sidelines of the new policy – behind the Great Wall.[36]

Despite definite achievements in bilateral relations, such an approach could not serve as the basis for solid cooperation with Russia's great neighbor. It also compromised Russia's position in its negotiations with the West. Even as Moscow leaders repeatedly argued that Russia's double-headed eagle should look toward both the East and the West, its foreign policy actually tilted back and forth in favor of one side or the other.

The View of China in Putin's Russia

After coming to power, Vladimir Putin continued to develop relations with Asia. In an article called "Russia: New Eastern Perspectives" that he published in November 2000, Putin noted: "We have never forgotten that the main part of the Russian territory is in Asia. Frankly, we have not always made good use of that advantage. I think the time has come for us, together with the Asia-Pacific countries, to move on from words to actions and to build up economic, political and other ties."[37]

Moscow began to regard Beijing as its most important Asian partner. In an interview with *People's Daily*, the Xinhua agency, and RTR TV during a visit to Beijing in July 2000, Putin said that Russia should "rely on two pillars, as it were, the European and the Asian." He explained: "We know that Russia is both a European and an Asian country. We respect both European pragmatism and Oriental wisdom. So, Russia will pursue a balanced foreign policy. In that sense, relations with the People's Republic of China will certainly be one of our main priorities." The Russian president reconfirmed China's role as a strategic partner and added: "China and the Russian Federation share positions on a wide range of international issues and adhere to similar principles. I am referring, above all, to our goal of maintaining and strengthening the multi-polar world, our joint efforts to preserve strategic equilibrium and balance in the world and to promote peaceful, progressive and effective development of both our states."[38]

The Putin administration acknowledged that Moscow had given little attention to developing practical ties with Asia, with the result that Russia was no longer perceived as a global power. Therefore the new Russian leader placed the initial emphasis on rapidly developing relations with Asian countries, giving it equal priority with traditional relations with the West.[39]

At a meeting of the Shanghai Forum in Dushanbe in Tajikistan in July 2000, a regional group which at that time included Russia, China, Tajikistan, Kazakhstan, and Kyrgyzstan, President Putin reiterated that "China is to us a strategic partner in every sense – from the standpoint of international security guarantees, friendly relations, and development of contacts in culture, the economy and every sphere of state activities."[40] That same year, foreign minister Igor Ivanov, while acknowledging that some problems existed in Russia's economic cooperation with China, said that "in a strategic sense, we have no problems now and do not expect any in the years to come." He also stressed that overall, "relations between Russia and China are steadily advancing."[41]

It was clearly very natural for Russia and China to seek rapprochement after years of hostility that ran counter to the fundamental interests of both countries. It was motivated largely by concerns that both Moscow and Beijing had regarding the impact the international situation would have on their main areas of mutual interest. Thus, according to Igor Ivanov, "Russian-Chinese cooperation has special importance in such key areas as enhancing the authority and role of the UN, defending the primacy of international law in international affairs, maintaining strategic stability and, above all, preserving the ABM [Anti-Ballistic Missile] treaty, creating a fair and equitable world economic order."[42] The common goals to which Ivanov drew attention no doubt stem from a common concern over the trend toward the dismantling of the existing system of international law and the creation of a center of international policy outside the framework of the UN – and without the participation of Moscow or Beijing. For Russia and China, the NATO bombardment of Yugoslavia in 1999 without UN Security Council approval was the most dangerous manifestation of this trend. Moscow and Beijing expressed common concern over Islamic terrorism and separatism. Referring to these problems on the eve of his visit to Beijing in July 2000, President Putin emphasized,

> Russia's main goal in international politics is to preserve the balance of forces and interests in the international arena. As you know, from time to time we are confronted with new threats, with what we believe are dangerous new concepts, such as alleged humanitarian interventions in the internal affairs of other states. We face such threats as international terrorism and such problems as religious extremism and separatism. . . . In this context, China is one of Russia's key partners in dealing with these problems and eliminating their possible negative consequences.[43]

Both Russia and China attached great importance to developing and signing a new framework agreement. Analyzing the reasons why it was necessary to sign the Russian-Chinese Treaty of Good-Neighborliness and Friendly Cooperation, Igor Rogachev wrote:

> The idea of developing a new treaty did not arise spontaneously: it was suggested by the very logic of life, the course of development of Russian-Chinese relations. The comprehensive build-up and deepening of cooperation in all areas in the 1990s led to the realization in Moscow and Beijing of the need to establish a strategic partnership on a fundamental and legal basis. The specific agreement to develop a new

foundational Treaty was reached during Vladimir Putin's state visit to China on July 17–19, 2000.

The Russian diplomat admitted that each side "had its own initial vision of the concept for its contents," but said that they were able to work out those differences during the formulation of the document.[44]

According to foreign minister Sergey Lavrov, the signing of the document

> laid a reliable political and legal foundation of stable, predictable, and multifaceted relations between the two countries. The Treaty imbibes the centuries-old experience in the development of relations between Russia and China, inherently combining it with the generally recognized principles and norms of international law. This basic international legal act, governing Russian-Chinese relations at present and for the foreseeable future, reflects in full measure the deep historical traditions of good-neighborliness and friendship between the Russian and Chinese peoples, and the peace-loving foreign policy of the two states.[45]

There was some concern in Moscow that the new generation of Chinese leaders would have a cooler attitude toward Russia than the generation of Deng Xiaoping and Jiang Zemin, many of whom frequented the Soviet Union in their youth and sometimes lived there, as either college students or employees. By contrast, Hu Jintao visited Russia for the first time only in 2001. However, those fears proved groundless. This is not simply because the new Chinese leader demonstrated his knowledge of Soviet literature during an interview, stating that the all-but-forgotten World War II Soviet patriotic piece *The Story of Zoya and Shura* was one of his favorite books, but because he purposely chose Russia as the destination of his first official visit abroad. Russia acquired importance for Chinese foreign policy not as a result of the personal predilections of Chinese leaders, but because of China's national interests and the way in which the situation in the world was developing.

Explaining the need for the signing of the treaty in a speech dedicated to the fifteenth anniversary of that event, Vladimir Putin underscored that it was the result of a long and incremental process of rapprochement. "The unprecedented level, achieved through mutual trust and understanding, allowed us to resolve complicated and fairly delicate issues that we inherited, and most importantly, we have opened opportunities for moving forward, for establishing multilateral relations in the most diverse areas," he stressed. He also recalled that in the run-up to the treaty, "hundreds of bilateral documents have been signed, favorable conditions were created for boosting the cooperation of government agencies, regions, public and business communities, representatives of science, culture and education."[46]

The Shanghai Cooperation Organization

The Shanghai Cooperation Organization, officially established in 2001, grew directly out of the process of the normalization of Soviet-Chinese relations. From the Russian point of view, the so-called "Shanghai Five" – the predecessor of the SCO – arose from the need among the former Soviet republics sharing a border with China to continue a series of negotiation processes with that country as a collective whole. Within that structure, the unified delegation representing Russia, Kazakhstan, Kyrgyzstan, and Tajikistan continued negotiations with China on confidence-building measures along their common borders. That was a temporary but necessary format. At the same time, it was not yet clear what form of integrative arrangement would remain after the collapse of the Soviet Union: the Russian government held out hope that some degree of political unity would endure within the CIS framework and that Moscow would act as its leader.

When these hopes did not pan out because the CIS retained only a few unifying mechanisms in the areas of economy and education, the search began for new forms. Several CIS states signed a collective security treaty that became the basis of the Collective Security Treaty Organization (CSTO). At the same time, the "Shanghai Five" and Uzbekistan found that their common interests in cooperating with China were not limited to border issues, but also included comprehensive coordination in such areas as security, the economy, science, education, and culture.

Russia and China actively promoted this project. There were several reasons why the SCO was important for the Russian leadership. First, the realists understood that China's influence in Central Asia was growing, and that it would be useless to try to stop it. The most reasonable policy, therefore, was to coordinate regional cooperation with China through an organization in which all member states would have equal rights, and which would make decisions by consensus. Second, as disagreements with the West increased, the SCO came to be seen, if not as an alternative to Western economic and political structures, then at least as something of a counterbalance to them – a function that Russia, alone, could not have served. Third, Moscow sought a mechanism for coordinating efforts with Beijing and Central Asian capitals in the struggle against the growing terrorist threat of

Islamic extremism in the region. Fourth, Russia wanted to utilize SCO mechanisms to harness China's economic power for the development of its own economy.

From the start, Russia most actively developed cooperation on security within the framework of the SCO. Following the events in the US in September 2001, Russia effectively supported US operations in Afghanistan and pursued a corresponding policy in the SCO. Expressing that opinion in an interview with *Vremya Novostey* newspaper (July 24, 2003), Alexander Losyukov, deputy minister of foreign affairs of Russia, spoke about the fight against the terrorist threat in Central Asia:

> Neither we nor China are glad that the American military presence appeared in Central Asia. That is a new and very serious element in the balance of forces in the region ... We could ... not cope with that [terrorist] threat either alone or with China's help. Afghanistan was in danger of becoming totally Taliban controlled. And then the instability would have flooded over the border ... An American presence emerged as a result of the struggle against that threat, with us being interested. By means of the US intervention it became possible to remove that threat, albeit not completely, and that is a significant achievement. We see the USA not as an adversary, but as a partner in this struggle, with whom we have interests coinciding in many respects. The Chinese also understand that.[47]

However, after the US and EU member states criticized the Uzbek government for the methods it used in suppressing antigovernment protests in 2005, the SCO became more wary of US intentions in Central Asia. In June of that year, Russia supported a point of the SCO declaration, put forward by Uzbekistan calling for members of the antiterrorist coalition to set deadlines for withdrawing their military contingents from the territories of the SCO member states. Despite that, however, Russia continued to cooperate with the US in Afghanistan until Washington ended it in response to events in Ukraine in 2014.

However, Russia took an ambivalent stance with regard to economic cooperation within the SCO. On one hand, in all of its official declarations Moscow advocated multilateral economic development and supported the adoption of various plans, documents, and declarations. On the other hand, when it came to implementing them, Russia behaved extremely passively, effectively hindering the development of multilateral cooperation as well as mechanisms that China had actively proposed for financing it. The unofficial explanation was that Russia was worried that China would dominate the SCO bank proposed by Beijing, with the result that the bank was never created. Russia and other SCO member states also had concerns about the free trade zone actively favored by China. As a result, those states responded to Chinese proposals not by rejecting them outright, but usually by offering only noncommittal statements – and this despite the fact that the SCO Charter calls for the creation of a free trade zone. In general, the economic bloc of the Russian government was of the opinion that Moscow should deepen economic cooperation with the countries of Central Asia through the Eurasian Economic Community (EurAsEC) where Russia held much greater influence than in the SCO.

Russia's position regarding the expansion of the SCO changed over time, a result of a change in Russia's overall approach to the international situation. Initially, Russia and China did not desire any expansion because they viewed it as a purely regional organization whose main task was to coordinate the policies of the two countries in Central Asia. However, as tensions with the West increased, Moscow began thinking more about expanding the functions of the SCO to make it a more effective, non-Western counterweight to Western structures. From this perspective, Russia saw that it could advance that goal if other major non-Western countries were to accede to the SCO and the organization could broaden its agenda. Moscow has therefore actively supported the accession of India, and managed to convince Beijing of its necessity on the proviso that Pakistan – which had applied for membership first – accede simultaneously. Russia became the main supporter of the SCO's enlargement. At the SCO summit in Dushanbe in 2008, it initiated the establishment of a special expert group, which later drafted the admission documents. At the Astana summit in 2011, Russia called for the termination of the temporary unofficial moratorium on the admission of new members. Russia's position stems from its strong support for India's candidacy, which was stated in the Joint Russian-Indian Declaration on Deepening the Strategic Partnership, signed by the leaders of the two countries during an official visit to Russia by Indian prime minister Manmohan Singh in December 2009.[48] Admitting such a large and successfully developing country as India would make the SCO the second largest international organization in the world after the United Nations in terms of the aggregate population of its members. India's admission in 2017 would significantly increase the SCO's political weight and economic attractiveness among developing countries.

One of the SCO's priorities is stepping up cooperation in Central Asia. Russia is actively cooperating with China within the SCO. In doing so, Russia welcomes China's stabilizing economic presence in Central Asia, while Beijing recognizes the traditional Russian interests in the region. Yet some analysts in Russia fear China's economic role in Central Asia will grow too rapidly. From this point of view, one could only welcome India's admission to the SCO, as this country can make a significant contribution to the development of Central Asian countries and help diversify their external economic relations.

Indian interests in Central Asia fully coincide with the interests of the SCO member states, and India's development goals meet the organization's objectives. India is a secular state and is actively combating ethnic nationalism, separatism, and religious extremism. It knows from its own experience what the threat of terrorism is. In the last few decades, India has been successfully developing its economy. Its unique economic model, which is oriented toward the domestic market and which showed its advantages during the recent global crisis, would supplement the other development models of SCO members. In addition, relations with Russia, China and Central Asian countries have always been a top priority for India.

Thus, from Moscow's point of view, admitting India would also help stabilize the situation in Central Asian countries and accelerate their economic development. India has a long history of mutual relations with the region. There were times when Central Asia, Afghanistan, and northern India were parts of one state. Today, India continues to actively develop trade and economic ties with Central Asia and make significant investments there. The strengthening of its economic positions in the region would not conflict with the interests of other SCO member states; moreover, it would serve the common goal of economic development of the region, while counterbalancing the growing economic influence of the West, especially the EU. One should also keep in mind the positive political influence of New Delhi, because India is the world's largest democracy, which at the same time has preserved many of its values and characteristics. India could also make a great contribution to the SCO's efforts to stabilize the situation in Afghanistan. India has already invested over US$1 billion in reconstruction projects in Afghanistan, and it could provide significant support to programs of the SCO and its members aimed at developing the Afghan economy. Geopolitically, India's full-scale membership in the SCO could result in a shift of its partnership interest from the West to Russia and Asian states.

After the US applied sanctions against Russia in 2014, Moscow began to support Iran's bid to join the SCO. It is important that Iran also suffered from Western sanctions. Russian foreign minister Sergey

Lavrov made it clear on several occasions that Russia was willing to support the accession of Iran to the SCO as a full member and that the lifting of UN Security Council sanctions would make that possible.[49] Speaking at a news conference in Lausanne on March 31, 2015, he said that sanctions against Iran should be lifted once the deal was reached, which means immediately and not gradually, as the US wants. In fact, Moscow's policy toward Tehran was always part of Russia's broader foreign policy. As Russia's relations with the West have deteriorated, Iran's importance has become increasingly clear. Sometimes Russia's relations with Iran were used to counterbalance its ties with the West. For instance, the media reported that after the 2008 war with Georgia, Moscow and Washington reached an informal agreement that the latter would turn a blind eye to Russia's recognition of Abkhazia and South Ossetia in exchange for Russian support for sanctions against Iran in the UN Security Council.

Today, the situation has changed. Russia has become disillusioned with the West and has no reason to follow along anymore. Relations between China and the West (particularly the United States) are also becoming increasingly strained. Against this background the importance of working with countries with an independent foreign policy, including Iran, is becoming clear. Its accession to the SCO is fully in line with the interests of Russia and China.

At the SCO summit held in 2015 in Ufa, Russia, all member states supported the Russian and Chinese proposal to admit India and Pakistan simultaneously to the organization. The decision was formalized at the next summit in Tashkent in 2016 and was formally realized at the June 2017 summit in Astana. The SCO will also consider requests by other countries intent on joining its work. In his comments, President Putin, while not directly mentioning Iran, said that the organization "will also consider the intentions of other countries to join our work."[50] Speaking at a a news conference following a meeting of the SCO foreign ministers in Astana in April 21, 2017, Lavrov said that after Iran had settled the problem of the UN Security Council sanctions, it fully meets the SCO membership criteria and stressed that it will be "the next country we will discuss to join."[51]

The Russian leadership does not exaggerate the successes of the SCO. However, it sees it as an important and popular mechanism of international cooperation in the region. "I would not say that we have made astonishing progress or carried out any high-profile activities; yet the Organization has become highly demanded and attractive in the region, and many countries of the world have expressed their willingness to join it," President Putin said in his June 2017 interview.[52]

President Putin earlier formulated the Russian vision of the SCO's future role in his message to the secretary-general of the Shanghai Cooperation Organization, Zhang Deguang. According to Putin, "the historical role of the SCO is to become a transcontinental bridge linking Europe and Asia. Its destiny is predetermined by the unique geopolitical situation of the SCO member countries, the SCO philosophy of respect for all cultures, religions and traditions, openness and determination for broad international cooperation."[53]

The Ukrainian Crisis and Russian Approach towards Relations with China

It would be difficult to overestimate the impact that the Ukrainian crisis and Russia's accelerated pivot to Asia have had on the structure of international relations. That reorientation, very much in line with the concept of a multipolar world, began long before the crisis. As already mentioned, Russia was seeking wider cooperation with the countries of the Asia-Pacific as a future center of world politics and economy. It also sought broader investments and high technologies from the most developed of those countries to boost the economies of Russia's Asian regions and to diversify political and economic cooperation to reduce its dependence on the West. However, before the clashes in Ukraine, leading Russian politicians were unanimous in their conviction that closer cooperation with Asia would complement rather than weaken Russia's partner relationships with the US and the EU.

In response to events in Ukraine, the West cut back on its cooperation with Moscow in order to force its retreat from its positions. This drove home the simple message to the Russian elite that there was no alternative to intensified cooperation with Asia. The continued rapprochement between Moscow and Beijing constituted the major component of Russia's pivot to Asia. That process has prompted a range of comments in Russia, some of them contradictory.

Russia's domestic supporters of orienting the country toward the West have raised concerns that this rapprochement with Beijing threatens to turn the weaker Russia into a "satellite" and a "raw materials appendage" of the more powerful and aggressive China. By contrast, those who welcome confrontation with the West have written about the necessity and inevitability of building an alliance with China, which in their view would strengthen Russia's position in its effort to chart an independent course. Both positions ultimately stem more from personal ideological preferences than from a sober analysis of the situation.

Both camps prefer to ignore the Chinese position of pursuing an independent foreign policy because it would interfere with their simplified picture of a bipolar world. What is clear is that since the start of the Ukrainian crisis, Russian government officials have begun to take significantly more interest in the Russian community of professional sinologists. In October 2014, the deputy editor of *Kommersant-Vlast*, Alexander Gabuev, published two articles devoted to the study of Russia in China and the study of China in Russia.[54] His argument rested on the observation that in China the study of Russia is heavily funded by the government, is constructed according to a well-defined system, and enjoys high demand from the government and business sectors, while in Russia the situation is reversed. In one illustrative example, even the six-volume work on "The Spiritual Culture of China,"[55] which received the 2011 Russian State Prize, was published with Chinese funding.

Similar articles had been published before but went unnoticed. Just two years earlier, in 2012, Gabuev wrote:

> This vicious cycle, in which sinologists complain about a lack of money while government and business representatives complain about a lack of China experts, has gone on for many years. Meanwhile young Russian sinologists, who should be in as much demand today as nuclear physicists were in the Soviet Union, cannot find work in their area of expertise and end up changing their profession or joining the ranks of those leaving Russia. The community of China experts in Russia is steadily declining, and with it the decision-making foundation for Russia's China policy. At the same time, China is actively developing its field of Russia studies.[56]

Gabuev's arguments elicited little response in 2012. However, by the end of 2014, when both the government and business sectors began to develop a great deal of interest in China, his latest articles provoked a stormy debate and were apparently noticed by the top leadership. China experts were suddenly in great demand. A group of experts affiliated with the Economic Development Ministry was created to discuss various options for greater cooperation with China, as well as ways to increase funding for Russian sinology. Stanislav Voskresensky, deputy minister for economic development, was appointed to coordinate new programs for cooperation with China, while deputy prime minister Igor Shuvalov, who was seen as having successfully organized the 2012 Asia-Pacific Economic Cooperation

(APEC) summit in Vladivostok, became the senior Russian government official in charge of overall Chinese and Asian policy.

So, at this point, the chill between Russia and the West is having its biggest impact not on specific agreements, but by compelling disparate circles of Russian society to seriously seek closer cooperation with China. The need to deepen this cooperation is increasingly viewed in Russia not as a declaration against the West, but as an urgent practical need. This new understanding is true of state bureaucrats and the business elite alike.

A notable development took place in March 2014 when Gennady Timchenko, a prominent businessman with close ties to Putin (in the words of the Russian president himself[57]), became the new head of the Russian-Chinese Business Council, an association of Russian businesspeople working with China. Prior to Timchenko's arrival, the council was more of a ceremonial body, organized from above and having little impact on practical cooperation. The new leadership brought about a sudden burst of activity. This coincided with Timchenko's inclusion in the US sanctions list in the wake of Russia's annexation of Crimea, which led him to sell his stake in the commodity trading company Gunvor Group (that he cofounded), and thus significantly reduce his operations in the West. The most important decision was the move to permit Chinese investors to purchase shares in Russian oil and gas companies – something that had not been formally prohibited, but was never allowed in practice. President Putin argued in 2016:

> China is increasing its presence in our energy market, it is a major shareholder in one of our significant projects, Yamal LNG, and it has acquired 10 percent of the shares in one of our leading chemical holdings, SIBUR. We welcome these Chinese investments not only as a means of placing financial resources but also as a means of further developing our partnership.[58]

This means that the current confrontation between Russia and West has laid the groundwork for a methodical and deeply rooted pivot to China based on cooperation on physical infrastructure and cultural and educational projects. Even more important is the pivot occurring in the minds of Russian officials and businesspeople: they are gradually accepting the fact that cooperation with the West cannot be fully restored, much less widened. The spiritual and axiological gap is growing wider while the hope that the Ukrainian conflict will end any time soon is dying, along with confidence in the West as a reliable partner. Cooperation with China is free from these hindrances, even though there are other, mostly manageable, problems: the very specific Chinese culture and psychology, the need to loosen Russia's traditional ties with Europe, the language barrier, etc.

This does not mean that Russia is unaware of possible complications in its cooperation with China: neither the government nor the expert community harbor any illusions. Nobody expects altruism from Beijing: everybody knows that China would not rescue Russia at its own expense or cooperate with Moscow against its own interests. Beijing has the right to insist on its own interests, and it does so on every applicable occasion – sometimes taking a very hard line. Oil and gas negotiations were long mired in haggling over terms and prices. Russia had learned from previous experience that China, as an exclusive customer, could become a headache. In 2003, as soon as the Blue Stream gas pipeline had been commissioned, Turkey demanded a reduction in the price of gas. If Russia shifts the source of its agricultural imports from Europe to China in response to its own countersanctions against Europe, trade turnover with China will increase, along with Russia's dependence on the Chinese market. Moscow knows that China needs the West to develop its own economy and that Beijing will not retreat from its relationship with the West for the sake of Moscow. The rapidly developing and politically very different China poses a challenge for economically stagnating Russia. It is no secret that growing nationalism in society and the army has been fueling China's increasingly assertive foreign policy activity.

Fully aware of this, under different conditions Moscow would have demonstrated greater restraint. A variety of approaches to China and the West have always been present in the Russian leadership and elite. Several groups favor continued close relations with the US and EU and wield a great deal of influence. They include the pro-Western bloc in the government and the groups closely linked to it, corrupt officials and allied businesspeople with major assets and real estate in Europe and the United States, and the business elite with serious business interests in the West. (Not infrequently, the same people belong to all these groups.) There is also a faction that wants Russia to deal firmly with the West, to actively promote Eurasian integration, and to establish closer ties with Asian countries. President Putin is maneuvering between the two extremes: Russia needs contacts with the West for economic reasons. At the same time, it must develop integration processes among the former Soviet republics and cooperate with China, on the one hand, and with South Korea, India, Iran, Turkey, and the ASEAN countries on the other. Putin is apparently convinced that Russia is an inalienable and yet independent part of Greater Eurasia (and has stated as much on numerous occasions), taking no commands from the Euro-Atlantic political center and acting without regard for the opinions of others. President Putin is doing his utmost to ensure such independence by diversifying foreign policy and establishing foreign economic ties in all directions, including with Eurasian countries and China. By dint of its anti-Russian policies, the West has already done much to undermine the positions of the pro-Western groups within Russia and has supplied their opponents with fresh arguments against cooperation. If the West eases its policies by lifting the sanctions – an eventuality that appears highly improbable at present – Russia would retreat somewhat from its present stance. That, in turn, would help the pro-Western group strengthen its position and to restore some of the ruptured ties with the West. There are several reasons, however, why it is impossible to return fully to the pre-Ukraine state of affairs. First, the widening contacts with China and other Asian states, as well as the new and profitable contracts with Chinese partners, are irreversible. Second, trust in Western partners has been undermined: there is nothing attractive about closing multimillion-dollar deals with companies in countries that do not hesitate to make political decisions which cause serious financial losses to overseas partners. Third, public opinion has passed the point of no return: the majority in Russia has learned to look at the US and the EU member states as enemies.

Conclusions: Reasons for Rapprochement with China, a Russian View

Like the Chinese pivot to Russia, Russia's pivot to China was the result of a long process of Moscow reassessing the nature of global processes and its own foreign policy. As a result, Russia abandoned its perception of China as a potential adversary or competitor on the world stage and came to understand the need for closer cooperation with Beijing on both global and regional issues. Changing perceptions of the intentions of the US and Europe, the abandonment of plans for a unified Europe stretching from Lisbon to Vladivostok, and the growing desire to make Russia an independent center of world politics played a significant role in this reassessment. That desire for independence also dissuaded the Russian leadership from efforts to enter into a formal alliance with China.

Russia has both political and economic reasons to maintain close and constructive relations with China in today's world. The following points summarize Moscow's motivations:

1. Cooperation with China is extremely important to Russia's geopolitical and international interests. China shares Russia's vision of a future multipolar international system. In practical terms, both countries would like a world that is not dominated by a single power, but one marked by cooperation between several centers of influence and guided by international law and the UN Charter. An obvious reality lies hidden behind the ideal of a multipolar world: Russia and China, as well as several other states, are large enough to have their own interests and their own approaches to issues of regional and global development. They are not satisfied with a world order completely dominated by a single major power that does not take their interests into account. However, they are fully content with the post–World War II world structure, its system of international law, and the role of supreme authority played by the UN Security Council. Their status as permanent members of the Security Council places them on equal footing with the United States – a state that in every other respect is more powerful and therefore naturally tries to alter a system that puts fetters on its possibilities. As President Putin put it, "The Chinese voice in the world is indeed growing ever more confident, and we welcome that, because Beijing shares our vision of the emerging equitable world order. We will continue to support each other in the international arena, to work together to solve acute regional and global problems, and to promote cooperation within the UN Security Council, BRICS, the SCO, the G20 and other multilateral forums."[59]
2. China is an important strategic partner for Russia. It is due to relations with China (as well as other Asian countries) that Russia's foreign policy becomes less one-sided, more developed and distinct, and Russia itself becomes a center of global influence. Russia's desire to become increasingly independent and powerful naturally makes it necessary to develop relations with China – that is, short of forming a military alliance with Beijing. That is something neither country wants because it can hinder their ability to cooperate with third-party countries as well.
3. Given Russia's confrontation with the West over Georgia and Ukraine, Moscow greatly appreciates even limited expressions of understanding from Beijing.
4. It is extremely important that Russia cooperate with China to

resolve such major regional issues as the North Korean and Iranian nuclear programs, the Syrian crisis, and many others – on the majority of which the approaches of the two countries coincide.
5. China is one of Russia's most important economic partners. Cooperation with China is necessary in order to compensate for economic losses resulting from hostile economic policies and Western sanctions, and at a more fundamental level, to achieve Russia's highly challenging strategic objective of developing Siberia and the Far East.
6. China is an important regional partner for Russia. Within the framework of the Shanghai Cooperation Organization, China works with Russia to help achieve their common objectives in Central Asia – fighting religious extremism and terrorism, supporting secular regimes, and facilitating the social and economic development of states in the region.
7. Russia needs China as a partner in the project of reforming the international financial system, in efforts to create a system for managing the International Monetary Fund and World Bank more equitably, and in searching for an alternative to the US dollar as the global currency. China fully supports Russia's proposals and objectives in these areas.
8. Within the context of the new and dynamic BRICS group, Russia and China cooperate on the very important task of shaping the agenda on global governance practices in defense of the interests of the non-Western world.

4

FROM NORMALIZATION TO STRATEGIC PARTNERSHIP

Russian-Chinese Relations under Yeltsin

Relations between the new, independent Russia and China formally began before Mikhail Gorbachev officially resigned as the president of the Soviet Union on December 30, 1991. Chinese and Russian deputy foreign ministers Tian Zengpei and Georgy Kunadze held talks in Moscow on December 27, 1991 on the principles of a new relationship between Beijing and Moscow. The talks resulted in the signing of a protocol in which China recognized Russia as the legal successor to the Soviet Union and reconfirmed all of the documents previously signed with the Soviet Union.

A framework intergovernmental agreement on trade and economic relations was concluded in Beijing in March 1992.[1] Moscow was glad to note that even as the economic situation in the country kept deteriorating, trade with China, especially cross-border trade, was booming, meeting the demands of people in the eastern regions of Russia. Later that month, during Russian foreign minister Andrey Kozyrev's visit to China, his Chinese counterpart announced the decision to open up several border towns to direct trade with Russian regions and suggested that Boris Yeltsin, as the Russian leader, visit China. The two countries also launched military cooperation, with the first shipment of Russian fighter aircraft transferred to China in 1992. According to official Russian reports provided to the United Nations, it consisted of 26 fighter jets, including 20 Su-27SK and Su-27UBK.[2]

The nature of the new relations between Moscow and Beijing was determined when Russian President Boris Yeltsin visited Beijing in December 1992. Yeltsin and the then PRC chairman Yang Shangkun firmly established those new principles by signing a joint declaration on the basis of mutual relations. That declaration proclaimed that Russia and China viewed each other as "friendly states" and would "develop relations of good-neighborliness, friendship, and mutually beneficial cooperation in accordance with the Charter of the United Nations, based on the principles of mutual respect and territorial integrity, non-aggression, non-interference in each others' internal affairs, equality and mutual benefit, peaceful coexistence, and other universally recognized norms of international rights."[3] Having agreed to leave ideological disputes behind them, the two sides stressed "the need to respect the right of the people of any country to freely choose the path of its internal development. Differences in the social systems and ideologies will not hinder normal development of interstate relations."[4] This statement basically recognizes the reality that emerged after the disintegration of the Soviet Union: Russia and China belong to different political systems but, at the same time, desire to develop normal good-neighborly relations based on the principles of international law despite these differences. Russia, which was eagerly embracing Western-type democracy, did not try to impose new values upon China, which, in turn, promised that its regrets about the collapse of the socialist elder brother would not affect interstate relations.

The declaration also formalized a number of other important points that formed the basis for further relations. Many of them were repeated in follow-up documents. The two countries pledged to resolve all bilateral problems peacefully, without resorting to force or threat of force, refrain from entering military-political alliances or agreements with third parties directed against each other, and prevent the use of their territory by third countries to the detriment of the state sovereignty and security of the other side. Russia once again recognized Taiwan as an integral part of China and promised to develop only unofficial ties with the island. Russia and China stressed the need for the United Nations to play a greater role and have more authority, and agreed to conduct active consultations at and outside the UN, and maintain regular political dialogue on different levels, including at the top. The sides also agreed to continue negotiations on the disputed sections of the border, build confidence in the border area, and develop military, trade, economic, scientific, technical, cultural, and other ties.[5]

The importance of the agreements reached in Beijing can hardly be overestimated. A Russian diplomat and one of the leading China experts, Georgy Zinoviev, wrote that the fact that there was no dramatic cooling of relations between Russia and China in 1992 can be regarded as an important victory of pragmatism and common sense in the foreign policies of the two countries. It clearly showed that both Moscow and Beijing had dropped ideological patterns and firmly understood the historically proven fact that the development of cooperation would fully serve their interests, while confrontation would entail exorbitant costs.[6]

Analyzing the reasons for the turn toward constructive cooperation, Russian ambassador to China Igor Rogachev concluded that "more than two decades of senseless and dangerous Soviet-Chinese confrontation helped the people, the public and the leaders of our countries develop some sort of 'anti-confrontational immunity' which essentially guarantees that this situation will not occur again and encourages us to take approaches that are fundamentally different from those used in the past."[7]

Russian-Chinese relations were progressing in the 1990s. Because of internal political problems in Russia, 1993 was the only year in the whole decade when the leaders of the two countries did not meet. China waited to see who would gain the upper hand in the confrontation between the executive and legislative branches of power in Russia, and the Russian leaders were preoccupied with internal political struggle. And yet, interstate exchanges intensified. In September 1994, during Chinese leader Jiang Zemin's visit to Russia, the two countries signed several documents: a bilateral declaration and a joint statement on no-first-use of nuclear weapons against each other and on mutual de-targeting of strategic nuclear missiles. The foreign ministers of the two countries signed an agreement on the western section of the Russian-Chinese border. The joint declaration defined bilateral relations as "truly equal relations of good-neighborliness, friendship and mutually advantageous cooperation based on the principles of peaceful coexistence."

This declaration included a mutual obligation of not targeting strategic nuclear missiles on each other and non-use of force against each other including non-use of nuclear weapons against each other as a first strike. The two sides agreed to continue and broaden exchanges and cooperation that were not targeted against third countries. They stated that they saw each other as "powers which are a major factor of maintaining peace and stability under the situation of emerging polycentric international system." They also called for "non-discriminatory participation in international affairs" and for prevention of expansionism, hegemonism and creation of political, military, or economic blocs." This was a clear criticism of the plans of NATO enlargement and the Western policy of using sanctions against China.[8] Trade was boosted when the Russian-Chinese (formerly Soviet-Chinese) Commission on Economic, Trade, Scientific and Technical Cooperation, headed by deputy prime ministers, resumed its work in August 1992. At about the same time, the two countries signed an agreement that laid out the terms for Chinese citizens moving to and being received in Russia. During deputy prime minister Alexander Shokhin's visit to Beijing in December of the same year, Russia and China concluded an agreement on the construction of a nuclear power plant in China. In 1992, bilateral trade turnover increased by 50 percent and exceeded US$5.8 billion, and gained another 30 percent in 1993, reaching almost US$7.7 billion. It declined again by more than 30 percent in 1994 and had settled at around US$5.5 billion by 1995. In May 1995, Chinese leader Jiang Zemin made a brief, but very symbolic trip to Moscow to attend celebrations marking the fiftieth anniversary of the victory over Nazi Germany in World War II. Chinese prime minister Li Peng was in Russia on June 25–8, but the Russian president's visit to China, scheduled for October, was canceled because of his illness.

Starting in the mid-1990s, the Russian leadership became increasingly inclined to step up its foreign policy in the East as a counterbalance to relations with the West, which were not always smooth. In their official documents, the Russian president and the Foreign Ministry began to pay more attention to the role the Asia-Pacific region and China played for Russia. While the Asia-Pacific region ranked sixth in Russia's foreign policy priorities in 1993 (after relations with the CIS, arms control, international security, economic reforms, and relations with the United States and Europe),[9] in February 1996 foreign minister Yevgeny Primakov moved it all the way up to third place (after the CIS and Eastern Europe).[10]

During his visit to China in April 1996, President Yeltsin, speaking in Shanghai, urged both sides to develop "equal and trustworthy partnership towards strategic interaction between the two countries in the twenty-first century."[11] This was stated in the joint declaration adopted during the visit. Interestingly, although the level of relations clearly required a new definition, the wording in the 1996 declaration was most likely spontaneous. Chinese diplomat Zhou Xiaopei, who took part in the negotiations, recalled that on his way to Beijing, President Yeltsin looked through the prepared draft declaration and disliked it, because it contained nothing fundamentally new that would reflect the direction of future relations between the two countries. He made corrections to change the phrase "to develop long-term, stable, good-neighborly, and mutually advantageous cooperation and constructive partner-like relations into the twenty-first century" to "equal and trustworthy partnership towards strategic interaction between the two countries in the twenty-first century." The words "strategic interaction" were the main novelty. Zhou recalls that some Russian diplomats had doubts as to whether the Chinese side would approve of such bold changes made regardless of protocol. In fact, the Chinese leader told Yeltsin that the changes had been given to him quite unexpectedly during a meeting he was chairing, but he had read and agreed with them without delay.[12] Since then, strategic interaction has been the official policy of the two countries.

The declaration reiterated their desire to "continue to strengthen cooperation in areas where our approaches are similar or identical, and look for ways to work together where our positions differ." Russia and China reaffirmed their readiness to develop ties at all levels, noting particularly the importance of regular high-level and top-level contacts between the leaders of the two countries, and announced the decision to set up a hotline between their governments.[13]

But the Russian-Chinese consensus was a far cry from the anti-American front hardline anti-Westerners desired to see for ideological reasons. While agreeing with Beijing on many issues, Russian government officials kept saying that "the development of the Russian-Chinese constructive partnership is not directed against the interests of any third country or group of countries, and it does not, and cannot, mean the creation of any bloc or alliance."[14] In their joint communiqué signed at the summit in November 1998, the two countries expressed their interest in cooperation with other countries, including the West and particularly the United States, and stressed again: "The emerging Russian-Chinese strategic partnership is not an alliance and is not aimed against third countries."[15]

Moscow and Beijing adopted a concept of a multipolar world and in Moscow in April 1997 Jiang Zemin and Boris Yeltsin signed the Russian-Chinese Joint Declaration on a Multipolar World and the Establishment of a New International Order. The declaration was not formally binding but was nevertheless important in that it reflected the goals the two countries were pursuing in developing their cooperation. The goal of creating a "multipolar world" revealed their common understanding of what kind of international order they should maintain. It was prompted by their serious concern about the strengthening of the United States, which threatened to undermine the world order created after World War II. The two countries voiced their concern, deepening in the late 1990s, about the desire of the US to establish "unipolarity," Washington's hegemonic policy (as China described it), the weakening of the United Nations and its Security Council, and attempts to keep those of its members which were not in US-led alliances (namely Russia and China) from participating in the adoption of decisions on key international issues.

Of several dozen documents signed by the two countries in the late 1990s, significantly expanding cooperation in all areas, some were particularly important. The joint declaration signed by the heads of state during Boris Yeltsin's visit to Beijing in April 1996 defined bilateral relations as an "equal and trustworthy partnership towards strategic interaction between the two countries in the twenty-first century." This became their official designation until 2001 when the Treaty of Good-Neighborliness and Friendly Cooperation was signed.

The Shanghai (April 1996) and Moscow (April 1997) agreements on confidence-building in the military field and mutual reduction of military forces along the border areas played a very constructive role. They were signed by China and former Soviet republics sharing a border with it. The agreement on the principles of cooperation between the administrations (governments) of Russian regions and the local Chinese authorities, signed by deputy prime minister Boris Nemtsov and vice premier Li Lanqing during Boris Yeltsin's visit to China in November 1997, established a legal framework for the further development of cooperation between Russian regions and Chinese provinces.

The Agreement on the Establishment of a Regular Meeting Mechanism between the Heads of Government and Its Organizational Principles (June 1997) and its four protocols created a permanent structure of economic cooperation, originally agreed to by the two countries in December 1996. Since then, annual meetings of the heads of government, focusing mainly on key issues of economic cooperation, have been prepared by a special commission co-chaired by deputy prime ministers of the two countries. The new mechanism replaced the Soviet-Chinese Commission on Economic, Trade, Scientific and Technical Cooperation formed in 1984. More than a dozen of its subcommissions, co-chaired by ministers and the heads of relevant agencies, have been meeting annually to evaluate the results of the work done and map out plans for the future. As of 2010, there were subcommissions on trade, economic, scientific, technical, interbank and customs cooperation; and on cooperation in the fields of energy, transport, nuclear issues, communications, information technology, civil aviation, and environmental protection.

Russian President Boris Yeltsin and Chinese leader Jiang Zemin established a good personal relationship. In November 1998, they held their first informal meeting in Moscow to discuss problems in bilateral relations. In December 1999, shortly before his resignation, Boris Yeltsin made his last visit to China as head of state. By that time, the two countries had signed and started implementing agreements on cooperation between parliaments, ministries and agencies, the armed forces, courts, the offices of the prosecutors general, research institutes, universities, and about 50 regions and cities in both countries. Hotlines between the heads of state and government of the two countries had become operational. The Russian and Chinese leaders talked to each other by phone on a regular basis. According to Igor Rogachev, by 1999 they had signed about 120 agreements at the levels of heads of state and heads of government and dozens of interagency agreements.[16]

Putin Becomes President

Russia's new president, Vladimir Putin, who took office in 2000, streamlined the government system in the country, which had a positive effect on relations with China. During his first visit to Beijing in July 2000, the two countries signed a declaration and a joint statement on missile defense, and a number of other documents on cooperation in specific areas, and agreed to draft and prepare a new basic Treaty of Good-Neighborliness and Friendly Cooperation.[17] In the same year, the two countries decided to set up a new intergovernmental commission on education, culture, health, and sports. Created within the framework of the regular meeting mechanism, the commission and its subcommissions have been working to deepen cooperation on a wide range of cultural issues.

The Treaty of 2001

The new Treaty of Good-Neighborliness and Friendly Cooperation, signed by President Putin and Jiang at their meeting in Moscow in July 2001, raised bilateral relations to a new level. This basic treaty, which is still in effect, is worth a closer look as it stirred much interest but also provoked controversial comments elsewhere in the world. Some claimed that the two former communist giants were marching toward a new alliance directed against the United States and the West as a whole. Others, on the contrary, said that it was a purely declarative document of no practical value.

Both opinions were quite superficial. The treaty did not create any alliance, let alone a military one. It contains no commitments regarding joint defense against aggression, unlike the Soviet-Chinese treaty signed by Moscow and the Chiang Kai-shek government in 1945, or the Treaty of Friendship, Alliance and Mutual Assistance signed by Moscow and the communist government of China in 1950, which set the stage for the "brothers forever" campaign. At the same time, the new treaty created a mechanism for consultations on joint actions in the face of a real threat.[18] The cautious wording of the treaty of 2001, a careful attempt to refrain from ideological declarations or knowingly unrealizable obligations, indicated that the leaders of the two countries were thinking long-term and tried to avoid mistakes made fifty years earlier. In fact, the previous treaties of 1945 and 1950 had stopped working in practical terms long before they officially expired. The treaty of 1950 was formally in effect when Moscow and Beijing considered each other enemies and armed skirmishes were taking place on their common border. This does not mean that the treaty of 2001 had no practical value, because it formalized an important tendency in modern international relations: the desire of two major world powers, members of the nuclear club and the UN Security Council, to establish closer cooperation with each other.

The treaty, just like Russian-Chinese cooperation in general, has two aspects: international and bilateral. The fact that the two countries have practically identical views on international issues is a major factor encouraging the improvement of bilateral relations. Moscow and Beijing have repeatedly said that their efforts to establish closer relations with each other are not directed against third countries, including the United States, which is absolutely true since neither China nor Russia considers the US and the West in general an immediate enemy. On the contrary, the two countries are deeply interested in economic and political cooperation with the West as an important factor in their development, and therefore it fully matches their strategic goals. But it is also true that the Russian-Chinese rapport was largely inspired by a number of negative (as seen by Moscow and Beijing) tendencies in international affairs, which were actively encouraged by Washington, especially at that time.

These included, above all, efforts to downplay the role of the United Nations and its bodies, NATO's attempts to assume the functions of the UN Security Council, interference in the internal affairs of sovereign states, support for separatist movements, NATO's expansion, the secession of the US from the ABM Treaty and refusal to join some other international agreements. By and large, there were two major tendencies in international affairs after the end of the Cold War. Having emerged from it much stronger, the United States sought the role of sole leader of the world, but felt restricted by existing international law, which was based on the principle of national sovereignty. Russia was weak and China had not yet become strong enough (it was large but not yet strong enough to resist US pressure, like several other states, such as India, Brazil, and Iran), so they sought to coordinate their efforts in order to defend the world of sovereign nations, which clearly suited them, and its bodies, primarily the United Nations. The Russian-Chinese treaty contained obligations to preserve the UN and its role, supported fundamental agreements underpinning strategic stability (such as the ABM Treaty), rejected attempts to interfere in the internal affairs of sovereign states, and thus provided a comprehensive program for safeguarding the postwar system of international law. The "multipolar world" concept pursued similar goals.

However, Russia and China were not at all interested in aggravating their relations with the United States or creating an anti-American alliance. Such an unnatural alliance could only have been possible if Moscow and Beijing had regarded the United States as a bigger threat than the one caused by their refusal to cooperate with the West. But the US stubbornly continued to move in the direction of creating this kind of fear.

The treaty also played an important role for bilateral relations. China appreciated the fact that it expressed respect for the chosen path of development, which signified Russia's refusal to lecture China about the advantages of a certain political system or human rights as it had tried to do in the early 1990s – that had been quite bizarre since at that time Russia itself was far from being a shining example to follow.

Article 8 prohibited the use of the territory of Russia or China by third countries to the detriment of the state sovereignty, security, and territorial integrity of either country, and banned the operation of organizations and groups that was detrimental to them. The implication was quite clear, involving the fight against separatist movements supported by international terrorist organizations or third countries. However, China subsequently invoked this article on several occasions in order to pressure Russia into restricting the activity of organizations that advocated the freedom of Tibet and Xinjiang or were linked to the Falun Gong sect, even though such activities were not forbidden by Russian legislation.

Article 6 was quite important for Russia as it recognized the existing state border with China and reiterated the need to keep the status quo on uncoordinated sections. The article put an end to speculation by the "fighters for Russian land," who asserted that China was allegedly preparing claims against Russian territories or was even carrying out a deliberate policy of populating the Russian Far East.

When assessing the treaty of 2001, it is important to remember that Beijing is generally reluctant to sign such basic documents with other countries. Therefore, its conclusion clearly reflects the significance China attaches to relations with Russia. Prior to 2001, China had similar treaties only with three other countries: Japan (on peace and friendship, signed in 1978), North Korea (on friendship, cooperation, and mutual assistance, signed in 1961), and Mongolia (on friendship and cooperation, signed in 1962; it was restated and extended in 1994). All of them were concluded before China adopted an independent foreign policy.

9/11 Attacks and Their Impact

The September 11, 2001 attacks in New York and the following antiterrorist operation did not have any long-term impact on the nature of relations between Russia and China. Moscow and Beijing did not have to gather strength for a new fight with international terrorism as they had already been fighting it for a long time. Russian-Chinese security cooperation became much more specific and effective, even though the initial reaction of the two countries differed, as has been described.

Beijing's concerns about Russia's possible rapprochement with the United States at China's expense were spurred by Moscow's increased diplomatic activity on the Western front and its lack of attention to Beijing. This is not to say that there were no contacts or consultations at all, but their intensity and promptness did not match the constantly touted "two-headed Russian eagle" policy. President Vladimir Putin was the first foreign leader to call US President George W. Bush to offer condolences and support. He talked with Chinese leader Jiang Zemin only when the latter called him on September 18.[19] Chinese official statements said it was a formal conversation during which the two leaders expressed their common opinion that international terrorism was becoming a serious threat to international peace and stability and a global evil, and called for joint international efforts to combat it. They agreed that China and Russia should coordinate their antiterrorism activities and contacts.[20] On the following day,

Putin called Jiang to inform him about his visit to the United States. The two leaders also discussed antimissile defense, the situation in Afghanistan, and more active antiterrorism efforts.[21]

The Russian and Chinese leaders met on October 20, 2001 at the APEC summit in Shanghai, but it was a formal meeting as China was trying hard to shift the attention of the Asia-Pacific leaders from counterterrorism to regional economic cooperation. Issues concerning the international situation after the 9/11 attacks and the ABM Treaty were also discussed during personal meetings and telephone calls, which were a continuation of those that had actually been held once a month or so before the terrorist attacks in America as well.

So, while Russia's contact with the United States, NATO, and Western Europe became increasingly intensive, its ties with China had in practice not changed. As a result, or so China believed, there arose the risk of a Russian-US deal on missile defense and NATO's expansion, in disregard of Beijing's interests.

In early 2002 Russia stepped up its diplomatic activity in the East and helped organize an unscheduled meeting of the foreign ministers of the Shanghai Cooperation Organization in Beijing. In their joint statement, the ministers stressed that they would like to see Afghanistan "free and neutral". They also said that a global counterterrorism system should be based on regional, subregional, and national structures.[22]

The latter was clearly at odds with Washington's plans as it preferred to act without consulting even its closest allies. But more moderate circles in America, and particularly officials connected with the previous administration, understood that the United States would most likely be unable to deal with international terrorism alone, and welcomed the idea of broad cooperation with regional organizations.[23] This adjustment in Russia's position served the interests of both China and Russia itself. As a result, bilateral relations continued to progress.

Shortly thereafter a new leader came to power in China: Hu Jintao. He made his first foreign trip to Russia on May 26–8, 2003. A couple of months before, on March 20, 2003, the United States had begun a military operation in Iraq, accusing it of not liquidating its chemical weapons.

Until the very last moment, Russia and China had been trying to find a peaceful solution to the crisis, insisting on strict compliance by both sides with UN Security Council Resolution 1441 which gave broad powers to the International Atomic Energy Agency (IAEA) and the United Nations Monitoring, Verification and Inspection

Commission (UNMOVIC) and required Iraq to cooperate with international inspectors but did not authorize armed intervention. This position was agreed during a telephone conversation between the leaders of the two countries on February 19, 2003.[24]

In a joint communiqué issued during Russian foreign minister Igor Ivanov's visit to China in late February 2003, both sides reiterated "their determination to render their full efforts for promoting a political solution to the Iraq issue" and stressed that "a war can and must be avoided." According to the document "Russia and China proceed from the assumption that inspection activities by the UNMOVIC and the IAEA play an important role in the matter of resolving the Iraqi question, have received definite progress and should proceed further." Moscow and Beijing called the United Nations Security Council to strengthen the guidance and support of inspection work. The two sides said that the UN Security Council "bears the main responsibility for the maintenance of international peace and security and, guided by the purposes and principles of the UN Charter, should continue to play a central role in resolving the Iraq problem. All of the UN member states must respect and protect the authority and powers of the UN Security Council."[25]

In a telephone conversation on March 23, Igor Ivanov and his Chinese counterpart Li Zhaoxing said:

> Russia and China resolutely advocate an immediate cessation of military actions against Iraq, which were undertaken in circumvention of the UN Security Council and have no legal basis ... Russia and China are firm in their stand that the UN Security Council alone can take decisions on the reconstruction of Iraq and on a settlement of the Iraq problem in accordance with the UN Security Council resolutions, and will actively strive for this.[26]

Russian-Chinese interaction was evolving to a new level amid increased disagreement with the United States. Apart from Iraq, there was another international problem to be resolved, the deterioration of the situation on the Korean Peninsula. In late 2002, having accused Pyongyang of clandestine uranium enrichment, the United States suspended fuel supplies to North Korean power plants under the bilateral framework agreement of 1994. In response, on December 12, 2002, North Korea officially resumed its nuclear program and sent IAEA inspectors out of the country. On January 10, 2003, Pyongyang officially seceded from the Nonproliferation Treaty, thus risking turning itself into a new hotspot in the world.

Moscow and Beijing wasted no time and began looking for ways to resolve the conflict diplomatically. In a special joint communiqué issued on February 27, 2003, the foreign ministers of the two countries voiced serious concern over the situation on the Korean Peninsula and urged all interested sides to exert maximum effort to find a peaceful and fair solution, called for the Korean Peninsula to have a nuclear-free status, and stressed that compliance with the nonproliferation regime, and preservation of peace, security, and stability there would meet the interests of the international community. They also called for the start of a "constructive and equal dialogue" between the United States and North Korea in order to resolve the "North Korean nuclear problem," and pledged every assistance and support to these efforts. Russia and China also stated their intention to "develop good-neighborly and friendly ties and cooperation with the Democratic People's Republic of Korea and the Republic of Korea."[27] Although this position condemned Pyongyang, it was at odds with the position assumed by the United States, which put all the blame for the crisis on the North Korean leaders and refused to begin negotiations with them.

On May 23, 2003, Russian Foreign Ministry spokesperson Alexander Yakovenko confirmed that the issues of peace and stability on the Korean Peninsula occupied a significant place in the Russian-Chinese dialogue, and reiterated the position of the two countries that "any forcible solution on the Korean Peninsula would be unacceptable."[28] This position was stated in the declaration signed by the Russian and Chinese leaders during Hu Jintao's visit to Moscow on May 26–8, 2003. It said that "peace and stability on the Korean Peninsula would meet the security interests of the two countries," and that parallel to creating a nuclear-free zone and ensuring the nonproliferation regime on the Korean Peninsula, steps must be taken to guarantee North Korea's security and create favorable conditions for its socioeconomic development.[29]

On August 27, 2003, largely due to China's and Russia's support, six-party talks on the North Korean nuclear program started in Beijing. Apart from North Korea, the United States, and China, also participating in the talks were Russia, Japan, and South Korea. China played the most instrumental mediating role in that they had hosted preliminary trilateral talks (China, North Korea, and the US) in April. This time the six-party format was proposed by Japan. Russia, which had put forward similar proposals in the mid-1990s, eagerly supported Japan's initiative but coordinated its position mainly with China and South Korea. In an interview after the first round of the talks in Beijing, the head of the Russian delegation,

Alexander Losyukov, said Russia regarded "the very fact of the talks in Beijing taking place as our common success that became possible not least because of the coordinated steps by Russia and China." He noted that their coordination had begun in January 2003, when the Russian president's special envoy visited Pyongyang, and continued in April during the trilateral talks in Beijing. "All this time we closely coordinated our actions on the Korean issues and are planning to do so in the future," the Russian first deputy foreign minister said.[30] Subsequently Moscow and Beijing continued close cooperation and consultations on the Korean issue. They always spoke jointly in favor of resuming the six-party talks whenever they stalled and for finding a diplomatic solution to the Korean nuclear problem.

The year 2004 was declared the Year of Friendship between the Young People of Russia and China. But its main event was undoubtedly Russian President Vladimir Putin's third (and first after reelection) visit to China on October 14–16, during which the two countries signed a joint declaration and several other documents. The declaration designated 2006 as the Year of Russia in China and 2007 as the Year of China in Russia. The sides approved an action plan to implement the Treaty of Good-Neighborliness and Friendly Cooperation between China and Russia in 2005–8. Russian deputy foreign minister Alexander Alexeyev said the action plan "became the first-ever comprehensive document in the history of bilateral relations that laid down a medium-term program of joint work in all areas from economic and cultural cooperation to such delicate matters as defense and security."[31]

The Additional Agreement on the Eastern Part of the Russian-Chinese Border undoubtedly became one of the most important documents signed. Chinese leader Hu Jintao stressed that the agreement meant "the final settlement of border issues between the two countries."[32] Putin said:

> An important political step has been taken: the border issue between our countries has been resolved. We spent 40 years solving this issue. Russia and China showed wisdom and reached a balanced decision that meets our mutual interests. For the first time in the history of Russian-Chinese relations, the border will be legally recorded and marked out on the ground.[33]

The agreement determined the border line on the two remaining disputed sections: near the Bolshoi Island in the upper reaches of the Argun River (Chita Region) and near the Tarabarov and Bolshoi

Ussuriisky (Heixiazidao) Islands at the confluence of the Amur and Ussuri rivers (near Khabarovsk), with both sections (about 375 square kilometers) divided approximately in equal halves.[34] Since Soviet times these sections had been controlled by the Soviet Union and later by Russia, but the legal grounds for such control were quite flimsy, especially after the signing in 1991 of the basic agreement on the eastern part of the border, which was drawn along the central fairway of the river in accordance with international law.

Initially, China had demanded control of the entire disputed territory, so the final decision was a real compromise. "Russia retained the most developed parts of the Bolshoi Ussuriysky Island with enterprises and Khabarovsk residents' summer houses. The church built there several years ago will remain on our side ... Nothing will hurt the interests of the people who live, work and go to church there," Vitaly Vorobyov, the head of the Russian delegation to the border talks, said.[35] Nevertheless, the agreement drew fire both in Russia and China. Their governments were accused of having given in to pressure and "sold out" national interests. Their critics spoke openly in the regional, and sometimes federal, press in Russia, and on the internet in China. But their opposition did not stir up mass protests, and the majority of serious experts welcomed the resolution of the last remaining territorial dispute between the two countries. The State Duma ratified the agreement on May 20, 2005. Six days later, it was endorsed by the Federation Council. The National People's Congress of China ratified the agreement on May 27.

The first joint military maneuvers codenamed Peace Mission 2005 and conducted on August 18–25 became one of the landmark events in 2005. The first command-and-staff phase took place in Russia's Far Eastern Military District, followed by real exercises on the Shandong Peninsula and in the adjacent parts of the Yellow Sea in China. About 10,000 military personnel, including 1,800 Russian men, from the two countries' air force, airborne, and land forces took part in the maneuvers commanded by the chiefs of the Russian and Chinese general staffs, General of the Army Yuri Baluyevsky, and Colonel General Liang Guanglie. The purpose of the exercises was to deepen mutual trust and friendship between China and Russia, strengthen cooperation and coordination between their armed forces in the field of security and defense, hone antiterror skills, improve crisis responses, and enhance the ability to counter new challenges and threats.

The end of 2005 was darkened by an environmental disaster in

China's Jilin Province bordering on Russia. On November 13, more than 100 tons of toxic substances containing benzene leaked into the Songhua River as a result of a series of explosions at a chemical plant owned by China's biggest state corporation. The benzene slick stretched for 80 kilometers, polluting the water 30 times above the adopted safety standards. Panic swept through Harbin, located downstream; its water supply system was shut down for several days, forcing people to buy drinking water at high prices. Since the Songhua is a tributary of the Amur, the toxic slick was expected to get into that river, bordered by several major Russian cities.

Russian experts said the Chinese authorities had obviously underestimated the danger and failed to act promptly enough. They officially informed Russia about the accident only nine days later, on November 22. But, after that, mutual coordination became more constructive. On November 26, Chinese foreign minister Li Zhaoxing received Russian ambassador Sergey Razov and briefed him in detail about the accident. Speaking in front of the press, the minister offered official apologies on behalf of his government for the environmental damage and delay in the provision of information. The sides agreed to set up hotlines between the environmental agencies of the two countries. Communication was established promptly,[36] and on December 4, Chinese prime minister Wen Jiabao sent an official letter of apologies to his Russian counterpart, Mikhail Fradkov.

Serious consequences were avoided in Russia owing to the joint efforts undertaken by the two countries, such as the construction of a dam near Khabarovsk and the supply of 150 tons of Chinese activated carbon for water purification facilities in Khabarovsk and Komsomolsk-on-Amur. But the accident raised serious concerns among Russian people about China's environmental practices. In fact, for a long time China refused to discuss the Russian draft agreement on cooperation in the protection and rational use of transboundary waters which had been repeatedly proposed by Moscow since 1997. It took a major environmental disaster to get this issue off the ground. The two countries also agreed to create a subcommission on environmental protection within the Commission for the Preparation of Regular Meetings of the Heads of Government.

The Russian mass media wrote about the dual effect of the Jilin chemical plant explosions. *Vremya Novostey* reporter M. Vorobyov said the accident

> reminded Russians that one of the key problems facing modern China – environmental pollution – directly affects its neighbors, including

Russia ... Needless to say that the explosions and the problems they caused did not help improve China's negative image in the Russian border regions. However, the constructive approach taken by the Chinese authorities in dealing with the aftermath of the accident somewhat smoothed out the initial reaction in Russia, and close joint work of the emergency and environmental services provided valuable experience of grassroots cooperation.[37]

The declaration of 2006 as the Year of Russia in China and 2007 as the Year of China in Russia was an important step in resolving the problem of mutual understanding between the broader populations of the two countries, a problem observed by many experts. Beijing and Moscow proposed a massive campaign for acquainting their respective populations with each other. The Years were prepared very thoroughly. The organizing committee was co-chaired by Russian prime minister Dmitry Medvedev, with vice premier Alexander Zhukov, responsible for cooperation with China, acting as his deputy, and by Chinese vice premier Wu Yi, co-head of the Russian-Chinese Commission for the Preparation of Regular Meetings of the Heads of Government. Chen Zhili, minister of education and chair of the Chinese part of the bilateral commission on cooperation in the field of education, culture, healthcare, and sports, and Tang Jiaxuan, responsible for foreign policy in the Chinese government, were appointed Wu Yi's deputies. Both events were opened by the leaders of the two countries and closed by the prime ministers.

Assessing the results of the Year of Russia in China at its closing ceremony on November 9, 2006, Russian prime minister Mikhail Fradkov said:

> We have every reason to speak about the success of the Russian national Year, which became possible largely due to the unprecedented intensity of our political contacts. The heads of state have already met five times this year. Practically all Russian senior government officials have visited China. About 250 events[38] have been held up to date, covering virtually all areas of Russian-Chinese cooperation. According to rough estimates, about half a million people in China participated in them, and hundreds of millions watched and read about them in the media. Tens of thousands of Russian people visited China during the events and even more helped prepare them in Russia. The Year of Russia in China was a truly mass project that engaged a large number of people in Russia and China.[39]

The most important events included the First Russian-Chinese Economic Forum attended by the top leaders, the Russian Culture

Festival, the Investment Week, and the Russian National Exhibition in Beijing.

The Year of China in Russia was officially opened on March 26, 2007 by the leaders of the two countries during Hu Jintao's visit, and ceremoniously closed by prime ministers Viktor Zubkov and Wen Jiabao in Moscow on November 6, 2007. The results of the Year of China in Russia were highly praised in Beijing. Speaking at the Second Russian-Chinese Economic Forum on November 6, Premier Wen said: "The success of the Year of Russia in China and the Year of China in Russia allowed the people of the two countries to experience even deeper the feeling of friendship and the desire to cooperate, and widened vistas for future bilateral cooperation on the basis of mutual benefit."[40] Evaluating the results of the Year of China in Russia, Ambassador Liu Guchang noted specifically increased volumes of bilateral trade and more intensive high-level contacts. He also spoke with satisfaction about the popularity of Chinese theater productions and other performances during the Year, as well as the fact that Russian mass media had covered all events promptly and thoroughly. He cited public opinion polls as indicating that Russian people considered China the friendliest country.[41]

The Year of Russia in China and the Year of China in Russia became a unique project in the history of bilateral relations. About 600 different political, trade, economic, military, scientific, technical, and cultural events were held. The success of the project convinced both sides to hold the most important of the events on a regular basis. It was decided to alternate cultural and student festivals, education, youth, and film weeks between Russia and China from 2008. The years 2009 and 2010 were declared the Year of the Russian Language in China and the Year of the Chinese Language in Russia, respectively.

The election of Dmitry Medvedev as Russian president in March 2008 did not lead to changes in Russia's policy toward China, which he had got to know well during the previous two years. On March 17, the Russian Foreign Ministry issued a special comment on unrest in Tibet. It reiterated that Russia "views Tibet as an integral part of China and considers the settlement of relationships with the Dalai Lama an internal matter for China." The ministry expressed the hope that "the Chinese authorities will take all necessary measures to stop illegal actions and ensure the earliest possible normalization of the situation in this autonomous region." In response to calls by some nongovernmental organizations to boycott the Beijing Olympics, Russia opposed politicizing the games.[42] This position was in sharp contrast to statements by Western countries which expressed concern for human rights violations in Tibet.

In 2008, the new Russian president and his Chinese counterpart, Hu Jintao, held five meetings. Their first personal meeting took place during the Russian leader's official visit to China on May 23–4, 2008. China was the first country outside the former Soviet Union to be visited by Medvedev after he took office as president on May 7. Following the talks, the two leaders signed a joint declaration in which they voiced their common position on major issues of world affairs. Medvedev praised the political dialogue between the two countries and said that the document "reflects the current level of cooperation within the frameworks of international and regional organizations and consolidates our positions on the most sensitive issues, including missile defense proliferation and bloc issues."[43] The visit showed that despite the change of power in Moscow, the similar attitudes of Russia and China to the policies of the United States and the West in general continued to be the driving force behind the two countries' rapprochement.

On July 8, 2009, the Russian Foreign Ministry issued a statement on riots in the capital of the Xinjiang Uyghur Autonomous Region, Urumqi, in which dozens of people were killed or injured. The statement supported China's official version of the events: "Riot initiators, using separatist slogans and provoking interethnic intolerance, attacked and beat civilians, overturned and set fire to cars, ransacked shops and public buildings." The statement emphasized that "the Russian side regards Xinjiang as an integral part of China, and what is happening there as an exclusively internal matter of the PRC."[44] This reaction contrasted with comments in the US and Europe, which kept emphasizing human rights violations by Beijing.

On July 11, Russia and China vetoed a UN Security Council draft resolution, proposed by the United States and supported by its allies, which called for sanctions against the Robert Mugabe regime in Zimbabwe. Their vetoes came as further evidence of the close coordination of the two countries' international positions. According to the Xinhua news agency, the ambassadors of Russia and China to the UN said after the voting that sanctions against Zimbabwe would undermine the mediation efforts of the African Union and the Southern African Development Community and endanger the negotiation process between the Zimbabwean government and the opposition.[45]

On August 7–9, 2008, Russian prime minister Vladimir Putin visited Beijing to attend the Olympic Games opening ceremony. The Russia–Georgia military conflict in South Ossetia, which took place in those days, and especially the subsequent Russian recognition of the independence of South Ossetia and Abkhazia, put Beijing in a difficult position. On the one hand, China could not but favor the frustration of NATO's eastward expansion plans, which would have drawn more territories into the US sphere of influence. On the other hand, Beijing could not renounce its support of the principle of territorial integrity of UN member states, because China itself was faced with the problem of separatism. As a result, China not only did not recognize Abkhazia and South Ossetia but also issued a very vague statement. Commenting on this decision, Chinese Foreign Ministry spokesperson Qin Gang expressed his concern "over the latest developments of the situation in South Ossetia and Abkhazia" and his hope that "relevant parties resolve the issue properly through dialogue and consultation."[46]

The way Chinese media stated the positions of the conflicting parties and other states and international organizations was pointedly objective and neutral, without any comments. At the same time, China provided humanitarian aid to victims in South Ossetia, a move that was highly appreciated by Russia.

In 2008, Russia and China completed the delineation of two eastern sections of their border. On July 21, 2008, during his visit to Beijing, Russian foreign minister Sergey Lavrov signed an additional protocol on the Russian-Chinese border. Upon completion of domestic approval procedures, the protocol entered into force on October 14, 2008.

In 2009, Medvedev and Hu met six times. During Hu's official visit to Russia in June, the two leaders paid special attention to important international problems, such as North Korea's nuclear program and the situation in Afghanistan. The parties denounced unilateral attempts to resolve international security issues, including by expanding military blocs and creating regional and global missile defense systems. Although none of the official documents adopted during the visit mentioned the United States, the target of this criticism was obviously Washington.

During Medvedev's official visit to China on September 26–8, 2010, the two countries signed a bilateral agreement on cooperation in combating terrorism, separatism, and extremism. The document showed the parties' complete agreement on the major issue of the linkage between international terrorism, on the one hand, and separatism and extremism, on the other. Both Moscow and Beijing view separatism and extremism (by which various antigovernment movements are usually meant) as a source of terrorism (for example, in Chechnya,

Xinjiang and Tibet, or Falun Gong practices), whereas the US and its Western allies often view such movements as struggles for national and religious freedom.

Russian-Chinese energy cooperation was marked by several landmarks, among them the signing of a contract for the supply of Russian oil to China through the Skovorodino–Daqing pipeline and an agreement on extended essential terms of natural gas supply from Russia to China. Other documents on energy cooperation included an agreement on strategic cooperation in peaceful uses of nuclear energy and a contract for the development of the technical design for units 3 and 4 of the Tianwan nuclear power plant.

On September 27, 2010, the leaders of the two countries attended the ceremony in Beijing celebrating the completion of the Skovorodino-Daqing oil pipeline. Commercial supplies of Russian oil through the pipeline began on January 1, 2011. On September 28, the Russian president had a conversation with China's deputy chairman Xi Jinping in Shanghai and then took part in the opening ceremony of Russia Day at the Expo 2010 Shanghai China.

Arab Revolutions

The tide of revolutions that spread across North Africa and the Middle East from 2011 caused concern in both Russia and China. Whereas Russia was mainly worried about the international consequences of those crises and the possible loss of its positions in the region, China also feared that this tide could reach Xinjiang and other areas of the country. Suffice it to say that after the success of the Jasmine Revolution in Tunisia the Chinese authorities banned the word "jasmine" on the internet.

The foreign ministers of the two countries discussed the situation in that region during their meeting in Beijing in May 2011. Lavrov said at a joint press conference after the meeting:

> We certainly did not ignore the situation that is evolving in the Middle East and North Africa. This situation is a great concern for us both – Russia and China. It is fraught with grave global upheavals. We have agreed, using the possibilities of our two states, to coordinate our actions in order to facilitate speedy stabilization of the situation, and the prevention of continuation of negative, unpredictable consequences. At the base of our joint position lies the principle according to which each people must themselves, without outside interference, determine their future. This is, in fact, a principle that is applicable to any area

of the world and which is embedded, by the way, in the Charter of the United Nations.[47]

Gradually, Russia and China developed a common approach to the revolutionary events in the Middle East and attempts by external forces to interfere in them. Lavrov wrote about this in his article published in the *People's Daily* newspaper on July 15, 2011.[48] The situation in the Middle East and North Africa, in particular in Libya and Syria, and the Middle East settlement was also discussed by Russian deputy foreign minister Mikhail Bogdanov and China's ambassador to Moscow Li Hui on July 29. According to the official report, "the parties noted the coincidence of Russia's and China's approaches to regional issues and reaffirmed the two countries' unending resolve to continue to coordinate their positions, including in the framework of the UN."[49]

This coordination resulted in a series of cases when Russia and China voted similarly in the UN Security Council. For example, on February 26, 2011, the two countries supported Resolution 1970 which imposed sanctions against Libya. On March 17, they abstained on Resolution 1973 which established a no-fly zone over that country and denounced NATO aviation for going beyond its mandate. In July and August, Russia and China proposed softening a resolution on Syria, and later took similar stances on the situation there.

Russia and China in Central Asia and the SCO

The Shanghai Cooperation Organization grew out of the so-called "Shanghai process," which initially involved five countries: Russia, China, Kazakhstan, Kyrgyzstan, and Tajikistan. The process originated from border negotiations between the Soviet Union and China. Member states of these countries, the so-called Shanghai Five, inherited unsolved problems of the former Soviet-Chinese border after the collapse of the USSR and made up the core of the SCO.

The "Shanghai process" was a continuation of the Soviet-Chinese negotiations, held in two tracks. First, Russia and China continued talks to specify confidence-building measures and reduce armaments along their border. In these negotiations, Russia was joined by Kazakhstan, Kyrgyzstan, and Tajikistan. Secondly, the negotiations also focused on the western part of the former Soviet-Chinese border, which the four post-Soviet countries inherited from the USSR.

The negotiations on confidence-building measures ended in two agreements among the five countries: the 1996 agreement on confidence building in the military field in the border area, and the 1997 agreement on the mutual reduction of armed forces in the border area. The agreements provided for a wide range of measures. The parties pledged to exchange information on the agreed components of the armed forces and border troops; to refrain from military exercises directed against the other party, and to limit the scale of military exercises; to reduce armed forces in the 100-kilometer zone on both sides of the border to agreed limits; not to deploy rivergoing combat vessels from their navies in this zone; to invite observers to military exercises on a reciprocal basis, etc.[50] It was in April 1996, at a summit in Shanghai, that the term "Shanghai Five" was first used. Simultaneously, the parties discussed unresolved border demarcation issues inherited from the past. By the beginning of the twenty-first century, the issue of the demarcation of the border between the former Soviet republics and China was largely resolved.

Having solved problems which stemmed from the legacy of the Soviet era, member states of the Shanghai Five went further. Realizing the need for broader cooperation, they established a new regional organization: the Shanghai Cooperation Organization. It turned out that countries in the region also had other common interests. Gradually, the members of the new international organization moved from resolving border issues to discussing a wide range of issues pertaining to security and economic and cultural cooperation. In other words, they found a sphere of common interests that went far beyond the initial tasks of the Shanghai Five.

On June 15, 2001 in Shanghai, the leaders of the six nations signed the Declaration on the Establishment of the SCO. Its members included the former Shanghai Five plus Uzbekistan. Uzbekistan's accession indicated that the Shanghai process went beyond issues related to the former Soviet-Chinese border: Uzbekistan does not border China, and it is other interests that bring it closer to the other five countries.

On June 7, 2002, the SCO summit in St. Petersburg adopted the SCO Charter, a basic document that set out the goals, tasks, and principles of the organization, its structure and major areas of activities. According to the Charter, the main tasks of the SCO are the strengthening of cooperation between the member states in all areas: security, economy, science, culture, and education, as well as a joint search for solutions to problems that may arise in the twenty-first century.[51]

The main principles of the SCO are mutual respect for sovereignty, the equality of all member states, openness, and no bias against other states and international organizations. All decisions in the SCO are taken by consensus, except for issues pertaining to the suspension or termination of membership in the organization. The SCO summit on May 29, 2003 in Moscow completed the organizational formation of the SCO. It adopted documents regulating the activities of the SCO statutory bodies, endorsed the organization's symbols (emblem and flag), approved the candidacy of the first SCO executive secretary (secretary-general since 2007), and signed an agreement on the procedure for the formation and implementation of the SCO budget.

With the creation of the legal framework and the introduction of working mechanisms, the SCO started to function as a full-fledged international organization. Its organizational and structural hierarchy was fully formed. The supreme body of the SCO is the Council of Heads of State (CHS), which sets priorities, outlines the main areas of the organization's activities, decides on fundamental issues of its internal structure, functioning, and interaction with other states and international organizations, and addresses important international issues. The Council of Heads of Government adopts the SCO budget and considers and decides on major issues of cooperation, especially in the economic sphere. The Council of Foreign Ministers is responsible for the preparation of CHS meetings and makes decisions on the holding of consultations in the SCO framework to discuss international issues. Regular meetings of the heads of ministries and other agencies of the SCO member states discuss cooperation in particular areas. There are also coordination mechanisms working through ministries in charge of foreign economic relations and foreign trade, transport, education, culture, defense, and emergency situations, as well as the Commission of senior officials and expert working groups. In addition, there are regular meetings of prosecutors general, the heads of antidrug agencies, customs services, and supreme and arbitration courts. In 2006, Moscow hosted the first meeting of the parliamentary speakers of the SCO member states. The Council of National Coordinators coordinates the organization's current activities and interaction among ministries and departments of the SCO members. The Secretariat of the SCO, headed by the executive secretary appointed by the CHS for a three-year term on a rotational basis, was established in January 2004 and is located in Beijing.

The SCO Charter was registered with the UN Secretariat, and the organization itself was registered as an observer at the UN General Assembly. At the CHS meeting in Bishkek on August 16, 2007, SCO leaders signed the Treaty on Long-Term Good-Neighborliness,

Friendship and Cooperation, which came as an important step in strengthening the legal framework of the organization. On April 5, 2010 in Tashkent, the SCO secretary-general Muratbek Imanaliyev and UN secretary-general Ban Ki-moon signed a Joint Declaration on Cooperation between the Secretariats of the UN and the SCO.

The June 17, 2004 meeting of the Council of Heads of State in Tashkent, which discussed ways to deepen multilateral cooperation in the SCO framework, was followed by the inauguration of the SCO's second permanent body, the Executive Committee of the Regional Anti-Terrorist Structure (RATS). This completed the formation of executive bodies of this international organization.

Cooperation in the field of security, above all in combating international terrorism, is one of the main areas of the SCO's activity. All the six members faced Islamic extremism and terrorism, often linked to separatist movements and international fundamentalist organizations, at the end of the twentieth and in the early twenty-first centuries. Russia and China are no exceptions. Russia has for many years been waging war on terrorism in the North Caucasus. In China, according to official Chinese data, from 1990 to 2001 alone, extremists advocating the secession of Xinjiang committed more than 200 acts of terrorism, killing more than 600 civilians and law enforcement officers.[52] Two years before the terrorist attacks on New York, the SCO began work on a Convention on Combating Terrorism, Separatism and Extremism, which was signed in June 2001 at the summit of the Shanghai Five in Shanghai.

Cooperation in the field of security is what the SCO is now focused on. The organization's approach to international security issues, particularly the fight against terrorism, is much broader than the approach used by the US and its allies. Washington assigns primary importance to military strikes against international terrorist centers and attacks against states supporting terrorism (these may be any regime Washington does not like), whereas the SCO members see a direct link between international terrorism, on the one hand, and separatism and religious extremism, on the other. The Convention on Combating Terrorism, Separatism and Extremism provides clear definitions of the three notions, and this at a time when there is still no generally accepted international definition of terrorism.

Guided by their broader understanding of the fight against terrorism, the SCO member states formulated their position on the presence of troops of the US and other countries of the so-called "antiterrorist coalition" stationed in Central Asia. The SCO took a pragmatic view of the foreign military presence in the region. On the one hand, Russia, China, and Central Asian countries understood that the military operation in Afghanistan contributed to the fight against terrorism. On the other, however, there were concerns that the US might perpetuate its presence in the region for its own political purposes. In this regard, the SCO foreign ministers adopted a joint statement in January 2002, saying that the US-led International Security Assistance Force (ISAF) in Afghanistan, established by the UN Security Council, "should operate in accordance with the UN Security Council's mandate and with the consent of the legitimate authorities of Afghanistan."[53] In 2003, NATO took command of ISAF, and in 2005, the SCO's CHS summit in Astana adopted a declaration which called on the ISAF command to set a deadline for the presence of its troops in Afghanistan.

After Barack Obama became US president, the tendency towards cooperation between the SCO and the West on the Afghanistan issue increased. The previous Republican administration of George W. Bush had ignored any advice from the outside and declined to cooperate with the SCO. The Obama administration concluded that it was essential for it to cooperate with all who could be involved in efforts to resolve the Afghan problem. Both the SCO and the US understood that the West's failure in Afghanistan would be a serious, perhaps irreparable, blow to the entire system of international relations. This is why the SCO countries, which are potential targets of terrorist and drug threats emanating from Afghanistan, are very interested in stabilizing the situation in that country. The SCO's active involvement in efforts to solve the Afghan problem was a major success of the organization. The Special Conference on Afghanistan, held in Moscow on March 27, 2009 under the SCO's aegis, was an important stage in the development of the organization and in the evolution of the international community's approach to regional issues. The conference was attended by UN secretary-general Ban Ki-moon, OSCE secretary general Marc Perrin de Brichambaut, NATO assistant secretary general Martin Howard, and representatives from SCO observer states, the Group of Eight, and international organizations such as the CSTO, EU, CIS, CICA, and the Organization of Islamic Cooperation. The participation of officials from NATO, the United States, and its main allies in the conference testified to changes in the West's attitude and its desire to really cooperate with the SCO and its members in Afghanistan.

After the Moscow conference, the SCO continued to address the Afghan problem. On January 25, 2010, the SCO held regional consultations on Afghanistan in Moscow, attended by deputy foreign ministers from Afghanistan, India, Iran, Kazakhstan, Kyrgyzstan, China, Pakistan, Russia, Tajikistan, and Uzbekistan, and representatives of the SCO Secretariat. However, the adoption of sanctions against Russia by the US and the EU in 2014 and 2015 resulted in scaling back these efforts.

The SCO members actively develop their military cooperation. Their defense ministries have joined in the efforts to combat terrorism, separatism, and extremism. In August 2003, the Interaction-2003 antiterrorist exercise was held in border areas of Kazakhstan and China. The exercise involved more than 1,000 troops from Kazakhstan, China, Kyrgyzstan, Russia, and Tajikistan; aviation, heavy armor, and artillery. In August 2005, the first Russian-Chinese military exercise, Peace Mission-2005, was attended, as observers, by the defense ministers of the SCO member states and representatives of SCO observer states. The Peace Mission-2007 exercise, held in August 2007, involved troops from all member states. The first stage of the exercise was held on August 9 in the capital of Xinjiang, Urumqi. The final stage took place on August 17 at training range 255 near Chebarkul (in Russia's Chelyabinsk region). The exercise scenario comprised 46 episodes of antiterrorist action, including repelling a terrorist attack and freeing hostages. The exercise involved 6,000 troops, including 2,000 troops from Russia and 1,700 from China, six Il-76 and eight attack aircraft, an air force airborne company, and 32 helicopters. The SCO defense ministers at their meeting in April 2009 approved a plan of cooperation between the defense ministries of the SCO member states for 2010–11. The plan provided for holding a series of multilateral and bilateral military exercises, largely intended to practice counterterrorism measures.

Another big step forward in security cooperation was made during Russia's presidency of the SCO in 2008–9. During this period, RATS drafted an SCO convention against terrorism and a program for cooperation among SCO states in combating terrorism, separatism, and extremism for 2010–12. These documents were adopted by the CHS in June 2009 in Yekaterinburg. The SCO members also signed an agreement on training SCO counterterrorism troops. All these documents have translated counterterrorism cooperation plans into practical action.

Another area where the SCO member states have an approach of their own is the fight against drug production and trafficking. These states have a strong view that the situation with drug production in Afghanistan has markedly deteriorated since the troops of the antiterrorist coalition entered the country. The new authorities of

Afghanistan and the foreign troops supporting them do not wish or are unable to improve the situation. The inflow of Afghan drugs into neighboring countries has increased and now poses a serious threat to their security. The SCO members signed the Agreement on Cooperation in Combating Illicit Trafficking of Narcotic Drugs, Psychotropic Substances and Their Precursors in June 2004 in Tashkent. Under the agreement, special services of the SCO states exchange information and conduct joint operations to eliminate drug trafficking channels.

The SCO members view their economic cooperation as a priority area in the organization's activities. At their first meeting on September 14, 2001 in Almaty, the SCO heads of governments signed the Memorandum on the Main Goals and Areas of Regional Economic Cooperation, which started the process of creating favorable conditions for trade and investment. In September 2003, the SCO Council of Heads of Government (prime ministers), who gathered in Beijing, endorsed the Program for Multilateral Trade and Economic Cooperation, which set guidelines and stages for economic integration of SCO countries for the period until 2020.

However, having adopted many important documents setting out plans for the development of multilateral economic cooperation and mechanisms for their implementation, the SCO member states have not gone any further. Not a single multilateral economic cooperation project has yet reached the stage of implementation. All reports by interested ministries only show the growth of bilateral cooperation. The same applies to loans given unilaterally by China to SCO countries that have seen no support from other members.

Experts draw different conclusions from this situation. One point of view, largely shared by Russian agencies responsible for economic cooperation, holds that the SCO should not be engaged in active implementation of multilateral projects. The main goal of the organization should be to develop a legal framework for cooperation between individual member states, harmonize customs, banking, and other legislation, and take other measures to promote the growth of economic activity within the SCO. As regards the numerous documents on cooperation projects that were adopted, this can be explained by an overly optimistic atmosphere that surrounded the establishment of the SCO. The SCO leaders did not take into account the complexity of the real economic situation in their countries and differences in their levels of development, and now a more pragmatic policy should be worked out. Another view, advocated by China, is that the SCO countries should speed up the development of multilateral projects, create a system for their financing, and move toward the creation of a free trade area.

The main reason for the slowdown in economic cooperation is the absence of a funding mechanism for multilateral projects. The SCO budget (about US$4 million) is too small and is not intended for this purpose. It has long been proposed to establish a SCO Development Fund or Bank, but this has never been done. China insists on the creation of a bank in which votes would be allocated according to the size of the contribution. Russia worries that China's contribution will be the greatest and that Beijing will control the bank and use its resources in its own interests.

Russia has proposed opening a special account as a mechanism for funding preproject studies, above all in areas such as energy, transport, and high technology. It is assumed that the implementation of projects would be funded by an SCO Interbank Association, a nongovernmental association of banks of the member states. However, this mechanism has not been created either.

Unlike the situation with economic cooperation, there are good prospects for cooperation among the SCO states in the fields of education, culture, and public health. Central Asian countries, China, and Russia have ancient and unique civilizations. As these countries become increasingly open and as they make the best achievements of world culture an integral part of their own culture, they are being faced with a problem of preserving their national traditions in the face of an inflow of low-standard mass culture from abroad.

As regards education, it is generally known that the Soviet educational system served as the basis for the educational systems of all SCO member states; therefore, they still have many common features. Now Russia has joined in the so-called Bologna process and is seeking to unify its educational standards with those in Europe. It is a common task for all SCO members to harmonize their educational standards with international ones, while preserving the advantages of the old system.

The main SCO project in the field of education, which has already been translated into practical action, was the creation of the SCO University. It operates as a network of existing universities in the SCO members and offers programs at different levels (bachelor's, master's and postgraduate degrees). The first students began their studies in 2010.

The clear position of the SCO, which stands for a multipolar world and the preservation of the decisive role of the UN and its Security Council in international affairs, evokes interest and respect in many parts of the world. Its international contacts are based on agreement on a temporary system of relations with other international organizations and states, adopted by the SCO foreign ministers in November 2002.

On the whole, despite some teething problems, the SCO is slowly but surely turning into a really functioning and authoritative international organization to be reckoned with, whether one likes it or not. The basis for its existence is simple. All its members value cooperation with the West and understand that their economic development is impossible without this cooperation. At the same time, they feel more comfortable in a world where there are alternative centers of power and where there are organizations that understand their fundamental problems better and more deeply than the West does. The same considerations and even the very existence of a serious international organization whose working languages are Russian and Chinese, but not English, attract to the SCO more and more new interested partners from other regions. In today's world, with its strong tendency toward uniformity in everything, including politics, the voice of countries advocating a multipolar world, pluralism, and tolerance in foreign policy must be heard.

In the early years of the SCO, all its members and most experts held that the number of members should not be increased for the time being, as the organization must first strengthen itself in its present composition, set its mechanisms going, and gain experience. That was why the SCO Council of Foreign Ministers reached a tacit understanding in May 2006 on a moratorium on the admission of new members. The understanding was tacit because it was at variance with the SCO Charter, which proclaims the organization open to other states. The moratorium was further confirmed at meetings of the SCO Council of Heads of State in June 2006 in Shanghai, in August 2007 in Bishkek, and in June 2010 in Tashkent.

Meanwhile, international interest in the SCO kept growing. Back in 2006, Pakistan, which had the status of observer state, requested full membership. Iran made similar requests in 2007 and 2008, and one more observer, India, expressed its wish to become full member in 2010. In 2009, the SCO summit in Yekaterinburg introduced "dialogue partner" status, which was granted to Sri Lanka and Belarus. Egypt, Nepal, Serbia, Qatar, Azerbaijan, Turkey, and some other countries also displayed interest in establishing contacts with the SCO. In 2011, Turkey asked the SCO secretary-general to be granted dialogue partner status. The United States, too, showed official interest in this status. Both countries are NATO members, which indicates that this alliance is very serious about the SCO.

The SCO gave technical reasons for its reluctance to accept new members, namely, the absence of mechanisms for joining the organization. However, by the end of the first decade of the twenty-first century, such a mechanism had been created, along with a legal basis and clear-cut procedures. The CHS at a June 2010 meeting in Tashkent approved Regulations on the Admission of New Members to the SCO, which formulated clear criteria that new members must meet. Under the regulations, a state wishing to become a full member of the SCO must be located in Eurasia, have diplomatic relations with all SCO member states, maintain active trade and economic ties with them, have the status of observer or dialogue partner, and not be under UN sanctions. The latter criterion makes Iran, one of the most active applicants, ineligible for full membership for an indefinite time. In the security field, the international obligations of states wishing to join the SCO must not conflict with international treaties and other documents adopted by the SCO. In addition, an applicant state must not be involved in an armed conflict with another state(s). The SCO summit in Astana in June 2011 adopted a model Memorandum on Obligations of an Applicant State Required for SCO Membership, which was the last step in creating the formal basis for admitting new members. Now there are no formal grounds for denying admission to other countries by pleading the absence of relevant procedural documents.

Officially, Beijing did not object to the enlargement, but it said that the conditions were "not ripe" for the SCO's expansion. However, as Russian-Chinese cooperation deepened and the international situation changed, Beijing changed its position, too, and agreed to the admission of India if China's old friend Pakistan also joins the organization simultaneously. As a result, the two countries formally joined the SCO at the summit in Astana in June 2017. In addition, Russia has officially supported the admission of Iran, which has become possible after international sanctions were lifted on Tehran.

The accession of India, Pakistan, and possibly Iran in the not-too-distant future will radically change the very nature of the SCO. The organization would then count all the leading non-Western powers of Eurasia among its members. Belarus, a European nation with a somewhat peculiar political system, has already become an SCO observer state. An increasingly Euroskeptic Turkey the same, and Sri Lanka, which has become disillusioned with the West for pointlessly defending Tamil separatists, has received the looser dialogue partner status.

With these new members, the SCO could be regarded as an emerging cornerstone of the multipolar world in the making, a platform offering a Eurasian alternative to Western Europe. If the BRICS group is about to become an alternative to Western structures in terms of global governance (narrowly speaking, an alternative to the Group of Seven within the Group of Twenty), the SCO could assume the role of a second, non-Western center of gravity in Eurasia (since Western Europe is also part of Eurasia).

Conclusion

The analysis of the evolution of official relations between Russia and China after the breakup of the Soviet Union clearly shows that the rapprochement between the two countries was not accidental or desired only by individual leaders. It continued under all leaders and gained momentum, because the two countries came to understand better each other's vital interests. This shared understanding, in turn, stemmed from fundamental changes in the international situation, as well as in the positions of Russia and China in the international arena. The increased influence of the United States and its allies in the world after the Soviet center of power ceased to exist, with the transformation of the US into the strongest center of power in world politics and its attempts to use its influence to impose its own values and development model on the whole world caused serious concern both in Beijing and Moscow. These factors helped Russia and China overcome their political differences of the early 1990s and begin their rapprochement. Later, the strengthening of the two countries, on the one hand, and US attempts to retain its absolute leadership through pressure and armed actions in various regions of the world, on the other, drew Moscow and Beijing still closer together and encouraged them to create a system of bilateral strategic cooperation. This system will be described in detail in chapter 5.

5

THE STRATEGIC PARTNERSHIP MATURES: MULTIDIMENSIONAL COOPERATION

Strategic Partnership System

There are various views on the strategic partnership and interaction between Russia and China, ranging from the idea that there is nothing behind it, to the opinion that this partnership is de facto an alliance. These two views do not correspond to the reality of their bilateral relations. As has been shown in the previous chapters, the creation of an alliance is neither an official nor a real goal of the Russian and Chinese leaderships. However, this does not mean that the strategic partnership between the two countries is devoid of content. It is true that China has signed strategic partnership agreements with more than fifty countries, which has raised doubts within the country about whether this institution makes any sense.[1] Indeed, some of these partnerships are devoid of serious content. However, Russian-Chinese relations, officially described as those "based on comprehensive partnership and strategic cooperation,"[2] are not an empty partnership.

First of all, over the years of their development, the proliferating structure of these relations has been institutionally consolidated. The summit of these relations is annual official meetings of the heads of state, held alternately in China and Russia, where the two leaders discuss fundamental issues of bilateral cooperation and sign basic documents and agreements. Also, during these visits, significant economic agreements are signed in the presence of the heads of state, thereby gaining additional legitimacy. In addition to annual summits, the leaders of Russia and China meet during and on the margins of various international events: summits of the G20, SCO, BRICS, APEC, etc. They usually hold four to five such meetings a year. However, it is the official mutual visits by the heads of state that are the peak of the bilateral cooperation system. There is no established mechanism or frequency for such visits, but they have become annual by default since 1996, the year when the strategic partnership was proclaimed.

Next down in the hierarchy of bilateral relations is the mechanism of regular meetings between the heads of government of Russia and China, established in December 1996 and regulated by the June 27, 1997 intergovernmental agreement. The meetings are held once a year. The countries have set up five commissions (for the preparation of regular meetings, cultural and educational cooperation, energy cooperation, investment cooperation, and cooperation concerning the development of Russia's Far East and Baikal region and Northeast China). The commissions are co-chaired by deputy prime ministers and convene annually prior to meetings of the heads of government. If necessary, meetings of the co-chairmen are organized.

The Russian-Chinese Commission for the preparation of regular meetings of the heads of government was established by the 1997 agreement. Currently, it is co-chaired by deputy prime minister Dmitry Rogozin of Russia and vice premier Wang Yang of China. The functions of the working secretariat are performed by Russia's Ministry of Economic Development and China's Ministry of Commerce.

The Russian-Chinese Commission for Cultural and Educational Cooperation was established by the July 13, 2007 protocol on amendments to the Additional Protocol to the Agreement. It has replaced the Russian-Chinese Commission for Cooperation in education, culture, health, and sports, set up by the Additional Protocol to the December 5, 2000 agreement. The commission is currently co-chaired by deputy prime minister Olga Golodets of Russia and vice premier Liu Yandong of China. The functions of the working secretariat are performed by Russia's Ministry of Education and Science and China's Ministry of Education.

The Russian-Chinese Intergovernmental commission for energy cooperation initially existed in the format of the Energy Dialogue, established by the May 23, 2008 agreement between presidents Dmitry Medvedev and Hu Jintao. Later, the parties agreed to include it in the mechanism of regular meetings of the heads of government. During the seventeenth regular meeting of the heads of government on December 6, 2012, the parties signed a protocol to the agreement which transformed the Energy Dialogue into an intergovernmental commission at the level of deputy prime ministers. Currently, the commission is co-chaired by deputy prime minister Arkady Dvorkovich of Russia and vice premier Zhang Gaoli of China. The functions of the working secretariat are performed by Russia's Ministry of Energy and China's National Energy Administration.

The Russian-Chinese Intergovernmental Commission for Investment Cooperation was created under an accord reached by Russian President Vladimir Putin and Chinese leader Xi Jinping on May 20, 2014 in Shanghai. The protocol to the agreement on the commission's establishment was signed at its first meeting in Beijing on September 9, 2014. It is now co-chaired by first deputy prime minister Igor Shuvalov of Russia and first vice premier Zhang Gaoli of China. The functions of the working secretariat are performed by Russia's Ministry of Economic Development and China's National Development and Reform Commission.

The mechanism of regular meetings of the heads of government includes twenty subcommissions (usually headed by ministers), as well as working groups (usually headed by deputy ministers) and special structures, which usually meet once a year.

The Commission for the Preparation of Regular Meetings of the Heads of Government includes the following eleven subcommissions, which are usually headed by ministers or their deputies:

1. Subcommission for Trade and economic cooperation, established in 1997. It includes the following working groups: for inter-regional and cross-border trade and economic cooperation; for cooperation in the protection of intellectual property rights; for issues concerning special economic areas; for standardization, metrology, certification, and supervisory control; and for forest development and use.
2. Subcommission for Scientific and Technological Cooperation, established in 1997. It includes working groups for cooperation between state research centers of Russia and leading state research institutions of China; for conversion technologies; and for high technology and innovation.
3. Subcommission for Transport Cooperation, established in 1997. It includes the following working groups: for border crossing; for sea, river, and road transport and for roads; for rail transport; for air transport; for transit; and for the study into a Eurasian Moscow–Beijing high speed corridor.
4. Subcommission for Nuclear Issues (which has replaced the Subcommission for Nuclear Energy Cooperation, created in 1997). It includes the following working groups: for scientific and technological cooperation; for the construction of nuclear power plants; for conversion; for the construction of an experi-

mental fast reactor; and for the search for mutually acceptable forms of cooperation.
5. Subcommission for Cooperation in Finance. It was established in 2000.
6. Subcommission for Cooperation in Space, set up by the November 3, 2000 protocol to the 1997 agreement. It includes a working group for the study of the moon and outer space.
7. Subcommission for Communication and Information Technology, established in 2001. It includes the following working groups: for cooperation in mobile communication; for cooperation in telecommunications; for cooperation in postal communication; for the coordination of radio frequencies; and for information technology and network security.
8. Subcommission for Cooperation in Environmental Protection. It was established in 2006 in the wake of an environmental disaster in Jilin Province in Northeast China, caused by an explosion at a chemical plant in November 2005. It includes the following working groups: for the prevention of environmental pollution and coordination in environmental emergencies; for the monitoring of water quality in transborder water bodies and their protection; and for nature reserves and the conservation of biodiversity.
9. Subcommission for Customs Cooperation, established in 2009. It includes the following working groups: for customs payments; for measures to improve customs clearance and customs control; for customs cooperation in law enforcement; for customs statistics; for the training and retraining of personnel; and for the preparation of proposals to minimize risks of violations of customs legislation and increase the efficiency of customs control and clearance in Russian-Chinese trade during the formation of the Customs Union.
10. Subcommission for Agriculture, established in 2014. It includes a working group for cooperation in veterinary and phytosanitary control and food safety.
11. Subcommission for Cooperation in Industry, established in 2015 (it has replaced the Subcommission for Cooperation in Civil Aviation and Civil Aircraft Building). It includes the following working groups: for equipment; for raw materials; for cooperation in civil aviation and civil aircraft building; and for radio electronics.

The Commission for Cultural and Educational Cooperation includes:

1. Subcommission for Cooperation in Education, established in 2000. Since July 2011, it has included a working group for cooperation in the study and teaching of the Russian and Chinese languages, the development of bilateral academic exchanges, and scientific and technological cooperation between Russian and Chinese universities.
2. Subcommission for Cooperation in Culture, established in 2000.
3. Subcommission for Cooperation in Public Health, established in 2000.
4. Subcommission for Cooperation in Sports, established in 2000.
5. Subcommission for Cooperation in Tourism, established in 2002. Since June 2010, it has included a coordination working group for tourism security.
6. Subcommission for Cooperation in Mass Media, established in 2007. Since June 2010, it has included a working group for the broadcasting of Russian TV channels in China, and Chinese TV channels in Russia.
7. Subcommission for Cooperation in Cinematography, established in 2007.
8. Subcommission for Cooperation in Youth policy, established in 2010.
9. Working Group for Cooperation in Archive Affairs, established in 2007. There are plans to promote it to the level of subcommission.

The Russian-Chinese Intergovernmental Commission for Energy Cooperation deals with comprehensive interaction in the oil, gas, coal, and power (including nuclear power) industries, new and renewable sources of energy, and other areas closely related to the fuel/energy sector. The commission includes a working group for cooperation in the coal sector. In 2014, the parties agreed to establish working groups for electricity and renewable energy at the level of deputy ministers. Under the commission's auspices, there is a working group for the assessment of the situation in international energy markets.

The main tasks of the Russian-Chinese Intergovernmental Commission for investment cooperation are to encourage favorable conditions for the development of investment and interregional cooperation between Russia and China; develop proposals to improve mechanisms for its implementation; and facilitate the implementation of bilateral investment projects and the development of contacts between businesses. The commission has set up the Advisory Committee of Entrepreneurs, which will focus on ways to improve the selection and promotion of promising long-term investment projects that require government support and coordination.

The youngest intergovernmental commission – the Commission for Cooperation and Development of Russia's Far East and Baikal region and Northeast China – was established at the twenty-first regular meeting of the heads of government of Russia and China, held on November 7, 2016 in St. Petersburg. The commission is co-chaired by deputy prime minister and presidential envoy to the Far Eastern Federal District, Yuri Trutnev of Russia, and vice premier Wang Yang of China. The commission is only beginning its work. It is intended to strengthen mutually beneficial cooperation in key areas such as investment, port logistics, resource development, the processing of agricultural products, and the modernization of transport infrastructure. The parties are now working on the organizational structure of the Council. More opportunities for interaction will be offered with the creation of areas of priority socioeconomic development in the Russian Far East and the implementation of the Free Port of Vladivostok project.

The coordination of cooperation between the two countries in international issues is maintained at the level of foreign ministries. In accordance with annual plans, the ministries hold bilateral consultations at the level of ministers or departments. Russia and China coordinate their positions before voting in the UN Security Council, and this is why they have almost always voted similarly of late. This was the case in July 2008, when China and Russia jointly vetoed a US-drafted resolution on sanctions against Zimbabwe; in March 2011, when both countries abstained from voting on a resolution on Libya; in December 2016, when Russia and China blocked a draft resolution on the humanitarian situation in Aleppo; in voting on resolutions on sanctions against Iran and North Korea; and in many other cases. Of course, this does not mean that the two countries vote similarly in all cases. For example, in October 2016, Russia vetoed a resolution on Syria, whereas China abstained. However, the two countries have not blocked each other's resolutions for a long time.

Sometimes there is some inconsistency between the actions of Moscow and Beijing. For example, as shown earlier, China did not fully agree with Russia's actions with respect to Ukraine in 2014, and had not been notified in advance, although it did express its understanding. The Russian press criticized Beijing when China and the US agreed on new tough sanctions against North Korea in November 2016. Russia complained that Beijing had not informed Moscow about the contents of this document.[3] Chinese diplomats privately acknowledged the inconsistency between their actions and those of Moscow, but eventually they took Russia's proposals into account.[4]

When the Permanent Court of Arbitration was examining the South China Sea dispute in 2016, Beijing was actively looking for international support of its position. In several cases, Chinese state media (most likely on purpose) misinterpreted the position of Russian and other international officials in China's favor. For example, in May 2016 top Chinese news agencies quoted a statement by the SCO Secretary-General Rashid Alimov, who allegedly expressed his organization's full support for China in the dispute.[5] The Russian Foreign Ministry had to publish its own comment, which stated that according to the press release of the SCO Foreign Ministers' Council meeting on May 24 in Tashkent, the SCO members insist on "preserving the principles of law and order at sea that are based on international law" and believe that any "dispute must be addressed peacefully through amicable negotiations and agreements between the interested parties," without any effort to internationalize these disputes and without external interference.[6] This meant that while supporting the Chinese position that the dispute should be settled between the disputing parties and without outside interference, Russia at the same time did not support China's or any other party's specific territorial claims.

After the ruling of the court, which was unfavorable to China, Russia moved further in the direction of Beijing and supported China's rejection of the ruling on the grounds that China had not initiated the arbitration and its position was not heard at the court.[7] But this still did not mean support for China's claims.

However, such inconsistencies are rare and the level of coordination of foreign policies between two large states that are not formal allies is unprecedented.

In addition to mechanisms of cooperation between the central governments and their agencies, the countries have an extensive system of interaction between their regions. Interregional cooperation is an important aspect of Russian-Chinese ties. Cooperation with China is becoming a priority for many Russian regions. Areas of cooperation include trade, economy, investment, and cultural and educational ties. The system is based on the November 10, 1997 intergovernmental agreement on principles of cooperation between the administrations (governments) of Russian regions and local governments of China.

To date, there are 234 Russian-Chinese partnerships, including 91 between federal level regions[8] and Chinese provinces (as well as administrative units at the provincial level) and 143 at the municipal level. Fifty-one Russian regions have cooperation agreements with

Chinese regions, and 91 Russian municipalities have twin cities or partners in China. In China, four autonomous regions (out of five), 18 provinces (out of 22), and all four municipalities have partnerships with Russian regions; and 97 Chinese towns, districts, or counties have partnerships with Russian municipalities.

In practical terms, cooperation between individual Russian and Chinese regions varies in intensity. It will depend on initiative, favorable economic conditions, and interest in the development of relations. Overall coordination of cooperation is exercised by the Permanent Working Group for Interregional and Cross-Border Cooperation of the Subcommission for Trade and Economic Cooperation of the Russian-Chinese Commission for the preparation of regular meetings of the heads of government.

Contacts between Russian and Chinese border areas continue to play a key role in bilateral interregional ties. To step up these contacts, in 2009 the leaders of Russia and China endorsed a Program for Cooperation between Russia's Eastern Siberia and Far East and China's Northeast for 2009–18. Russia's Ministry of Economic Development and China's National Development and Reform Commission were charged with its implementation. The program covers various aspects of interaction, including the construction and reconstruction of border crossings, transport infrastructure, the development of cooperation areas, cooperation in manpower and tourism, and cultural and educational contacts. However, its main element is a list of investment projects. In Russia, of 92 projects, 14 are being implemented, 18 are under negotiation or being prepared for implementation, and five are at the stage of the preparation of technical documentation. More than 20 projects have lost their relevance and are to be excluded from the program.

An important step in the development of this kind of cooperation was the launch in 2013 of a Volga–Yangtze interregional cooperation mechanism, which involved fourteen regions in Russia's Volga Federal District and six Chinese regions in the upper and middle Yangtze River (Anhui, Sichuan, Hubei, Hunan, Jiangxi, and Chongqing municipality). In 2015, a decision was made to reformat the existing mechanism into the Volga–Yangtze Interregional Cooperation Council, co-chaired, as before, by Russia's presidential envoy to the Volga Federal District, Mikhail Babich, and state councilor Yang Jiechi of China. The first meeting of the council was held in July 2016 in Ulyanovsk. Interaction under this project is based on the List of Investment Projects and the Road Map for Cooperation in the Cultural and Educational Sphere, signed in Shanghai in May 2014. In

March 2016, the list was updated by the Mechanism Working Group, which met in Beijing.

There are plans to involve the North Caucasus in interregional cooperation. Russia's Ministry of North Caucasus Affairs, set up in 2014, is already working on it with China's State Ethnic Affairs Commission.

Regions take an active part in trade and economic forums, exhibitions and fairs held in Russia and China, among them the Eastern Economic Forum in Vladivostok, the St. Petersburg International Economic Forum, and the China-Northeast Asia Expo (Changchun, Jilin province).

Cultural and educational contacts are an important factor in forming a positive atmosphere for bilateral interregional exchanges. Russian and Chinese regions have made it a tradition to hold joint sporting and cultural events on the occasion of holidays and shared anniversaries. In 2015, the parties held joint events to mark the seventieth anniversary of victory in World War II.

The two countries also actively develop interparliamentary ties, which are very intensive. In recent years, the leaders of the houses of Russia's Federal Assembly and China's National People's Congress have met at least once a year. Delegations of parliamentary committees and commissions of Russia and China and deputy groups of Russian-Chinese friendship pay regular mutual visits, which indicates their keen interest in each other's lawmaking experience. The main role in strengthening bilateral parliamentary cooperation is played by joint parliamentary commissions of the State Duma/Federation Council and the National People's Congress, created in 2005. In 2014, they were united into the Commission for Cooperation between Russia's Federal Assembly and the National People's Congress of China.

The intensity of Russian-Chinese ties at lower levels is also growing. Today, it is difficult to find a large company, research center, or university in Russia without partners in China. Various bilateral parastatal and nongovernmental organizations actively promote the development of ties between the two countries. The most important of them are the Russian-Chinese Committee of Friendship, Peace and Development, the Russian-Chinese Friendship Society and the China–Russia Friendship Association, the Russian-Chinese Business Council, and the Russian-Chinese Chamber for the Promotion of Commerce in Machinery and Innovative Products.

The boom in ties with China has made Chinese the second most popular foreign language after English in many Russian universities. Chinese is also widely taught in secondary schools. In 2016, there were twenty applicants for every seat in the Chinese language department of Moscow State Pedagogical University, which trains teachers for secondary schools. In September 2016, Russia's Federal Education and Science Supervision Service tested about 1,500 high school students learning Chinese in twelve Russian regions to evaluate their knowledge of the language. From 2017, Russian high school graduates seeking admission to a university will be able to take the Unified State Exam in Chinese (until now, they could take the foreign language exam only in a European language: English, French, German, or Spanish). Chinese is taught in 123 educational institutions in 34 regions of Russia. The total number of students studying Chinese is more than 17,000, including about 5,000 high school students.[9]

The popularity of the Russian language in China is also growing after a decline in the 1990s. This is due primarily to the growth of Russian-Chinese trade and economic ties. In many cities and provinces of China (Beijing, many cities in Xinjiang and the northeastern provinces, Beidaihe in Hebei Province, and Sanya in Hainan province), there are large enclaves serving trade with Russia and other post-Soviet countries and Russian-speaking tourists: all traders there can communicate in Russian, and signs and product names are in both Chinese and Russian. The number of students studying Russian in Chinese schools and universities is increasing.

Figures like these show that the Russian-Chinese strategic partnership is based on an ever growing and developing cooperation network, and this growth has continued regardless of changes of leaders in Russia and China or changes in the international situation. It is significant that neither China nor Russia has a similar system of cooperation with any other country, or even with their closest allies (formally, China has one ally, North Korea). This network is a serious guarantee of the stability of friendly relations. Of course, some changes in attitudes in the upper echelons of power or the world may influence it, but it is hard to imagine that it can be quickly dismantled at the pleasure of individual leaders or due to a sudden international change.

Practical Cooperation

The structure of cooperation is essentially a mechanism for achieving a result. To understand the actual results, we need to consider the state of practical cooperation in its main areas.

Trade and Economic Cooperation

Stable interstate relations are always based on real mutual interests. Both Russia and China have such interests – in the economic as well as the political field. Economic cooperation is an important part of Russian-Chinese relations. Both parties understand that it can serve as an impetus to economic growth in Russia, including its Far Eastern regions, and in China's border provinces. Both Moscow and Beijing are aware that economic cooperation should be included in the focus of their attention, because without reliance on real common interests in this area their "strategic cooperation" may prove to be short-lived. But the economy somewhat lags behind politics in bilateral relations.

In the 1990s, the generally poor state of the Russian economy and chaos in the country stood in the way of the development of economic ties. At the beginning of the twenty-first century, the situation began to improve, and the economic aspect of bilateral relations became more stable and tended toward growth. This does not mean, however, that there are no problems in this sphere. First of all, in previous decades the scope of economic cooperation between the two neighboring great powers, separated by one of the world's longest land borders, did not correspond to its potential. President Boris Yeltsin set the task of increasing the volume of Russian-Chinese trade to US$20 billion by the year 2000. In reality, throughout the 1990s, this figure never reached US$8 billion, and at the end of the decade it even decreased as a result of the 1998 crisis. This was much less than China's trade with the US, and China did not rank high among Russia's trade partners either.

In many ways, it was Russia that was to blame for that: the legislative chaos and corruption in the country and the general crisis in the economy gave little hope for serious cooperation with foreign partners. The Chinese complained that Russian suppliers were unreliable and did not meet delivery dates. They also complained about the difficulty of doing business in Russia, where Chinese businesspeople suffered from the arbitrariness of law enforcement bodies and the mafia. Russian businesspeople often were not pleased with their Chinese partners, either. Large Russian companies complained that tenders in China were held only for show and that Russian firms were treated with disregard and were often denied contracts, even though their bids were more favorable than those of Western companies. The most obvious example is the 1997 tender for the supply of generators and turbines for the Three Gorges Dam, estimated at between US$3 billion and US$5 billion, which Russia lost to a consortium of Western European companies. In addition, Russia was concerned about the propensity of some Chinese companies and individual businesspeople operating in the country to engage in illegal activities or evade taxes, and about overly harsh rules for Russian investors in China.

Nevertheless, Russian companies gained a foothold in the Chinese nuclear energy market. At the turn of 1997–8, Russia and China signed a general contract for cooperation in the construction of the Lianyungang nuclear power plant in Jiangsu Province. The original project was estimated at US$3 billion. In 2000, trade between Russia and China reached US$8 billion, almost 40 percent more than in 1999. The two countries also developed trade in technologies, provided manpower and contract construction services, and promoted reciprocal investment, although not on a large scale.

In the first decade of the twenty-first century, the situation in trade and economic cooperation remained mixed. The turn of the century saw a breakthrough in Russian-Chinese trade, and its volume began to grow fast. However, this growth was accompanied by a sharp decline in the share of machinery, equipment, and products with high added value in general in bilateral trade, and by a decrease in Russia's export–import ratio. So, whereas bilateral trade in the 1990s was small but fairly balanced, with industrial products accounting for a large share of Russian exports, in the 2000s these were replaced by energy resources. Although Russian exports to China were still more diversified than exports to Europe due to their traditional structure, the diversification steadily decreased, and machinery and equipment gave way to goods with low added value.[10]

There were several reasons for these tendencies. On the one hand, the stabilization of the political and economic situation in Russia during Vladimir Putin's presidency contributed to a growth in Russia's trade with most countries. However, the emphasis on the development of energy industries at the expense of other sectors led to a situation where Russia simply had nothing to offer to China except for its oil and other fossil fuels. Meanwhile, Chinese manufacturers gradually learned to produce the bulk of the common types of machinery and equipment which Russian producers had been used to offering for export. Importantly, many of the Chinese-made analogues were cheaper and more competitive – first in the Chinese market and then in the markets of Russia and third countries. In addition, Russia was faced with increased competition from companies in the United States, Japan, the EU, South Korea and other countries, which offered more favorable financial terms (government support, preferential loans, payments by installment, etc.) and actively participated in the creation of joint ventures in China.

These factors required that Russian exporters of engineering products use new, flexible methods of work, boost market research, take a more active part in tenders and promotional activities, and provide aftersales services. Most exporters failed to cope with this task. Meanwhile, China skillfully used various restrictive measures to protect its own market, among them customs duties and antidumping investigations. Now and then it expressed its displeasure over the confiscation of goods smuggled by Chinese small and medium-sized companies into Russia to be sold on its markets.

The problem of illegal trade in smuggled goods arose in the 1990s, largely because of corruption at Russian customs and in law enforcement agencies, and the general managerial chaos in the country. Many Chinese traders willingly joined in corrupt practices. Instead of complying with legal procedures and paying customs duties (which was not easy to do, though, because corrupt officials impeded the work of those who did not pay bribes), they voluntarily used the services of intermediary firms which proposed that traders pay delivery fees together with customs duties in smaller amounts and leave it in their hands. The reduced payments resulted from informal economy practices where exporters understated the value of their goods at customs: computers turned into calculators, clothes turned into cloth, etc. In addition, goods were registered as belonging to Russian intermediaries rather than their real Chinese owners, who received them in Moscow. Rare inspections revealed that these owners had no documents for the goods.

Officially, China always supported Russia's efforts to restore order to trade.[11] All these problems were addressed by various intergovernmental agencies in charge of economic cooperation and at the level of heads of government. These meetings brought tangible positive results. This was largely due to the general political and economic stabilization in Russia. Another factor was that both countries had gained experience and learned to move away from empty declarations and better address specific cooperation issues. Improvements were evidenced in the fact that the gap in figures for bilateral trade markedly decreased by the end of the first decade of the twenty-first century. In 2010, Russia's official trade balance statistics for the first time even exceeded those of China. The customs and law enforcement agencies of the two countries actively cooperated with each other.

Prior to the global financial and economic crisis, bilateral trade grew fast. The annual growth rate from 2000 to 2008 was approximately

30 percent. In the precrisis peak year 2008, trade reached US$56.8 billion (according to Chinese figures). In 2009, due to the global crisis, trade decreased significantly, but in 2010 it almost returned to the precrisis level – US$55.45 billion, according to Chinese customs statistics. Russian exports to China amounted to US$25.94 billion, an increase of 21.7 percent on the previous year. At the same time, imports from China grew by 69 percent to US$29.61 billion. As a result, bilateral trade again showed a negative balance for Russia, at US$3.78 billion. Although the leaders of Russia and China set the goal of bringing bilateral trade to US$60–80 billion by the year 2010, the goal was not achieved, although it was closely approached.

However, there was only a year's delay – in 2011, bilateral trade grew by 42.7 percent to US$79.25 billion, according to Chinese figures. China's exports increased by 31.4 percent to US$38.9 billion, and imports grew by 55.6 percent to US$40.35 billion. The balance of trade was again positive for Russia, and this country became China's tenth-ranked trading partner.

In the late 2000s, Russian-Chinese trade also saw other trends that were unfavorable to Russia. Before 2007, Russia was one of the few countries in the world to have a positive trade balance with China. However, in 2007 the situation drastically changed, resulting in a trade deficit for Russia. The reduction of trade in 2009 again led to a surplus. This factor shows that high growth rates of bilateral trade were largely due to boosts in Chinese exports to Russia, and this despite the significant oil price increases which were behind the growth of Russian exports.

The range of Russian exports to China also steadily declined. There was a time when more than 40 percent of China's imports from the Soviet Union were machinery and equipment. By the end of the 2000s, their share dropped to several percent, and raw materials (mainly oil and timber) made up the bulk of Russian exports to China. For example, in 2004, 84.2 percent of Russian exports included such commodity groups as mineral fuel, timber, fertilizers, fish and seafood, ferrous and nonferrous metals, pulp and ores. In 2005, this figure rose to 88.7 percent, and in 2006 to 90.5 percent. The share of machinery and equipment fell to 1–2 percent.

By 2010, the structure of Russian-Chinese trade had not changed significantly: Russian exports to China were dominated by raw materials, while China exported mainly consumer goods to Russia.[12] According to the Russian Ministry of Economic Development, the bulk of Russian exports to China included the following commodity groups: mineral products (mainly fuel and energy resources), 55.6

percent; timber and pulp-and-paper products, 14.2 percent; and chemicals (mainly fertilizers), 14.0 percent. The share of machinery, equipment, and vehicles had increased to 7.9 percent, that of metals and metal products was 3.4 percent, and food products and agricultural raw materials were 4.7 percent.

The slight increase in the share of machinery and equipment in Russian exports was due to mutual efforts of the parties, with China playing an equally active role. To this end, in 2007 the two countries established the Russian-Chinese Chamber for the Promotion of Commerce in Machinery and Innovative Products.

Another important change in bilateral trade was a gradual enhancement of China's role in Russia's foreign trade, while Russia's role in the foreign trade of China decreased. In the 1990s, China never ranked higher than fifth in Russia's foreign trade (for example, in 1995 its share was 4.3 percent, less than the shares of Germany, the US, Japan, and Ukraine), whereas in 2007–8 it already ranked third, and in 2010 China for the first time became Russia's largest trading partner, accounting for 10 percent of its foreign trade. During the same period, Russia moved down the list of China's trading partners from seventh to thirteenth (in 2010), falling behind not only its traditional rivals, Japan, the US, Hong Kong, South Korea, Taiwan, Germany, and Singapore, but also Australia, India, Brazil, and Malaysia.

During Hu Jintao's state visit to Moscow in mid-June 2011, the two countries agreed to increase bilateral trade to US$100 billion by the year 2015, and to US$200 billion by 2020. In 2011, Russia's place as China's trading partner went up to tenth. However, the countries failed to achieve the first goal in 2015 and will hardly achieve the second in 2020.

Despite the problems, Russian-Chinese trade continued to grow and reached its peak in 2013–14. Later, however, it was seriously affected by the fall in world oil prices and economic problems in both countries (see Table 1). According to the Russian Federal Customs Service, Russian-Chinese trade in 2015 decreased by 28.1 percent from 2014 to US$63.6 billion. In 2016, bilateral trade increased by 3.9 percent compared to 2015 and reached US$66.1 billion. Russia's exports decreased by 2.1 percent to US$28.0 billion, while China's imports grew by 8.9 percent, reaching US$38.1 billion. Russia's trade deficit increased to US$10.1 billion.

The first four months of 2017 saw a sharp increase in trade. In January–April 2017, it reached US$24.5 billion, a growth of 37 percent compared to the same period in 2016. Russian exports grew to US$11.9 billion (+46.2 percent), Russia's imports to US$12.6

Table 1 Russian–Chinese trade, 2010–17 (US$ billion)

	2010	2011	2012	2013	2014	2015	2016	January–April 2016	January–April 2017
Turnover	59.3	83.5	87.5	88.8	88.4	63.6	66.1	17.9	24.5
Compared to previous year (%)	*150.3*	*140.8*	*105.2*	*101.6*	*99.5*	*71.9*	*103.9*		*137.0*
Russia's exports	20.3	35.2	35.7	35.6	37.5	28.6	28.0	8.1	11.9
Compared to previous year (%)	*121.8*	*173.4*	*102.0*	*99.6*	*105.7*	*76.3*	*97.9*		*146.2*
Russia's imports	39.0	48.3	51.8	53.1	50.9	35.0	38.1	9.8	12.6
Compared to previous year (%)	*171.2*	*123.9*	*107.6*	*102.9*	*95.7*	*68.7*	*108.9*		*129.3*
Balance	−18.7	−13.1	−16.1	−17.5	−13.4	−6.3	−10.1	−1.7	−0.7

Source: Russian Federal Customs Service.

billion (+12.3 percent). If this tendency continues (although it largely depends on rising oil prices), Russia's trade deficit should eventually decrease.

The Chinese figures are slightly different. According to China's General Administration of Customs, Russian-Chinese trade in 2016 reached US$69.53 billion, which is a 2.2 percent increase compared to 2015. Russian exports to China in 2016 decreased by 3.1 percent compared to 2015, to US$32.2 billion, while imports from China increased by 7.3 percent and reached US$37.23 billion. According to this Chinese source, Russian-Chinese trade in January–April 2017 grew by 26.2 percent compared to the same period in 2016 and reached US$24.7 billion. This includes US$13.1 billion of Russia's exports to China (+30.1 percent) and US$11.7 billion of Russia's imports from that country. This means that, according to Chinese statistics, it was not Russia, but China that was in deficit, by US$1.4 billion. Regardless of the differences in the figures, which are caused by different calculating methods, the tendency is clear: bilateral trade is growing again after a period of decrease and Russia's trade deficit is decreasing as well.

China's share in Russia's foreign trade in 2015 reached 12.1 percent, and in 2016, 14.1 percent. Conversely, in 2015, Russia ranked only sixteenth among China's major trading partners, accounting for 1.7 percent of China's foreign trade. The bulk of Russian exports to China in January–April 2017 included mineral products (mainly fuel, oil, oil-refining products, bitumen and mineral wax products), 71.7 percent (in January–April 2016, 64.6 percent); timber and pulp-and-paper products, 10.6 percent (13.0 percent); machinery, equipment, and vehicles, 6.1 percent (6.4 percent); food products and agricultural raw materials, 5.1 percent (7.3 percent); pearls and gemstones, 0.7 percent (0.3 percent); and metals and metal products, 0.4 percent (1.0 percent).

Imports from China in January–April 2017 included machinery, equipment, and vehicles, 55.4 percent (in January–April 2016, 53.1 percent); textiles and footwear, 11.7 percent (13.1 percent); chemicals, 10.0 percent (10.9 percent); metals and metal products, 7.2 percent (6.9 percent); food products and agricultural raw materials, 4.3 percent (5.1 percent); raw hides, furs, and fur products, 1.1 percent (1.1 percent); and timber and pulp-and-paper products, 0.9 percent (1.1 percent).

Overall, Russian-Chinese trade shows the following tendencies: the decline in trade volume, caused by the fall in commodity prices and difficulties faced by both economies, is gradually reversing. The old problems – the decrease of Russia's share in China's foreign trade and the growth of China's share in Russia's trade; the domination of raw materials in Russia's exports and the growing share of machinery and equipment in imports from China; and Russia's trade deficit, albeit small – persist, yet they have not worsened. At the same time, there have been some positive tendencies for Russia, caused by the sharp decline in the ruble exchange rate, which made Russian goods cheaper for Chinese customers, with growth in the export of food and agricultural products, machinery, and equipment.

However, analysts warn against exaggerating the decline in trade in terms of prices, because if the prices of commodities, above all hydrocarbons, had not collapsed in 2015, the target of US$100 billion would have been achieved. In addition, trade decreased in terms of value, not volume, and in some categories of goods it even increased. For example, Russia came first in oil sales to China in 2016, ahead of Saudi Arabia.[13]

Investment Cooperation

According to official figures, mutual investment between the two countries is not yet high, with Chinese investment in the Russian economy by far exceeding that of Russia in China. In the 1990s, mutual investment was insignificant because of the general state of the Russian economy at the time. The situation improved somewhat with the creation of the intergovernmental permanent Working Group for Investment Cooperation in 2004. China began to show great interest in increasing investment in Russia and adopted a plan to increase it to US$12 billion by the year 2020.

There is a problem in that Russian and Chinese figures differ considerably. The Bank of Russia estimated Chinese direct investment stock in Russia at US$2.8 billion in early 2015, and about US$1.7 billion in mid-2016. These figures can hardly be considered credible, since the existing projects cost much more in total. According to China's National Statistics Bureau and Ministry of Commerce, Chinese direct investment stock in the Russian economy reached US$8.96 billion by mid-2016 (Table 2, up 2.9 percent from the equivalent period a year before). However, the Chinese government must have doubted these figures and reportedly did an informal count of projects implemented by Chinese companies operating in Russia. The survey boosted the figure to US$33 billion.[14] The difference could be explained by the fact that a large part of the Chinese investment in

Table 2 China's direct investment stock in Russia, 2012–16 (at the end of the period, US$ million)

Data source	2012	2013	2014	2015	January–June 2016
General Administration of Customs, China	4888.49	7581.6	8380.0	8940.0	8963
Bank of Russia		1987.0	4547.0	2810.0	1693.0	1688

Table 3 Chinese direct investment inflow into Russia, 2012–16 (US$ million)

	2012	2013	2014	2015	January–June 2016
Investment inflow	784.6	1022.2	794.0	560.0	346.0

Source: China's National Statistics Bureau.

Russia comes not directly from China but from other jurisdictions, including offshore territories, and is not registered as Chinese. In fact, this is possible. According to official Russian figures, China ranks between eleventh and twentieth among major investors in Russia, far behind the British Virgin Islands, the Bahamas, Bermuda, and Saint Kitts and Nevis. If the unofficial Chinese figures are even partially true (which, of course, needs to be checked), China might turn out to be the largest investor in the Russian economy.

According to China's National Statistics Bureau and Ministry of Commerce, the inflow of Chinese direct investment into the Russian economy in the first half of 2016 amounted to US$346 million (Table 3, up 4.8 percent from the equivalent period a year before).

By mid-2016, Russia's direct investment stock in the Chinese economy had reached US$913.58 million (down 0.5 percent from the equivalent period a year before). According to the improbable figures of the Bank of Russia, by the beginning of 2015, Russian direct investment in China had amounted to US$195 million, and in early 2016 it stood at US$174 million (table 4). According to China's National Statistics Bureau and Ministry of Commerce, Russia's direct investment inflow in the Chinese economy in the first half of 2016 was only US$1.28 million (down 83.8 percent from the same period a year before).

In any case, whichever figures we accept, the total mutual investment, far from decreasing significantly, is growing, although the results may vary depending on the year.

Factors preventing growth of mutual investments are also tradi-

Table 4 Russia's direct investment stock in China, 2012–16 (at the end of the period, US$ million)

Data source	2012	2013	2014	2015	January–June 2016
General Administration of Customs, China	847.7	869.8	910.8	946.88	913.58
Bank of Russia	249.0	186.0	195.0	174.0	157.0

tional. According to an opinion poll, 91 percent of large Chinese companies view the Russian market as attractive for their business, and most of them have specific plans for investment projects in Russia: 61 percent of those polled plan to implement them within the next five years, and another 21 percent during the next year. More than 10 percent expect high returns on their investment in Russia. At the same time, the survey showed that 67 percent of respondents think that their knowledge in this area is insufficient; 66 percent are attracted by Russia's natural resources, and 62 percent by the size of its domestic market. Of companies already operating in Russia, 67 percent complain about law enforcement problems in the country, 63 percent about the deteriorating macroeconomic situation in Russia, and 59 percent about insufficient guarantees for investment.[15] Russian businesspeople complain about the incomprehensibility of Chinese legislation, Chinese protectionist measures against some categories of Russian goods, and the complex decision-making system used by their Chinese partners.

Russian and Chinese authorities understand the existing problems and try to solve them. The governments of both countries constantly encourage their businesspeople to cooperate with each other. Regular contacts are maintained between the border guard and customs services of the two countries. The Russia's Ministry of Economic Development and the China's National Development and Reform Commission have begun to hold regular Russian-Chinese investment forums. During Xi Jinping's visit to Moscow in early July 2017, the Russian Direct Investment Fund and China Development Bank agreed to create a Russian-Chinese Investment Cooperation Fund with a capital of 65 billion yuan (about US$10 billion), which would simplify mutual direct investment procedures and encourage payments in Russian and Chinese national currencies. Several dozen new investment and cooperation contracts were also signed.

Figures on the dynamics of Chinese investment in Russia suggest the following conclusions. Investment flows from China to Russia are growing, but in recent years they have been increasing more slowly than Chinese investment in other countries. Yet China's role as a foreign investor in the Russian economy cannot be compared to Russia's role as an investor in China. Russian investment in China has been negligible in comparison to all Russian investment abroad and all foreign investment in the Chinese economy. At the same time, the deterioration of Russia's relations with the West has led to a serious deepening of investment cooperation between Russia and China, which will be discussed further.

Energy Cooperation

Russian-Chinese energy cooperation is growing steadily despite some problems. A recent study "highlighted the Chinese–Russian systemic dimension of the bilateral energy interdependence being constructed." The authors conclude that for the Russian part, "this constitutes an answer to the difficulties encountered with the model of organization and exchange that the EU intends to promote with its main suppliers. On the Chinese side, it corresponds to its preference for international regulations, consolidating its political space for development."[16]

Bilateral economic relations were seriously damaged by the scandal over the privatization of the Russian stake in the Russian-Belarusian oil company Slavneft, when in 2003 the Russian government made every effort to bar China National Petroleum Corporation (CNPC) from the auction – despite the fact that the Chinese company could reputedly offer US$1–1.5 billion more than the winners did. As a result, the auction was won by Russia's Sibneft together with TNK, the Russian state budget lost a lump sum of money, and the Russian oil industry remained without significant investment.

Opponents of China's presence in the Russian oil market again raised the "China threat" issue. Some media and politicians proposed barring foreign companies from Russia's energy sector. However, several weeks after CNPC's failure, British Petroleum received a large segment of the Russian oil market after it reached a deal with TNK.

In July 2001, during Jiang Zemin's visit to Russia, China and Russia agreed to build an oil pipeline between the two countries and prepare a feasibility study for the project. In September of the same year, during the sixth regular meeting of the heads of government in St. Petersburg, Russian companies Yukos and Transneft signed a general agreement with CNPC on the oil pipeline's construction. China needed the pipeline badly because of the increased requirement for energy resources as its economy grew, and the depletion of its own oil reserves in Daqing, which could result in the loss of many jobs in the oil industry. But this project was advantageous to Russia, too, as it sought to diversify its exports and get rid of its total dependence on Western markets.

At the same time, some experts in Russia expressed concerns about its possible dependence on one consumer and proposed building a pipeline to a Russian port, which would allow the country to choose consumer countries depending on the price offered. As a result, discussions began in Russia in 2002 on a project for building an oil pipeline to the Pacific coast. During a visit to Russia by Japanese prime minister Junichiro Koizumi in January 2003, the parties reached an agreement to prepare a feasibility study for an oil pipeline project promoted by Japan.

In May 2003, the Chinese and Japanese projects were combined into the Eastern Siberia–Pacific Ocean (ESPO) oil pipeline. It was proposed to build the main pipeline from Angarsk to Nakhodka and a branch pipeline 1,030 kilometers long from Skovorodino through Mohe to Daqing. After the first stage of ESPO was built in April 2009, Russia began to lay the branch pipeline to the Chinese border, which was completed in late 2010. Regular shipments of Russian oil through the Skovorodino–Daqing pipeline started on January 1, 2011.

In October 2009, Rosneft and CNPC agreed to start joint construction in 2010 of an oil refinery in Tianjin, with a capacity of 10 million tons. The US$3 billion project was planned to be completed in 2012. However, its implementation took more time than planned. CNPC chairman Wang Yilin told the Russia-24 TV channel in May 2016 that the feasibility study for the project had been submitted for corporate approval. In January 2017, Rosneft announced the completion of the feasibility study and approval by the parties of the technological configuration of the refinery and a complex for the production of aromatic hydrocarbons.[17]

By the end of the 2000s, Russia had changed its attitude to opening its energy market to Chinese companies. Whereas earlier the market had been almost completely closed to them, in 2005–10 there emerged various forms of partnerships, including direct investment by Chinese companies in the Russian energy sector. However, these were only the first tentative moves. According to the ChinaPRO website,[18] on October 19, 2009, China Investment Corporation acquired a 45 percent stake in Russia's Nobel Oil, which develops oil and gas fields and whose raw material assets are estimated at US$300 million. Nobel Oil maintained a controlling stake.

However, Russia's approach changed more radically after the deterioration of relations with the West over Ukraine in 2014 and the introduction of anti-Russian sanctions. Already in May 2014, during Putin's visit to China, the parties had signed two major contracts for Russian gas supplies. One of them, the memorandum of understanding on gas supplies via the eastern route, was signed by Russian energy minister Alexander Novak and Wu Xinxiong, director of China's National Energy Administration, in Shanghai in the presence of the leaders of the two countries. The other document was the Purchase and Sale Agreement for the supply of Russian gas to China concluded by Gazprom and China National Petroleum Corporation and signed by Alexei Miller, chairman of the Gazprom Management Committee, and PetroChina CEO Zhou Jiping. The 30-year contract, the largest in the history of Gazprom, is worth US$400 billion.[19] Of course, the contract had been prepared before 2014, but the fact that the parties decided to sign it at that very time, and the fast pace of the negotiations, suggested that the parties wanted to demonstrate their solidarity and the existence of an alternative to Russian gas exports to Europe.

In September 2014, Gazprom started the construction of the first section of the Power of Siberia gas pipeline from the Chayanda field in Yakutia to Blagoveshchensk on the border with China. The 2,200 kilometer pipeline will deliver natural gas to China.[20] In February 2015, Russian deputy prime minister Arkady Dvorkovich said that the Russian government was ready to consider applications from Chinese companies for the purchase of controlling stakes in strategic oil and gas fields in Russia.[21] Earlier, Russia had not encouraged, and had even blocked such applications from Chinese partners. In the final days of 2015, Russian and Chinese companies signed several major deals: the Chinese committed €730 million to a fifteen-year loan for the liquefaction of natural gas for export in the Yamal LNG project in Russia, an enterprise in which the China National Petroleum Corporation already owns a 20 percent stake;[22] and the Sinopec Group acquired a 10 percent stake in Russia's largest gas processing and petrochemical group, SIBUR, along with the option of purchasing another 10 percent after three years. In April 2016, Yamal LNG announced that it had been granted a new loan of €9.3 billion and 9.8 billion yuan for 15 years by China's Export-Import Bank and China Development bank.[23]

On July 7, 2017, during Xi Jinping's visit to Russia, Leonid Mikhelson, chairman of the Board of Russia's operator Yamal LNG, "Novatek," announced that the first line should begin production by the end of 2017, while the second and third line would be built in 2018–19. According to Mikhelson, after the project is finished, Russia will move from ninth to fifth place among the world's largest LNG producers.[24] Mikhelson also mentioned that "Novatek" was also working on an "Arctic-LNG" project which would produce LNG at Gydansky peninsular in Western Siberia and export it to the countries of Asia-Pacific, including China. It will be using the Arctic ocean shipping route (Northeast passage), which will make it cheaper than the American LNG. In an interview to the Russian press in July 2017, Xi Jinping expressed interest in making joint efforts to develop and utilize maritime passageways, particularly the Northern Sea Route, and realizing the "Silk Road on ice."[25]

These projects were the largest Chinese investments in the Russian economy in the history of bilateral relations.

The main Russian-Chinese project in nuclear power engineering is the Tianwan nuclear power plant located 30 kilometers from Lianyungang in Jiangsu province. The Tianwan nuclear power plant is the largest in China in terms of per-unit capacity. Its master plan provides for the construction of eight power units generating 1,000 megawatts each. The construction contract was signed in December 1997. Despite Chinese complaints about delays and the quality of some work, the startup of the first unit took place on December 20, 2005, and in June 2007 the unit was commissioned. The second unit was commissioned on August 16, 2007. Simultaneously, the warranty operation of the nuclear power plant began. Since 2009, the plant has been operating in the normal mode. On March 23, 2010, Jiangsu Nuclear Power Corporation signed a framework agreement with Atomstroyexport for the construction of the second stage of the Tianwan nuclear power plant. The construction of units 3 and 4, at a cost estimated at US$2–2.5 billion per unit,[26] began in 2012 and 2013, respectively.

In late July 2014, Rusatom Overseas, which is part of Rosatom, and China's CNNC NEV Energy signed a memorandum for the construction of floating nuclear power plants for China. Rosatom also received a proposal to build a two-unit nuclear power plant in Harbin. In November 2016, during the 21st regular meeting of the heads of government, Russian prime minister Dmitry Medvedev and Chinese premier Li Keqiang adopted a declaration on the development of strategic cooperation in the field of nuclear energy.[27] In July 2017, Rosatom announced that four more contracts on further projects in China will soon be signed.[28]

Another area of nuclear energy cooperation is the production of enriched uranium on the territory of China for its nuclear power plants. On July 1, 2014, the two countries signed a document in Beijing on the completion of the warranty period of operation of the fourth stage of a gas centrifuge enrichment plant. Russia's TENEX built four stages of the plant (three in Hanzhong, Shaahxi province and one in Lanzhou, Gansu Province), with a total annual capacity of 1.5 million separative work units. Russia fully complied with its obligations under the intergovernmental agreement of 1992 on the construction of a gas centrifuge enrichment plant.[29]

Along with cooperation in developing nuclear power engineering, China buys electricity from Russia. In 2006, China's State Grid Corporation requested the supply of 60 billion kilowatt-hours per year from Russia by 2020. In 2015, the main Russian exporter, Eastern Energy Company, exported 3.299 billion kilowatt-hours of electricity to China.

Cooperation in Science and Technology

In bilateral cooperation in science and technology, the parties give priority attention to the development of innovations and support for mega-projects. The two countries are now implementing more than 30 joint projects related to basic and applied research in new materials, eco-friendly and energy-saving technologies, biotechnology, high-energy physics, chemistry and petrochemistry, mechanical engineering, instrumentation and automation, telecommunications, electronics and computer science, seismology, and others. The parties develop interaction through the Russian Academy of Sciences and its regional branches within the framework of direct interinstitutional agreements, and cooperate in microelectronics, energy, new materials and nanostructures, organic and inorganic chemistry, laser technology, plasma physics, ecology, and space sciences. In 2014–16, the parties provided support for nine projects to the tune of 305.5 million rubles. Of these, three projects have received funding of 47.7 million rubles under the federal target program Research and development in priority areas in Developing the Science and Technology Sector of Russia in 2014–20.

During President Vladimir Putin's visit to China in September 2015, the Russian holding company En+Group, which combines Oleg Deripaska's aluminum, steel, energy, mining, and logistics companies, reached an agreement with Chinese corporations CentrinData Systems and Huawei on joint construction of several data processing centers in Irkutsk. This is noteworthy because earlier, during a meeting on high technology held in Novosibirsk in January 2005, when Russian Academy of Sciences Siberian branch chairman Nikolai Dobretsov suggested that Russia create a Siberian center for information technologies in cooperation with Chinese partners, Putin asked him: "Why with China?" President Putin pointed to the need to be careful with regard to strategic partners, asking to ensure "that these zones do not later give the Chinese access to . . . well, it's clear . . ."[30] The change in attitude since then is obvious.

During President Putin's official visit to China in July 2016 more than 30 new cooperation deals were signed, including agreements on building a high-speed Moscow–Kazan railroad as part of the future Moscow–Beijing line, joint production of railroad freight cars in Russia, a factory for Advanced Heavy Lifter (AHL) type helicopters in China, a joint long-range passenger plane, and others.

Space exploration is a major area of Russian-Chinese cooperation in science and technology. Russia is still at the forefront in this sphere and is significantly ahead of China, but China is implementing a costly and ambitious development program. According to Russian expert Vassily Kashin, Russia used to be a key partner of China in space exploration and played a special role in the 1990s in developing China's manned space program, known as Project 921 (launched in 1992). Moscow helped Beijing with organizing astronaut training and designing spacesuits and Shenzhou spacecraft, with its first manned flight taking place in 2003.

Kashin notes that the Ukrainian crisis led to some intensification of Russian-Chinese space cooperation, which had significantly slowed down since the 1990s and early 2000s. According to Russian and Chinese experts, the more promising areas in this sphere are the integration of the BeiDou and GLONASS navigation satellite systems, possible supplies of RD-180 engines to China, purchases of Chinese electronic components, and joint projects related to the exploration of the moon and deep space. For now, all these complex technical projects are under study or at early stages of implementation and require long negotiations; thus, the results of the new joint space programs will only be seen in a few years.[31]

Arms Trade

In the 1990s, armaments made up a significant part of Russian exports (15–20 percent, although they were not included in trade figures). This was not accidental because China could purchase from Russia goods to which it had no access in the West due to the sanctions imposed on it after the 1989 events. Russia, too, was very interested in selling armaments to China. The Russian defense industry was in pieces as a result of the economic policy of the first half of the 1990s. The Russian government had to cut the defense budget and was unable to pay for defense orders, which threatened to leave hundreds of thousands of defense industry workers without means of support. Export was the only reliable source of finance for the Russian defense industry, and China showed great interest in purchasing Russian weapons. According to an arms trade expert, Pavel Felgengauer, as early as 1992 "China became one of the main targets of Russia's efforts to promote its weapons in new, 'non-traditional' foreign markets."[32] As reported by the former head of Russia's main arms exporter Rosvooruzhenie, Alexander Kotelkin, more than half of Russian defense production was financed from arms export revenues. Arms sales to China accounted for a large part of these revenues.[33]

During the turmoil of Yeltsin's times, Russian arms producers had a simple program: "Sell anything to anyone."[34] Formally, Russia had an arms export control system,[35] and the Ministry of Foreign Affairs claimed that "the military-technical cooperation with China is developing on the basis of full compliance with Russia's international obligations and its own security interests"[36] however, experts argue that "the Ministry of Defense and Russian special services are unable to establish exactly what was exported and what was not, especially in 1992, when, supposedly, there was virtually no control."[37]

For Russia, this trade was very important as it helped it solve vital social problems (specifically, it provided jobs and income for tens of thousands of defense industry workers) and made it possible to develop a technological potential concentrated in the defense sector in conditions when the state did not have enough funds. According to some estimates, two countries – China and India – accounted for 90 percent of Russia's arms trade in the 1990s.[38] According to leading Russian expert Konstantin Makiyenko, over 15 years (1992–2007), China was the recipient of "40 to 50 percent of all Russian military exports," and "the Russian defense industry survived mainly, if not exclusively, due to Chinese and Indian purchases." The expert noted that orders for conventional weaponry placed by the Russian Defense Ministry with domestic companies "began to influence the situation in the defense sector only since 2004."[39] China's defense imports from Russia included mostly warplanes, ships, and air defense systems.

Throughout those years, some Russian observers expressed concern that Russian weapons sold to China might change the strategic balance of power in East Asia, provoke an arms race, and even, in case of deterioration of relations, be used against Russia. Advocates of developing military-technical cooperation with China argued that the Chinese army was too far behind that of Russia to pose any threat to it in the foreseeable future, and that its main efforts were focused on the solution of the Taiwan problem, which might take decades; so it would be shortsighted to forgo lucrative contracts in this situation.[40]

China's official position is that, while modernizing its armed forces, China does not seek to compete with or threaten anyone; it only seeks to reduce its technological gap with other countries and the world level. Defense minister Liang Guanglie explained: "Military and military-technical cooperation between the two countries is an important content of the Sino-Russian relations and strategic partnership. It fully embodies a high level of mutual trust and relations of strategic partnership, playing an important role in maintaining international strategic balance, establishing a multipolar world and promoting peace and stability on the planet."[41]

Russia's official approach was formulated by deputy foreign minister Alexander Losyukov:

> The armed forces of China have slowed down in development and do not correspond to the level of modern China. This is why China now pays more attention to their development. Naturally, this situation requires modernizing the technological basis of the armed forces and purchasing some types of weapons. This is what China is doing now and will probably do in the coming years. The question is how China will do it, and where it will buy these modern weapons. We believe that in this situation selling certain types of modern weapons to China is in our interests, because our military-industrial complex is facing difficulties. We need money to support our industrial base, and not only in the defense sector, and modernize industrial facilities. One way to get this money is to sell armaments. In particular, given the friendly nature of our relations with China, we are interested in selling modern weaponry to it. At the same time, we do it so as not to upset the balance of military capabilities in the region and not to undermine stability. We understand that modern weapons are available for purchase not only in Russia but also in other countries, and that other countries, too, are interested in a market such as China. It is not only Russian weapons that are to be found on the world market. If we did not sell advanced weapons to China, it would buy these weapons somewhere else.[42]

The mid-2000s saw a decline in China's purchases of Russian armaments. This was for several reasons. On the one hand, Russia diversified its arms exports, with Algeria, Venezuela, Vietnam, and Syria joining China and India as their main buyers. On the other hand, Russian arms manufacturers faced serious competition from China's fast-developing defense industry. According to media reports, "Russian experts, who have had the opportunity to get acquainted with the Chinese aircraft, engine and shipbuilding industries, always point out their first-class level. In addition, after the Chinese receive our weapons, they immediately try to copy them." Referring to Makiyenko's assessment, the author of the report wrote:

> So far, these efforts have met with limited success. But the experience of reproducing and infinitely improving Soviet-made second-generation systems (especially the MiG-21) shows that the Chinese will solve this problem sooner or later. This is why China now demands a sharp increase in the technological level of Russian weapons offered for sale and insists on the purchase of very limited batches. At the same time, unlike India, China has no interest in joint projects for the development and production of new generation systems.[43]

Despite the difficulties, the arms trade remained an important part of bilateral cooperation, and China was among the five top importers of Russian weapons. Russia's Center for Analysis of World Arms Trade estimated all Russian arms exports to China in 2002–9 at US$14.055 billion.[44] China never fully stopped importing armaments. In 2009, Chinese purchases of weapons and military equipment accounted for 9 percent of Russian arms exports; in 2012, this figure increased to 12 percent. In early 2011, Rosoboronexport signed a contract with the Chinese Ministry of Defense for the supply of 150 AL-31F aircraft engines to China. They were used to replace outdated engines in Russian-supplied Su-27 and Su-30 twin-engine fighter aircraft and their Chinese copies, J-11 and J-16. In the summer of 2011, a contract was signed for the delivery of 123 AL-31FN engines (used in the J-10 fighter, developed in China with the assistance of Israel and Russia). In autumn 2011, another contract was concluded for the supply of 184 D-30 KP-2 engines to replace engines of Il-76 transport aircraft and for installment in H-6 bombers. In early 2012, Rosoboronexport signed a contract with the Chinese Ministry of Defense to supply 140 AL-31F aircraft engines.

According to the Rosoboronexport general director, Russia and China achieved great understanding on many issues. In particular,

Russia agreed to joint development and technology transfers to build up bilateral cooperation. China showed interest in technologies and state-of-the-art equipment that had just begun to come into service in Russia. In March 2013, the two countries signed a framework agreement for the supply of 24 Su-35 aircraft and four Lada-class submarines.[45]

But it was only after the beginning of the Ukrainian crisis that Russia agreed to sell to China the most advanced weapon, which it was reluctant to do earlier. In early autumn 2014 a contract was signed to sell to China S-400 surface-to-air missile systems that were estimated to be worth at least US$1.9 billion, with delivery in 2017. And in 2015, Russia finally agreed to deliver the 24 Su-35 fighter jets to China. Kashin, claims that "neither deal should be seen as a consequence of the Ukraine crisis: negotiations on both deals began before the crisis, and most points of contention were resolved by 2014,"[46] yet it seems that, as in the case of Chinese investment in the energy sector, the confrontation with the West has speeded up the negotiations and weakened the position of skeptics in the Russian government concerned with possible strategic challenges from China.

According to Kashin, "though the sale is relatively small, it may have a considerable impact on regional security: even a single regiment of Su-35s may be enough to affect the balance of power in Taiwan. Irbis radar systems can detect airborne targets at a range of up to 400 kilometers, which will allow Beijing to monitor Taiwanese airspace from Mainland China."[47] During his visit to China in November 2016, Russian defense minister Sergey Shoigu said that the arms trade with China reached US$3 billion per year, which was comparable with the level of the 1990s.[48]

Military Cooperation

Military cooperation between China and Russia is developing in many areas, including the training of Chinese military specialists: about 140 Chinese service personnel attend Russian universities, and crews of Chinese submarines, surface ships, and air defense systems, as well as pilots, are undergoing training in Russian training centers.

Russia and China regularly hold joint military exercises as part of the strategic partnership and coordination of their forces, among them annual joint sea and land exercises. Annual exercises of their ground troops Peace Mission practice joint responses in case there is an aggravation of the situation in Central Asia. Although Peace Mission exercises are officially called antiterrorist, they look not so much like operations against terrorist groups but more widely as preparations for possible joint armed actions on a local scale.

There are also other events within the framework of bilateral military cooperation. For example, in 2014 the Chinese military for the first time participated in a tank biathlon competition and in an Air Darts contest, after which they decided to continue participating in events like this.

But of more interest are exercises held after the beginning of the Ukrainian crisis. In May 2015, Russia and China for the first time held the Joint Sea exercise in the Mediterranean Sea. The exercise caused quite a stir in the Western press. Russia and China were accused of creating a new naval alliance against the United States and its allies. But, of course, the main shock was caused by the site of the exercise and the two countries' desire to demonstrate the joint presence of their navies in the sea where the fleets of NATO countries had dominated since the Soviet Union's breakup. In addition, in 2015 and 2016, Chinese warships visited the Russian Black Sea port of Novorossiysk, located near Crimea; and in September 2016, the Joint Sea exercise was held in the South China Sea and in July 2017 in the Baltic Sea.

Despite some divergence of the two countries' positions on Crimea and the South China Sea islands, the military of Russia and China demonstrate their mutual support and willingness to cooperate. As Russian deputy defense minister Anatoly Antonov explained, this cooperation is based on common challenges and threats. He said during a visit by Sergey Shoigu to China in May 2015: "Our Chinese colleagues have stressed the coincidence of our positions on the issue of challenges and threats. They have noted the need to rebuild the present world order, depart from double standards and strengthen equal and mutually beneficial relations in the world."[49] On June 7, 2017, Russian and Chinese defense ministers signed a roadmap on military cooperation for 2017–20. According to China's Defense Ministry spokesman,

> the roadmap makes top-level design and general plan for the military cooperation between China and Russia in 2017–2020. It shows the high level mutual trust and strategic cooperation; it is conducive for both sides to face new threats and challenges in the security field and to jointly safeguard regional peace and stability. In the next step, the two sides will formulate a concrete plan to promote the military cooperation.[50]

Korea

Russia and China also jointly opposed the US plans to deploy Terminal High Altitude Area Defense (THAAD) missile system in South Korea. Officials of both countries condemned this plan on many occasions in 2015 and 2016. In March 2016, foreign ministers Sergey Lavrov and Wang Yi warned at a joint press conference that they would respond. Wang Yi said that Beijing believed these plans "to be directly damaging to Russian and Chinese strategic security" and that "such plans go beyond the defense requirements in the region, violate the strategic balance and would lead to a new arms race." Lavrov called the US and South Korea "not to shelter behind the excuse that this [deployment] is taking place because of the North Korean reckless ventures."[51]

In a joint statement on the current world situation and important international problems signed by the foreign ministers of the two countries during Xi Jinping's visit to Russia in early July 2017, Russian and China stressed that the deployment of THAAD "will cause serious harm to the strategic security interests of regional states, including Russia and China." They called on "the relevant countries to immediately halt and cancel the process of deployment." Instead they put forward a plan for easing tensions over North Korea, suggesting that Pyongyang declare a moratorium on nuclear and missile tests while the United States and South Korea refrain from large-scale military exercises. They also called on "the confronting parties" to start talks on the basis of a refusal to use force and a pledge to make the Korean Peninsula free of nuclear weapons.[52] These proposals clearly show the failure of Trump's attempts to use China to press North Korea without making any concessions on the part of the United States.

Most Chinese experts believe that while the THAAD in South Korea is useless against Pyongyang or Russia, the sophisticated radar capabilities it includes could be used to track China's missile systems. This would give the United States a major advantage in any future conflict with China.[53] According to Major General Luo Yuan, a researcher at the Chinese Military Science Academy, the US is "building an encirclement of anti-missile systems around China, and the only missing link is the Korean Peninsula."[54] So this is an obvious case of the US anti-Chinese military strategy stimulating Russia's support for China and Russian-Chinese military cooperation.

Cooperation in Culture, Education, and Sports

Cultural cooperation is an important part of Chinese-Russian bilateral relations, crucial for better understanding between the two nations. In the 1990s it developed under the Agreement on Cultural Cooperation which was signed on December 18, 1992 and laid the legal groundwork for bilateral ties in this sphere.

Cultural exchanges between Russia and China took place on all levels, including governmental, interdepartmental, regional, and commercial. Moscow and Beijing pay special attention to such key aspects of cultural cooperation as broader student exchanges, joint bachelor's degree programs, regular education exhibitions, popularization of Russian language studies in China and of Chinese language studies in Russia, creation of cultural centers, and organization of cultural and film festivals; infectious disease prevention, traditional medicine, and tighter pharmaceutical drug control; facilitation of tourist exchanges and better tourist services; and more intensive contacts between mass media.

The legal framework of current Russian-Chinese cooperation in the field of education is based on the following intergovernmental agreements: On Cultural Cooperation, signed on December 18, 1992; On Mutual Recognition and Equivalency of Education Diplomas and Academic Degrees, signed on June 26, 1995; On Russian Language Studies in China and Chinese Language Studies in Russia, signed on November 3, 2005; Agreement between the Ministry of Education of Russia and the Ministry of Education of China on Cooperation in the Field of Education, signed on November 9, 2006. In addition, there are other working documents such as notes of annual meetings of the Russian-Chinese Intergovernmental Subcommission for Cooperation in Education.

Within this education subcommission, operating since 2001, there is a Working Group for Interaction in the Study and Teaching of the Russian and Chinese Languages, Development of Bilateral Academic Exchanges and Scientific Cooperation between Universities. The working group is tasked with monitoring bilateral cooperation in the field of education and drafting recommendations for the subcommission and universities. The two countries are planning to increase exchanges to 100,000 students and postgraduate students by 2020 and have already worked out an action plan.

To maintain the high level of interaction and promote the Russian and Chinese languages among young people, the two countries held the Year of the Russian Language in China and the Year of the Chinese Language in Russia in 2009–10. Their results are particularly important for improving the training of sinologists and Russian specialists for Russian and Chinese organizations and agencies as well as for strengthening practical and academic Chinese Studies. To date, more than 900 partner ties have been established between Russian and Chinese universities and organizations, involving 120 Russian and about 600 Chinese universities. Some 1,000 Chinese students study in Russia annually on government grants. Russian and Chinese universities set up summer schools for each other's students.

There are 20 Confucius Institutes in Russia, and 11 Russkiy Mir Foundation centers and offices in China. Russian and Chinese educational institutions organize regular exhibitions of educational services, exchanges of students and schoolchildren, and student festivals. In 2008, 53 leading universities in Shanghai Cooperation Organisation countries, including 16 Russian and ten Chinese universities, announced the creation of the SCO University.

China is among the countries with the largest number of their students studying in Russia. According to official Russian statistics, it was second only to Kazakhstan in 2012–14. However, data vary. A report from the Knight Frank real estate company does not have Russia among the top ten countries with the largest number of Chinese students in 2015,[55] while Russian data indicate that 18,200 Chinese students studied in Russia in 2013–14, which would have made it ninth in the Knight Frank ranking (above New Zealand but below Germany). In turn, Russia ranked fifth in 2015 by the number of its students studying in China. Of more than 397,000 foreign students from 202 countries and regions who studied in China, 66,672 came from South Korea, 21,2975 from the United States, 19,976 from Thailand, 16,694 from India, and 16,197 from Russia.[56] In any case, among the ten countries considered by Chinese students to be the most attractive for study abroad, Russia is at the bottom of the list. There is practically no information on the comparative attractiveness of China for Russian students, but one thing is clear: the number of Russian students in China keeps growing, including those who enroll in English language programs in that country.

Tourism is on the rise. In November 1993, the two countries signed an intergovernmental agreement on cooperation in the field of tourism. By the beginning of the twenty-first century, China had become one of the most popular travel destinations for Russians. In 2001, the Chinese government included Russia in the list of countries where Chinese citizens could travel for tourism purposes. As a result, the number of Chinese tourists in Russia increased significantly. At the same time, the number of Russian tourists visiting China was much larger. China is among the most visited destinations for Russian tourists, along with Finland and Turkey. Every year, some 1.5–2 million Russian tourists visit China, and 1–1.5 million Chinese tourists go to Russia.[57]

In 2001, Russia and China for the first time signed a sports exchange plan. Chinese traditional medicine is also becoming increasingly popular in Russia.

Numerous events held as part of the Year of Russia in China (2006) and the Year of China in Russia (2007) as well as the Year of the Russian Language in China (2009) and the Year of the Chinese Language in Russia (2010) gave a boost to the development of cultural ties between the two countries. They helped more people, especially young people, become better acquainted with the culture of their neighboring country. In 2012 and 2013, respectively, the Year of Russian Tourism in China and the Year of Chinese Tourism in Russia were held. Years of Russian Media in China and China's Media in Russia took place in 2016 and 2017. As RT's editor-in-chief Margarita Simonyan explained during a meeting with Putin and Xi Jinping in Moscow on July 4, 2017, in the situation of the world domination of Western media, spreading fake news about both Russia and China, Russian-Chinese mutual support in that field "is a question of survival of our resources, your resources as different from the mainstream."[58]

Chinese Demographic Expansion Myth

Rumors about the Chinese "demographic expansion" have arisen on and off in Russia for more than 15 years. The Russian and foreign press claim that hundreds of thousands or even millions of Chinese migrants have moved to Russia; that the Chinese government allegedly encourages such migration as part of its plans to populate and seize Russian territories; that China subsidizes travel expenses for its migrants heading to Russia; that the Chinese mafia, also manipulated by Beijing, controls Russia; and that China is grabbing Russia's strategic resources and buying modern Russian weapons in order to use them later against Russia.

Contrary to reality, these scary tales about the Chinese invasion are quite popular in society and some political circles, both "liberal" and "patriotic." One of the reasons is the absence of accurate information about the actual number of Chinese citizens, or foreign citizens in general, in Russia. Government agencies responsible for immigration and law and order keep no such statistics, while law enforcement agencies, which are supposed to have such information, appear to be the least knowledgeable.

According to the Russian national census of 2002, there were 34,577 people in Russia who identified themselves as Chinese.[59] The census of 2010 put their number at 28,943.[60] These figures seem to be close to reality: there are certainly not hundreds of thousands of Chinese living in Russia permanently, let alone millions. As a matter of fact, the census of 2002 clearly showed that there were five times more Koreans in Russia than Chinese, four times more Tajiks, twice as many Poles, and almost as many Finns.

It is quite natural that at any given moment there are a significant number of Chinese in Russia and Russians in China, because the two countries are friendly neighboring countries whose economic cooperation with each other is on the rise. According to data from the Russian Federal Migration Service, cited by its head, Konstantin Romodanovsky, at a meeting on customs and migration issues in border regions held in Blagoveshchensk on July 3, 2010, there were 248,000 Chinese citizens in Russia at that moment, including 86,000 in the Russian Far East. Replying to a question from prime minister Dmitry Medvedev, who chaired the meeting, Romodanovsky said that these figures might exclude only those who had entered Russia before the end of 2008 and had stayed in Russia illegally. But their number could not be large.[61] These official figures are not at odds with the census data as they include not only permanently residing persons, but also those staying in the country at a given moment, including tourists, entrepreneurs, and people on a private visit.

According to the Federal Migration Service, there were 11 million foreigners in Russia in May 2015, mainly labor migrants. Chinese accounted for a mere 3 percent of that number (about 330,000), ranking tenth after Ukraine (23 percent), Uzbekistan (19 percent), Tajikistan (9 percent), Kazakhstan (6 percent), Belarus, Azerbaijan, Moldova, Armenia, and Kyrgyzstan (about 5 percent each). Responding to alarming media reports about "Chinese expansion," Romodanovsky said there was no such threat as there were only 10,000–20,000 more Chinese migrants in Russia than there were Germans.[62]

Almost none of the Chinese citizens to be met in Moscow, Novosibirsk, Khabarovsk, or Vladivostok (their number is relatively small compared to other major cities in other countries) will have entered Russia by illegally crossing the border, which has been effectively guarded since Soviet times, crossing the Amur, or using roundabout paths through the Ussuri taiga (in contrast to immigrants from Africa to the EU countries, who illegally cross a border which is poorly guarded or not guarded at all).

The Chinese in Russia can be divided into several groups: tourists, officially invited contract laborers, entrepreneurs, and students (some of whom actually run businesses in Russia). These groups account for 90 percent of all Chinese citizens in Russia, but none of them can strictly be defined as immigrants since all these categories stay in Russia legally and for a particular period of time (from several days to several years). Real (legal) immigrants are those who have received residence permits or citizenship. There are few of them in Russia (census data apparently represent the total number of Chinese who legally live in Russia on a permanent basis). Most Chinese do not want to live in Russia permanently (according to polls, they do not like the Russian climate, confusing legislation, hostile attitude from the authorities and people, and corruption). Most of them prefer to make money and then return to China, where life is much more comfortable and calmer today for people with money.

There are, of course, those who live in Russia illegally without registration, on expired visas, in trailers at massive Chinese flea markets, or in Chinese hostels or rented flats, reluctant to go out for fear of running into the authorities. But they do not number hundreds of thousands. Besides, they are constantly detained and deported and, in that event, denied new entrance for five years. So, there is no such thing as mass Chinese immigration to Russia, but only a growing flow of Chinese visitors.

Other fears about China are groundless. The PRC has never made official territorial claims against Russia even in the most strained periods of Soviet-Chinese relations, and there is no evidence to prove that the Chinese authorities encourage migration to Russia. On the contrary, the Chinese authorities constantly advise their citizens already in Russia or other countries to respect local laws and contribute to their economic development.

There are many Russians in China as well. There are significantly more Russian tourists visiting China than there are Chinese traveling to Russia. Chinese border towns are filled with Russian tourists and merchants, some of whom live there permanently or come and go several times a month. According to press reports, a large number of Russians, many of them pensioners, go from adjacent regions to Heihe, Suifenhe, and other towns in China where property costs half or a third of that in Russia and is of better quality. After selling their apartments or houses at home, pensioners can buy a new property in China, saving a hefty sum of money, not so far from their own country. Chinese resorts such as Dalian or Beidaihe, and even the remote Hainan Island, have turned into Russian enclaves where Russians own restaurants, stores, clubs, travel agencies, apartments, and summer houses. All merchants at Beijing's famous Yabaolu Market speak Russian, and many of its restaurants, hotels, and dozens of transport companies are owned by Russians. Many major Russian companies have opened offices in China. The Russian-speaking social network VKontakte alone has about 100,000 registered users who are in China. Although not all of them are Russians (some are citizens of other CIS countries and Chinese who speak Russian), most are Russians, and their number is quite impressive.

Why is the myth about the Chinese demographic expansion so persistent? Inside Russia it is hyped up by the opponents of closer relations with China, both pro-Western ones who view China as a force that pulls Russia into backward and authoritarian Asian savagery, and extreme nationalists who see enemies everywhere. Outside the country, it is fed by those who consider the Russian-Chinese rapport dangerous and view China as a threat. The latter include mass media and politicians in the United States and Europe, who are trying to convince Russia that it has no other way to go but to be subordinate to the progressive West, but also similar groups in some of the countries that surround China, such as Indonesia, Vietnam, and India.

Myth of the Russian-Chinese Struggle for Influence in Central Asia

Another theory, quite popular both in Russia and abroad, is that Russia and China are destined to fight for influence in Central Asia. Conceived by Western political scientists such as Zbigniew Brzezinski and Samuel Huntington, who build abstract constructs like "chessboards," "great games," or "the clash of civilizations," it has become quite widespread in academic circles in the post-Soviet space. The popularity of such ideas in the United States, where they are not at all dominant, can be explained by the wishful thinking of anti-Russian and anti-Chinese conservatives who believe that conflicts and struggle between Moscow and Beijing could benefit Washington. In the post-Soviet space, it is based partly on the piety for Western theories, and partly on political approaches. In Russia, it is usually outright Westernizers who speak about the danger of China, thus seeking to encourage Russia to follow the United States and Europe, as well as radical nationalists who see threats to Russia everywhere, with China no exception.

The theory of Russian-Chinese rivalry in Central Asia can assume different forms. One of them questions the benefits that Russia can get from participating in the Shanghai Cooperation Organization, which is generally viewed as a Chinese project designed to subjugate Russia to Beijing's interests. Some Russian experts have claimed that the SCO is dominated by China, which is seeking to solve its own strategic tasks at the expense of other partners, primarily Russia. Yuri Galenovich, of the Institute of Far Eastern Studies, wrote that the agreement on confidence-building measures with China was "a step towards realizing its strategy of restoring so-called historical justice and 'reviving the zhong hua nation' by regaining both territories that were allegedly taken away from China in the past and pieces of the divided nationhood which Beijing considers parts of the Chinese nation that was forcibly torn apart." Based on this understanding of the Chinese strategy, Galenovich concluded: "In a situation where Beijing has the overwhelming superiority in conventional weapons, conventional armed forces and potential size of the army, and when our own country is weak, this can only benefit Beijing." He further claimed that the Chinese approach toward talks with Russia on this issue is "an ultimatum to the enemy defeated in a war," "revenge for the fictional past" and "firm adherence to the theory that our country has always been a threat to continental China," and drew the conclusion that by having agreed to limit the number of troops within 100 kilometers of the border, Russia "infringed upon its own sovereignty in the field of defense and allowed foreign inspections by military representatives from the neighboring country."[63]

Professor Vilya Gelbras of the Institute of Asian and African Studies at Moscow State University also noted that, for China, such notions as "good-neighborliness" and "cooperation" were synonymous with agreement with a "one-way traffic" approach. He wrote: "Russia is among the historical antagonists of the Chinese nation. Beijing has assumed an active offensive position with regard to Moscow, pressing consistently and very persistently for more and more concessions." Gelbras believes that the creation of the SCO, where China holds "leading positions," illustrates the success of this "good-neighborly" and "friendly" pressure:

For example, the creation of the Shanghai Cooperation Organization, which was very nearly glorified by all of its members, actually means that Russia and its CIS partners have publicly and politically recognized the expansion of China's vital interests to the whole of Central Asia. By so doing they objectively made their share of contribution to the "great revival of the Chinese nation."

Gelbras stated that "there is no need to look for any reason for mistrust of China" as "there has been no trust among member states since the very first day of the SCO's existence." To make his point, Gelbras names the creation of the Collective Security Treaty Organization among CIS states as proof.[64]

Analyzing Russia's approach toward Central Asia, Vasily Mikheev, deputy director of the Institute of World Economy and International Relations, lists Russia's concerns about China's role in the SCO. He says that the general belief in Russia (he does not specify among whom exactly) is that not all members of the Chinese leadership are so positive about cooperation with Russia in the SCO, that the two countries disagree over the organization's development strategy, and that China may use for its own benefit disagreements between Russia and Central Asian countries over the development of their energy resources. He further says that Beijing is also concerned about Moscow's attempts to use the SCO in order to control China's activity in Central Asia. The Chinese leadership has doubts about the organization's capacity and efficiency and is becoming increasingly disappointed with the work of its bodies.[65]

More recently, Alexander Gabuev of Carnegie Moscow Center commented on the SCO enlargement on which Russia insisted, saying that it would turn the organization into a useless discussion club because of the lack of common interests and various differences among the members. In his view, the reason for Russia putting forward the "Greater Eurasia" idea, as well as inviting India into the SCO, was to limit "Chinese expansion into Eurasia by wrapping up Beijing's initiatives (such as One Belt, One Road) within even larger-scale projects."[66] These opinions, expressed by some Russian as well as foreign experts,[67] are groundless and partly based on manifest errors. As far as confidence-building measures on the former Soviet-Chinese border are concerned, first, all such measures provided for in the agreements of 1996 and 1997 are reciprocal, and thus there can be no question of unilateral concessions. Second, Russia has agreements on confidence-building measures which limit the number of troops in certain areas (including border regions) not only with China (as Galenovich claims) but with some other countries as well. It is a standard international practice designed to improve interstate relations. For example, until recently Russia was bound by a system of confidence-building measures with NATO countries under the Treaty on Conventional Armed Forces in Europe, signed in 1990. Confidence-building and mutual verification measures accompanied Soviet-American strategic arms reduction treaties signed from the 1970s. Finally, and this is the most important point, because Russia's conventional forces were cut for domestic reasons and their actual strength within the 100 kilometer area was already below the limits determined by the treaties at the time of signature, these agreements were more beneficial for Russia than they were for China. In fact, it is China that may exceed these limits. In other words, it is China that is affected by the restrictions.

Most specialists are confident that, given the economic and demographic situation in Russia and the state of its conventional forces, in any conflict in the foreseeable future Russia will have an advantage in nuclear, not conventional, weapons which puts it far ahead of China. Generally speaking, Galenovich and other authors sharing his views have so far failed to provide any proof of China's aggressive plans with regard to Russia or other SCO countries. In fact, Galenovich does not cite any documents, but talks in general terms. However, documents and reality prove otherwise. For example, Beijing has voluntarily pledged not to deploy any armed forces within the 100 kilometer area, except for border regions; it has never made any official territorial claims against Russia (or the Soviet Union); and it has always recognized the inviolability of the border with Russia under the Treaty of Good-Neighborliness and Friendly Cooperation signed in 2001.

As for China's dominance in the SCO and its purportedly leading role in this organization, there is no corroborating evidence. Representatives of the member states hold senior positions on a rotational basis. Russia's contribution to the SCO budget is equal to that of China. SCO members agreed to have the secretariat in Beijing because China had offered better conditions. However, the organization's key body, the Regional Anti-Terrorist Structure, operates in Tashkent. In fact, the location of the headquarters is not so important. One can hardly say that the United States dominates the United Nations only because most of its bodies are located in New York. On the contrary, the US considers the UN a necessary evil, especially since the UN Security Council and particularly the General Assembly often hold views that disagree with those of America.

In reality, China's interests in Central Asia coincide with those of Russia. The following are three key factors:

1. Maintaining political stability (no one wants a political eruption that can bring radical Islamist movements to power).
2. Keeping the power of secular regimes.
3. Accelerating the economic development of countries in the region as the only political basis for stability.

In this sense, economic or any other activity carried out by either China or Russia in Central Asia should not be regarded as threatening the interests of other countries (as diehard conservatives of the Cold War era sometimes claim). If China invests in Central Asia's economy and supports cultural and research work there, it does not necessarily seek to harm the interests of Russia in the region, because its efforts will eventually lead to the economic and cultural development of these countries. It would be silly to oppose such activity. Being a dog in the manger irritates people in Central Asia and is hardly possible in the modern world. What is true is that Russia itself should be more active in implementing such programs.

But, of course, the coincidence of vital state interests does not mean the absence of economic competition between companies from different countries. Many of them, including large state-owned power and other corporations, obviously compete for the Central Asian markets and often get support from their own governments. But economic competition between companies should not be confused with rivalry between states, particularly close allies. This was shown by the potato war between the US and Canada in 1982–3, the banana war affecting the interests of the US, the United Kingdom, the EU, and some Latin American countries, or the constant trade tensions between the US and Japan. Those were acute economic conflicts, but they did not spoil political relations based on a solid allied foundation.

Real Areas of Potential Disagreement

Both China and Russia base their policies on their own interests. This is the reason why some of their approaches toward international issues or bilateral cooperation differ or only partly overlap. The following are some examples.

China has no plans to join nuclear arms reduction agreements, as it believes that Russia and the United States should be the first to cut their nuclear arsenals to a lower level, which it does not specify. This may slow down nuclear arms reduction talks at some point.

While generally supporting Russia's multipolar policy, China cannot support the recognition of Abkhazia and South Ossetia or the reincorporation of Crimea. Moreover, the issue itself irritates Beijing, because territorial integrity is a very sensitive matter for China, especially in light of the events in Tibet in 2008 and Xinjiang in 2009. China has no intention of cutting its arsenal of medium- and short-range missiles and actually tries to acquire as many of them as possible in case of a possible war with Taiwan.

As the world's largest consumer goods manufacturer, China supports market liberalization and free trade and advocates them in APEC, the SCO, and other international organizations. In this respect, it is more of an ally for the West and the "North" than for the rising "South" and, to some extent, Russia, where "the protection of domestic manufacturers" is becoming an increasingly relevant issue. But Russia's position on the issue changed after the dramatic fall of the ruble, which lost almost half of its market value in 2014–15, and the ensuing decline in prices for its exports. In May 2016, first deputy prime minister Igor Shuvalov said at a news briefing after a meeting of the Supreme Eurasian Economic Council in Astana, Kazakhstan, that Russia was planning to begin talks on a comprehensive trade and economic partnership with China. He said that nontariff barriers in bilateral trade would be the first to fall.[68] The first phase of the talks on a free trade area between the Eurasian Economic Union and China was held in the middle of October 2016. This issue was also discussed during a meeting between Russian prime minister Dmitry Medvedev and his Chinese counterpart Li Keqiang in St. Petersburg on November 7–8, 2016. It was then raised again when trade and economic cooperation was discussed as part of a broad Eurasian partnership which could embrace EAEU states, India, China, Pakistan, and other countries that may be interested in joining this project. An agreement on a free trade area between Russia and China could be the first step toward this goal. Press reports said that a free trade area, initiated by Russia and China and encompassing the EAEU, India, and Pakistan, could become an effective response to the US-led Trans-Pacific Partnership (TPP).[69]

China competes with Russia for foreign investment and the development of border regions (Russia's Far East and Northeast China), and it needs Russia as a supplier of resources and a market for its goods. Russia, in turn, needs Chinese labor, capital, and technologies for the development of its own Far Eastern regions and could offer China not only raw materials but also machines and technologies. Currently, some of the Chinese machinery and equipment directly supplied to Russia competes with their Russian analogues (for example, automobiles).

Another challenge is that it is hard for Russian and Chinese entrepreneurs to work with each other because of differences in culture and decision-making mechanisms. This largely explains why the initial enthusiasm of Russian businesspeople and their unfounded hopes that Chinese colleagues would become a complete replacement for Western counterparts after the imposition of anti-Russian sanctions quickly gave way to some disappointment and even a desire to work with other Asian partners, such as Japan or South Korea, which are easier to understand.

In some fields, there is no reciprocity. For example, Chinese television, newspapers, and magazines are easily available in Russia, while foreign mass media are banned in China by law. It took a lot of effort and persuasion to convince the Chinese authorities to allow Russian television channels even in hotels, permitted now in several hundred. However, this situation may change, since it was announced during Xi Jinping's visit to Russia in July 2017 that a new Russian TV channel, Katyusha, will soon start operating in China.

None of these examples constitute problems that can cause a dramatic worsening of bilateral relations similar to the ideological differences of the 1960s. The present basis of the Russian-Chinese strategic partnership is so strong and solid that any differences can be effectively resolved through the existing mechanism of consultations and constructive cooperation.

CONCLUSION: BEYOND STRATEGIC PARTNERSHIP? MANAGING RELATIONS IN AN INSECURE WORLD

The Impact of the Ukrainian Crisis

Initially, the deterioration of relations between Russia and the West and the growing tensions between China and the US over the South China Sea led to increased expectations that Russia and China would deepen their cooperation and possibly even form an alliance. However, that mood gradually gave way to a series of disappointments and a more cautious outlook.

The decrease in Russia's trade with major Asian partners in 2015 sparked a new debate over Moscow's Asia policy. Critics in both Russian and Western media concluded that the economic crises in Russia and China spelled an end to Moscow's pivot to Asia. Two rival camps in Russia teamed up in this campaign: the pro-Western media – which always exaggerate the dangers China and cooperation with Beijing supposedly pose – along with their opponents, who claimed that China is not really criticizing Russia as a whole, but the monetarist pro-Western part of the government in charge of economic policy. In the West, there was a renewed attempt to prove to Moscow that it has no other option than to cooperate with the US and Europe on their terms.

That outpouring of rather low-quality information in turn sparked a more serious debate. In summing up the results of Russia's "pivot to Asia," a number of commentators who ostensibly took a more balanced approach to the issue were actually just as critical of Russia as their colleagues.[1] Their arguments are summarized in the following points.

CONCLUSION: BEYOND STRATEGIC PARTNERSHIP?

1. Once relations with the West soured, Russia had heightened expectations that its Asian partners would almost completely replace those in Europe. Those expectations were not fulfilled.
2. The Asian partners, and particularly China, turned out to be tough negotiators, and in many cases took advantage of the difficult situation in Russia to secure better terms for themselves.
3. The Chinese partners are only interested in Russian raw materials. Simply selling Chinese products to Russia and sending Chinese laborers will not help Russia achieve greater production, import substitution, and investment.
4. Chinese banks do not extend sufficient credit to Russia over concerns about the effects of US sanctions.
5. Russia's trade with China and other Asian countries fell sharply in 2015.
6. Disappointed Russian leaders have lost interest in cooperating with Asia-Pacific countries, as evidenced by President Vladimir Putin's decision not to participate in the 10th session of the East Asia Summit in Kuala-Lumpur, the APEC summit in Manila and a meeting with Asian businesspeople at the Eastern Economic Forum in Vladivostok in 2015.

Considering all of these arguments, commentators concluded that, despite some positive developments, the scope of cooperation with China and other Asian states has not reached the level expected, that Asia could not replace Europe, and that Russian leaders had been mistaken in placing their bets on Asian partners. From that point onward, their opinions diverge. Some argue that the current situation indicates that Russia should not have quarreled with the West and that Moscow should have made concessions in order to align itself with the "civilized world." Others suggest that the Russian leadership should change course and make even more determined overtures to Asia, adapting to its demands as necessary.

Various Russian political and economic groups holding a range of vested interests stand behind this criticism of the "pivot to Asia." On one hand, those with business interests and property in the West are trying to show the danger and harm in collaborating with the "unpredictable" and "egoistic" East. On the other hand, proponents of a more "nationally oriented" domestic policy are attempting to force out the existing government that they consider the successors to the pro-Western course taken under Yegor Gaydar and Anatoly Chubais in the 1990s. However, even knowing this should not stop us from analyzing their arguments on their own merits.

CONCLUSION: BEYOND STRATEGIC PARTNERSHIP?

It is striking that, despite their many differences, most of the critics share several rather questionable assumptions. First, most of the critical articles link Moscow's pivot to Asia with the recent deterioration of Russia's relations with the West over the Ukrainian crisis. Second, they view the pivot to Asia as a strictly economic process. Third, the critics give excessive weight to Russia's cooperation with China. Fourth, the "pivot to Asia" is portrayed as an alternative to relations with the West, with the possibility of preserving those ties necessarily precluding deeper ties with the East.

In fact, Russia – and previously, the Soviet Union – has been talking for decades about the need to develop relations in the Asia-Pacific Region. Analysts from academic institutions first suggested as much in their writings during the rule of Leonid Brezhnev. Later, during a famous speech in Vladivostok in 1986, Mikhail Gorbachev spoke of a new policy in the Asia-Pacific Region. And Yevgeny Primakov took significant steps to strengthen the focus on Asia during his years both as foreign minister and prime minister. In 1998 he was the first to formulate the idea that Russia, China, and India coordinate their actions. Also, long before the Ukrainian crisis, Vladimir Putin spoke repeatedly about the need to increase activity in Asia. What's more, from the outset, the "pivot to Asia" was a response not to a worsening of relations with the West, but to two purely objective challenges: the need to establish relations with a region that is gradually becoming the center of world economics and politics, and Russia's strategic goal of developing its Siberian and Far Eastern regions.

Of course, progress has been slow in accomplishing those goals. Numerous government programs remain unrealized, the population of the eastern regions has decreased, and Russia's economic presence in the Asia-Pacific Region remains at negligible levels. But thanks to President Putin, efforts in the region have met with some success recently: the APEC summit in Vladivostok in 2012 significantly improved the local infrastructure, and legislators introduced a law in 2014 on territories of advanced social and economic development that has already had an impact, along with a number of other measures.

In fact, the normalization of Russian-Chinese relations began in the 1980s and evolved steadily throughout successive changes in leadership in both countries. They have passed through the stages of inception and normalization to what has become a close strategic partnership today. That indicates that both countries have an interest in seeing relations improve and in ensuring that those relations remain unaffected by the larger political situation or their individual relations with other countries.

CONCLUSION: BEYOND STRATEGIC PARTNERSHIP?

Economic cooperation is one, but not the major reason behind Russia's deepening ties with China and its "pivot to Asia" in general. Geopolitical considerations have played a greater role in that shift, especially during the initial stages. Having lost the competition with the West, Soviet leaders sought the normalization of relations with Beijing in order to use the "China card" against the United States – just as Washington had previously played it against Moscow – hoping thereby to at least partially break what the Chinese call the "united anti-hegemonic front" comprising China along with the US and its allies against Soviet hegemony.

In the early 1990s, Russia initially pursued a one-sided pro-Western course, but was driven by economic necessity to return, after some vacillation, to developing relations with China and other Asian states that were not oriented to the West. It turned out that without arms exports to China and India, Russia's entire military-industrial complex could grind to a halt. That would cause serious discontent among the hundreds of thousands of employees of those factories (the country's own military might was not a consideration at the time). When, in 1996, Yegor Gaydar called for Russia to focus its Asia policy on Japan and to create a military cordon against China,[2] his supporters were pushed aside – at least with regard to foreign policy. And no sooner had Yevgeny Primakov become foreign minister than he began speaking of the importance of the Asia-Pacific Region for Russia.[3]

Later, seeing more and more clearly that it had misunderstood the West, Moscow began viewing cooperation with China, India, and other burgeoning non-Western power centers primarily as an alternative to the idea of creating a united Europe stretching from Lisbon to Vladivostok – a single, powerful "civilized" bloc that would become a major center of world politics. It had turned out that the West was offering Russia only a subordinate position in that scheme, a role that Moscow found less than inviting. Therefore, while maintaining economic ties with Europe and political relations with the US in the form of a "reset," Moscow began searching for partners with whom it would stand on equal terms, and who might form a counterweight to its Western course and help free Russia from its excessive dependence on the West.

The basis for developing relations with states such as China and India lay not in economic interests, but in their similar vision of a future, multipolar world as an alternative to a unipolar world in which the West decides every question at its sole discretion. Moscow strove to support the central role of the United Nations in an effort to preserve the system of international law as it had developed since World War II, as well as the democratization of international relations – that is, the consideration of the opinions and interests of non-Western states in a move away from the dictatorship of the West and toward pluralism in international affairs. In fact, it was on this basis that the BRICS group formed, rather than for economic reasons as Western analysts have claimed. It grew not out of bilateral economic cooperation among its members, but from the geopolitical rapprochement between Moscow and Beijing, which New Delhi, and later, Brasilia and Pretoria also joined. The desire of the BRICS states to change international economic institutions and to gain greater influence in them is closely linked to their own geopolitical ambitions.

In the view of most US experts and politicians, the idea of a multipolar world stems from the desire of new growing powers, especially Russia and China, to secure spheres of influence around their borders, insulating them from international law and where universal values would not be fully implemented. According to Jacob Stokes, once the shared political vision of Russian and China is realized, "each nation would command an effective sphere of influence in Asia and eastern Europe, respectively," and this should not be permitted.[4] In the view of Moscow and Beijing, it is the US which is trying to make the entire world unipolar and turn it into its own monopolistic sphere of influence by imposing on others its own values, which it proclaims universal. Moreover, the US strives to maintain that hegemony by accusing Russia and China of violating international laws that Western capitals instituted for others but refuse to observe themselves.

What Moscow and Beijing are trying to achieve is not spheres of exclusive influence where they will be able to do as they please without any interference from the outside world, but an international agreement on a new set of rules which would suit the interests not only of the US and its allies but also of other major international players, and which would therefore be observed by all sides.

The Ukrainian crisis and the subsequent sharp deterioration in Russia's relations with the West were a natural consequence of long-standing and deepening disagreements that accelerated, but did not initiate Moscow's pivot to Asia. The main result of this crisis has been a change in the psychology of the Russian elite, rather than a shift in its rhetoric or plans. According to a leading Russian foreign policy expert, Sergey Karaganov,

> In 2015, almost the entire Russian elite understood that the confrontation with the West would continue for a long time, that it did not arise

CONCLUSION: BEYOND STRATEGIC PARTNERSHIP?

by chance and that Russia would have to live with a different reality than that which starry-eyed dreams had suggested of integration with the West while also maintaining its independence and sovereignty. They prevailed among the Russian political class almost to the end of the 2000s.[5]

Representatives of major Russian businesses who are accustomed to traveling to the EU and US as if to a second home, purchasing houses in the West, sending their children to study there and doing business with Western companies on an equal footing have understood from the Russian leadership that the current situation is no joke, and that they should not expect any improvement in relations with the West. And because most of these businesspeople have close ties to the Russian leadership and are dependent on its attitude toward them, they have had to give serious consideration to refocusing on the East. What's more, Russia has lost its trust in the West as a partner: some individuals were prevented by the sanctions from traveling to the West and doing business there, while others felt their turn might come soon. In short, many began to feel that the political risks of economic cooperation with the West had become too high.

No such political risks are connected with the Asian states. But other limiting factors come into play here: the inertia of Russia's familiar orientation to the West, its poor knowledge of Asian markets and the Asian business culture, and a shortage of pertinent specialists. It is therefore natural that the economic pivot to Asia is occurring gradually, so anyone who had high expectations that China would quickly replace the West as a trading partner, investor, and source of bank credit was greatly mistaken. However, only very poorly informed businesspeople could have harbored such hopes. Russian experts have always warned against excessive optimism, explaining that the countries of Asia – and even Russia's strategic partner China – would never be moved by fraternal feeling to step in to "save" Russia to the detriment of its own interests, that is, by trading at a loss or investing in poorly conceptualized projects that promise little or no profit. However, China does value its cooperation with Russia. It is primarily important for geopolitical reasons, and less so for economic considerations. Beijing has repeatedly shown its willingness to take Russia's interests into account and to make certain compromises. However, it will only agree to compromises that both sides find mutually beneficial rather than those that involve unacceptable losses for China – especially given the difficult economic situation in which that country now finds itself.

CONCLUSION: BEYOND STRATEGIC PARTNERSHIP?

Chinese businesspeople must first be convinced that Russia is offering them mutually beneficial projects – a challenging task given that many of them still clearly remember the disappointing attempts at cooperation in the 1990s. Russians must study the Chinese market and understand the Chinese business culture, with its decidedly hard-hitting negotiating style. It is also necessary to understand China's mindset, particularly the fact that Beijing values its cooperation with the West, considers it important for achieving its development goals, definitely does not want a confrontation with the West, and is unwilling to do anything that might seriously undermine that cooperation. While it considers the US a geopolitical opponent and accuses it of trying to contain China's growing political and economic influence in the world, for now the Beijing leadership believes that it can take its rightful place in the global system without serious conflict, by applying consistent pressure, by clarifying its position, and by gradually making corrections to the existing system of global governance without resorting to destroying it by revolutionary means. Beijing is playing a nuanced diplomatic game, not waging a war against US imperialism on all fronts – as it might seem to some poorly informed Russian politicians and experts who want to drag China into the same self-defeating course that they would like Moscow to follow.

Also, the argument that a decrease in the value of Russia's trade indicates that it is not pivoting to Asia is unfounded. First, Russia's trade levels have fallen not only with Asia, but with all countries. This is due to its own economic problems – and in the case of China, the problems faced by that country – as well as the falling prices of its main export commodity: energy. The same was true after the crises of 1998 and 2008, but the subsequent upswings in Russia's economic situation have always led to a resurgence and even a sharp increase in those indicators, with the result that China has ranked as Russia's largest trading partner since 2010. Moreover, trade volumes decreased in 2015 not only between Russia and its partners, but also for many countries of the world. Speaking at the seventh Gaydar Forum in Moscow on January 13, 2016, Russian deputy economic development minister Stanislav Voskresensky presented the following figures for 2015: exports between countries in the Organization for Economic Co-operation and Development fell by 20.4% and imports by 20.8%. The same indicators fell in Europe [EU] [by 13.2% and 14.5% respectively, while Germany's trade fell by 12%, Japan's by 18%, Brazil's by 16% and Australia's by 21%.[6] Thus, there is nothing unusual about Russian-Chinese trade levels.

As it happens, positive trends arose even as Russia experienced a fall in trade. Even as the share of mineral raw materials exported by Russia to China fell from 78% to 71% in 2015, food exports rose by 23% and chemical products by 8%.[7] However, as noted earlier, trade statistics are only one indicator, and far from the most important in gauging the strength of this partnership. Far more significant changes are taking place in the trade and economic partnership between Russia and China – namely, a radical shift in the psychology of the Russian elite that has permitted bilateral cooperation to reach areas that the elite had previously considered off limits. In fact, the Xinhua news agency put forward nearly the same arguments in an article published on January 28, 2016 that sharply criticizes those who argue that a decrease in trade with Russia is proof of a broader decline in bilateral relations. The author expresses confidence that the Russian-Chinese partnership will withstand the current challenges and states that "among the countries [Chinese leader] Xi Jinping has visited in the past three years, visits to Russia have produced the most significant benefits."[8]

Major steps have been taken to remove barriers to trade and economic cooperation as well. Officials signed a protocol amending the Agreement between the Governments of Russia and China on the Avoidance of Double Taxation on October 13, 2014 that would prevent double taxation and tax evasion. That document aims to reorient borrowed capital away from European markets and toward the Asian capital market.[9]

And, of course, the major achievement of 2015 occurred during a visit to Russia in May by Chinese leader Xi Jinping: the signing of the statement on cooperation in coordinating the development of the Eurasian Economic Union and the Silk Road Economic Belt, which Xinhua called "a historic milestone that will inject vigorous impetus into relations between the two sides and bring them to a new height."[10] That made it possible to prepare cooperative projects between Beijing and not only Russia, but also the EAEU as a unified partner. In fulfillment of that accord, current projects include joint investment in transportation corridors, efforts to remove trade barriers, and cooperation in the field of high technology. This agreement was the first step toward formulating the concept of a "Greater Eurasia."

Xi Jinping's visit to Russia in early July 2017 did not lead to any spectacular new deals. However, more than forty new bilateral documents and contracts were signed, so even the usual Russian skeptics began to talk about a new stage in Russian-Chinese relations. This will be a stage with fewer slogans and big plans but more practical work on harmonization of the two countries' economies, customs rules, investment opportunities, etc.[11] This shows that the Russian-Chinese rapprochement is taking a less sensational but a more practical, routine, solid, and irreversible form.

Asia – Not Only China

Russia's pivot to Asia does not mean developing cooperation only with China. This is to dissent from Marcin Kaczmarski's argument that Russia's rapprochement is a Sinocentric policy.[12] Changes are also underway in Russia's approach to other parts of Asia. While Moscow is developing increasingly close relations with Beijing, it is also trying to develop and deepen cooperation with other countries in the region. This tendency to diversification, which has always been part of Russia's official discourse, only strengthened in 2016 when it became clear that deepening cooperation with China alone cannot fully compensate for the losses caused by Western sanctions and hostility. This by no means implies any kind of distrust of or disillusionment with China, but a pragmatic policy of increasing benefits pursued by a country which is striving to become an independent power center in a multipolar world.

East Asia as a region is the closest to Russia and, naturally, is always in the focus of its attention. Here Russia continues to actively develop relations with Japan and South Korea, its major Asian trading partners. Much success has been achieved in relations with Japan, especially during Shinzo Abe's premiership. The strong position of Shinzo Abe increased his interest in stepping up talks on concluding a peace treaty with Russia which had not been signed after World War II. Russia responded positively. This new interest in developing comprehensive cooperation was expressed in a joint declaration signed during Abe's visit to Russia in April 2013.

However, the next year Japan joined Western sanctions against Russia, which significantly damaged the bilateral relationship. Russian-Japanese trade dropped 31.4 percent in 2015 compared to 2014, because of sanctions and Russia's economic difficulties, but Japan remains Russia's second trade partner in Asia. In 2016, trade turnover dropped again to only US$16 billion, which was a 25 percent decrease. Direct investments by Japan in Russia also went down: in the first three quarters of 2016, Japanese investments in Russia dropped by 80 percent.[13] Japanese diplomats privately point out that Japan's action on sanctions was taken under pressure from Washington and

CONCLUSION: BEYOND STRATEGIC PARTNERSHIP?

was against Tokyo's interest, but Russia had to react by applying its countersanctions against Japan. However, talks continued and in May 2016 Abe became one of the few leaders of the states allied to the US who visited Moscow, where he presented his "Cooperation Plan." The talks were formalized and furthered during President Vladimir Putin's visit to Japan in December 2016, when apart from major progress in trade, economic, and investment cooperation, the leaders of the two countries also made a statement concerning joint business activities on the disputed South Kuril Islands, which Japan calls its Northern Territories.

During Abe's visit to Moscow at the end of April 2017, the Japanese prime minister and Putin agreed to make a list of joint projects for the disputed islands and to send a delegation of Japanese officials and businesspeople there on a fact-finding mission. The two leaders also agreed to work on a peace treaty, although they stressed that there was no need to wait for its signature before deepening cooperation.[14] This has been Russia's position for a long time. According to a senior Japanese defense expert, Shinji Hyodo, "Given apparently stable governments in both countries, the political environment appears conducive to concluding a peace treaty."[15]

As for South Korea, Russia is very appreciative of its refusal to join in anti-Russian sanctions and is developing cooperation with it in all areas. One of the most important of these involves joint efforts to find a solution to the nuclear issue on the Korean peninsula.

Where India is concerned, Moscow took a number of steps to enhance cooperation during the visit by Indian prime minister Narendra Modi to Russia in late December 2015. They included the signing of an agreement to supply oil for the following ten years, preparation of an agreement on military equipment production, a plan for joint investments totaling US$1 billion, a decision to combine efforts to combat terrorism, and the signing of an intergovernmental protocol to expedite visas for businesspeople. Prime minister Modi also announced plans to increase trade to US$30 billion by 2025.[16] Although Russia's trade and economic cooperation with India is far less than with China, Moscow and New Delhi share geopolitical goals and a common vision for structuring the world. Furthermore, it would be difficult to find any Russians who harbor doubts or hostility toward India, or Indians with such feelings toward Russia. The annual summit meeting between the president of the Russian Federation and the prime minister of India is the highest institutionalized dialogue mechanism under the Strategic Partnership between India and Russia.

CONCLUSION: BEYOND STRATEGIC PARTNERSHIP?

Prime minister Modi and President Putin met again in Tashkent on June 24, 2016 on the sidelines of the SCO summit (Uzbekistan), where they had a separate bilateral meeting. In mid-October 2016, Putin went to India on an official visit. He visited Goa on October 15–16 for the 17th Annual Summit, which produced nineteen documents covering cooperation in defense, space, information security, foreign policy, trade and investment, hydrocarbons, shipbuilding, railways, and science and technology. Prime minister Modi and President Putin also adopted a joint statement, "Partnership for Global Peace and Stability," and a Roadmap of Events to celebrate the seventieth anniversary of the establishment of diplomatic relations between India and Russia.[17]

Russia is also actively developing its cooperation with ASEAN as an organization and with its individual members. Russia and Iran have been particularly active in pursuing rapprochement. The crisis in Russia's relations with the West has significantly increased the value of Moscow's cooperation with Tehran. This acceleration came as a result of Russia's changing approach toward the Middle East, as well its new understanding of the geopolitical situation. On the whole, Russia's policy in Asia dovetails well with its larger policy of creating partnerships with independent non-Western players on the world stage – including China, India, Brazil, and South Africa. Iran is a fitting addition to their ranks.

Russia's pivot to Asia is a reality, one that is motivated by both political and economic interests. Although that shift is not progressing as quickly as some might want, and occasionally encounters difficulties, the process has definitely begun and is, in all likelihood, irreversible. Of course, Russia has had varied relations with the West over the years. And although today's extremely confrontational relations might later give way to a more tranquil period, it is probably not possible that relations will ever fully return to their previous state. Only a small, marginal segment of Russian society continues to dream of unity with Europe – which itself has entered a period of severe crisis. Most of the Russian elite, as well as the majority of Russian citizens, understand that nobody is waiting for them there with open arms. Therefore, while it does not want confrontation and seeks to maintain working relations, Russia – under any leader – is unlikely to pursue a relationship based on a common outlook. A "peaceful coexistence" that involves reaching agreement on some points while maintaining differences on others – such will be the basis of Russia's relations with the West. That, in turn, will move Russia ever closer to the non-Western world, primarily to the Asian giants that have long pursued such a course. That constitutes the solid foundation of Russia's pivot to Asia.

Russian-Chinese Cooperation and the Emergence of Greater Eurasia

Russian expert circles developed the concept of a "Greater Eurasia" in 2015 after concluding that the deterioration in relations with the West over the Ukrainian crisis was irreversible. In May 2015, Dmitri Trenin, director of the Carnegie Moscow Center, published an article titled "From Greater Europe to Greater Asia? The Sino-Russian Entente." In it, he noted that, because of Russian-Chinese rapprochement, "Putin's vision of a 'greater Europe' from Lisbon to Vladivostok, made up of the European Union and the Russian-led Eurasian Economic Union, is being replaced by a 'greater Asia' from Shanghai to St. Petersburg."[18] He also mentioned that the SCO and BRICS might play a role in that scheme.

In August of the same year, in an article "Russia, China and the Emerging Greater Eurasia," published first in the South Korean journal *The Asan Forum* and later in Russia, I wrote about Greater Eurasia not as a goal of Russian and Chinese diplomacy, but as an objective reality reflecting fundamental processes in world politics. Speaking of the formation of a system based on Russian-Chinese rapprochement and the linkage that began at that time between the Eurasian Economic Union and China's planned Silk Road Economic Belt, along with the expansion of the SCO, with its planned inclusion of India and Pakistan, as well as BRICS and ASEAN, I noted:

> The above and other groups over time will comprise the system of Greater Eurasia, the states of which will not be tied by alliance relations, as are the United States and its European satellites. Some of them may turn to different centers of power; however, on the whole, they will form a unity, brought together by core interests. Precisely, this kind of democratic unity of Greater Europe could not be established by the United States and its allies. Attempting to subordinate every state to their dictates, they have united allies from most of Eastern Europe but lost Russia and Central Asia, and are increasingly antagonizing China and India, forcing them to draw closer to each other even in spite of significant contradictions. Only the future will tell who will succeed and who will not.[19]

Experts from the Valdai International Discussion Club and Higher School of Economics summarized these ideas in several reports and recommendations drawn up for Russia's leadership. As a result, President Vladimir Putin incorporated the idea into his speech and interview at the St. Petersburg International Economic Forum in June 2016. The Russian president used more discreet phrasing, referring to the emerging system as a "Eurasian partnership." He attributed the idea to Kazakh President Nursultan Nazarbayev, with whom Putin had discussed it on the eve of the forum. Putin mentioned that over 40 states and international organizations had expressed the desire to establish a free trade zone with the Eurasian Economic Union and suggested that the EAEU could become one of the centers of an emergent greater integration area. On that basis, he proposed to consider "the prospects for more extensive Eurasian partnership involving the EAEU and countries with which we already have close partnership – China, India, Pakistan and Iran – and certainly our CIS partners, and other interested countries and associations."[20]

Putin's formulation was incorporated into the Russian-Chinese declaration signed by the leaders of the two countries during the Russian president's visit to China later in June 2016. That document stressed the paramount importance attached by the two sides to implementing the Russian-Chinese agreement on linking the formation of the EAEU with the realization of the SREB. The document also called for creating a "comprehensive Eurasian partnership based on the principles of openness, transparency, and mutual interests, and including the possible involvement of EAEU, SCO, and ASEAN member countries." The governments of the two countries were tasked with developing measures to implement the initiative.[21]

During the visit to Russia by Chinese premier Li Keqiang in November 2016, Russian prime minister Dmitry Medvedev said that Russia was continuing to work with China on forming a comprehensive Eurasian partnership that would include EAEU and SCO member states. According to Medvedev, Russia and China had conducted a joint study on what should serve as the basis of that partnership. He and Li Keqiang discussed and approved the results of that study during their meeting and instructed experts from the two countries to formulate the economic basis of the project.[22]

In mid-May 2017, President Putin was the main guest at the Beijing top-level Belt and Road Forum for International Cooperation, where he fully supported Chinese initiatives. At a meeting with President Putin in Moscow on May 25, 2017, Chinese foreign minister Wang Yi said that China welcomed and supported "Mr President's personal initiative on creating a Eurasian partnership." According to Wang, the Chinese Commerce Ministry and the Russian Economic

CONCLUSION: BEYOND STRATEGIC PARTNERSHIP?

Development Ministry are currently examining possibilities for developing a Eurasian trade partnership and are preparing a relevant agreement.[23]

In July 2017, during Xi Jinping's visit to Russia, the Chinese minister of commerce, Zhong Shan, and the Russian minister of economic development, Maksim Oreshkin, signed a joint declaration of a feasibility study on a Eurasian Economic Partnership Agreement. According to an official Chinese comment, the signing of the declaration

> is a significant trade and economic achievement of President Xi Jinping's visit to Russia, showing the steadfast determination of China and Russia to deepen their mutual beneficial cooperation and promote trade liberalization and regional economic integration. It also shows the common willingness for a comprehensive and high-level trade and investment liberalization arrangement which opens to other economies in the future. It will inject new strength for the comprehensive strategic partnership of the two countries.[24]

Most Russian and Chinese experts see a Eurasian Economic Partnership as just part of a larger, comprehensive Eurasian partnership, or Greater Eurasia. The media and expert community literature all began referring to a "Greater Eurasia." Thus, according to Sergey Karaganov, "Russia's pivot to Asia, which had been announced many times but really only began in 2011–2012, was for the most part completed."[25] This made it necessary to go further. "Russia and China came up, jointly and officially, with the concept of a Greater Eurasia partnership or community as a common space for economic, logistic and information cooperation, peace and security from Shanghai to Lisbon and from New Delhi to Murmansk." In his view, the reason was the crisis of the world order, "which the West tried to impose since the 1990s," and which "was badly aggravated in the 2010s when it was challenged, rather straightforwardly by Russia and less so by China and other new leaders but still quite openly, as unfair, disadvantageous for them and dangerous for the world, and, on top of it all, dysfunctional. That's when a new alternative was proposed."[26] Ruan Zongze, executive vice president of the China Institute of International Studies, a Chinese Foreign Ministry think tank, commented:

> Promotion of the "One belt, one road" initiative has had a significant impact on Russia. In Russia, they are also thinking about how to achieve linkage. There is some overlap between the "One belt, one road" and Putin's recent proposal to establish a partnership in Greater Eurasia. In effect, they create an opportunity for cooperation between

CONCLUSION: BEYOND STRATEGIC PARTNERSHIP?

China and Russia on the Eurasian mainland region, to expand the reach of Sino-Russian cooperation.

According to Ruan Zongze, the concept of a "Greater Eurasian partnership" "is the result of the ongoing Russian effort to improve its strategic environment by constantly adjusting its general strategy – a course that at various times has led it to promote such projects as the 'North-South transport corridor' and the Eurasian Economic Union."[27]

The authors of the idea see the following as the main features of a "Greater Eurasia":

1. "Greater Eurasia," as a new unified international entity of some kind, is arising from Russian-Chinese rapprochement and efforts to link the EAEU and SREB.
2. Other non-Western organizations and groups – primarily the SCO, ASEAN, and BRICS – will play a major role in this process.
3. "Greater Eurasia" is not yet a formal organization or even a group. It is a partnership of sorts based on the common interests of non-Western states.
4. The states involved share two types of interests: political and economic. The former is based on the concerns over a unipolar world in which the US and its allies attempt to play a dictatorial role and fail to respect the interests – and, often, the sovereignty – of other states. In this respect, "Greater Eurasia" is developing a fundamentally different approach to world politics, one based on respect for international law as it took shape following World War II, the leading role of the United Nations and its Security Council, respect for various cultural traditions and the political systems to which they gave form, and pluralism and democracy not only within countries, but also in international relations. These principles are very similar to the principles of "peaceful coexistence" that developing countries first expressed as far back as the Bandung Conference in 1955, and to the so-called "Shanghai spirit" of the SCO. They are also clearly formulated in the Russian-Chinese Joint Declaration on Promotion and Principles of International Law, signed on June 25, 2016 and the Joint Statement on the Current World Situation and Important International Problems.[28]
5. Economic interests could serve as the basis of a broad partnership. These interests include the linkage of the EAEU and SREB and the strengthening of the economic component of the SCO following accession by India and Pakistan, and possibly Iran. The future

creation of a broad free trade area (FTA) is also a possibility. It is important to note that Russia and China already proposed the creation of a bilateral FTA in 2016. In addition, China has already created such areas with several ASEAN countries, and a single market was also created within the Eurasian Economic Space that preceded the EAEU. As a result, all of those FTAs could expand or even merge, possibly based on the Regional Comprehensive Economic Partnership proposed by China and ASEAN. Another important economic interest is the creation of new transport routes through Central Asia to Europe as part of the linkage with the SREB, and as part of the Maritime Silk Road initiative that would connect Eurasia with ASEAN countries.

6. "Greater Eurasia" will be an open partnership for everyone, including Europe. Individual European countries or the EU as an organization would be most welcome to cooperate with "Greater Eurasia" if they are willing to uphold its pluralistic principles. The interest that European states have shown in China's proposed Asian Infrastructure Investment Bank, the SREB, and more recently, the EAEU, indicate that such an eventuality is possible. However, the new Eurasian system will not be centered in Europe or include the condition that all participants adopt so-called "European values," but will be located in Eurasia and operate on the principles of pluralism and multipolarity.

The concept of a "Greater Eurasia" is still under development and its exact boundaries remain undefined. Experts from a number of countries, Russia and China foremost among them, are working to flesh it out. They have encountered a number of difficulties on the path to its creation: the destructive policies of the United States, international terrorism, and the differing interests and disagreements between major Eurasian players and organizations. However, global trends favor the creation of a "Greater Eurasia," indicating that the process is irreversible.

Donald Trump and the Future of Russian-Chinese Relations

Donald Trump's rise to power and his new approach to relations with Russia and China raise questions about the prospects for Russian-Chinese rapprochement. Trump has stated opposing goals with regard to each of the two countries, promising to improve cooperation with

CONCLUSION: BEYOND STRATEGIC PARTNERSHIP?

Russia, primarily to fight international terrorism, while promising to apply heavy pressure on China to force concessions from it on a number of issues.

It seems this approach is very deliberate and stems from the outlook of Trump and the political forces he represents. Whereas in the first decade after the end of the Cold War, both major US political parties pursued the ideology of "democratization" – the global spread of US values through the imposition of varying degrees of political control over other states, at times at the expense of US taxpayers – Trump and his supporters now hold that the main objective is just the opposite: to selfishly improve the standard of living and the economy in the US and to force the whole world to either serve that purpose or stay out of the way.

The US leadership considers Muslim terrorism the main outside threat to the country. This takes the form of radical Islamists who threaten US interests abroad, while also infiltrating US territory under the guise of refugees and migrants to undermine the country from within. From this perspective, it is logical that Russia, which is not a serious economic rival of the US but possesses considerable military might, could prove a useful ally in the fight against Islamism. Feuding with Russia is pointless: as Trump says, it makes more sense to mend fences with Moscow.

The situation with regard to US-Chinese relations is more complex. Trump has set the goal of achieving economic success for the US and Russia is not a competitor in this regard, only an obstacle in Washington's pursuit of global domination – a course whose main advocates lost in the US presidential election. China, with its economic might, does present a challenge to the US – a challenge that Trump does not like.

It is difficult at present to predict how relations between Russia and the US will develop under President Trump. In either case, his campaign promises will most likely run up against reality, as well as resistance and even sabotage from the state bureaucracy and the Washington elite if his proposals deviate too far from the usual path, run contrary to ideological clichés, and especially, if they undermine the financial interests of the ruling establishment. This is already happening: Trump has had to soften his position on both fronts. In the case of Russia, Trump has effectively refused to lift sanctions, and with regard to China, he has acknowledged the inviolability of the "One China" principle. Thus, although US-Russian relations might undergo a moderate warming and find opportunity for cooperation on some isolated issues, an overall strategic rapprochement such as

CONCLUSION: BEYOND STRATEGIC PARTNERSHIP?

occurred in the 1990s is hardly possible. The disagreements have become too entrenched and the mutual distrust too deep.

At the same time, Moscow will not go out of its way to seek rapprochement with Washington, as it did in the 1990s. It will wait for concrete proposals and actions from Trump. If he has the desire and ability to make progress, Moscow will meet him halfway. If not, Moscow will not waste any effort in hoping. In that case, the current confrontation will continue, but Russia will not return to the practice of making unilateral concessions while the US conducts negotiations according to the famous Soviet principle of "What's mine is mine, and what's yours is up for discussion."

A serious break between the US and China is also hardly possible for the abovementioned reasons. It remains unclear whether Trump can make any fundamental changes to Washington's relationship with Beijing. Because the interconnections between the Chinese and US economies run so deep, any drastic moves could prove disadvantageous and injurious to both – something the authorities in Beijing and Washington will have to keep in mind. Beijing, at least, would go to great lengths to avoid a conflict, and would engage in one only if the US were to encroach directly on its sovereignty over Taiwan or challenge it with a direct military confrontation in the South China Sea. The numerous articles critical of Trump published by the tabloids controlled by the Communist Party of China, such as the *Global Times* – sometimes taking a harsh or rude tone – were probably more of a warning, a kind of initial negotiating position than they were an indication of possible political moves by the Chinese leadership. (In the same way, Trump's threat to abandon the "One China" principle was most likely a negotiating position and not an expression of actual policy.)

But even if relations were to improve considerably between Moscow and Washington and the confrontation between China and the US were to deepen, it would have little influence on Russian-Chinese relations overall. Of course, Moscow would not want to find itself in a position of having to choose between the two partners, but if forced, it would unquestionably choose China.

One thing is certain: if anyone in Washington thinks the US can use Russia as a pawn in its confrontation with Beijing, they are sorely mistaken. As China's foreign minister Wang Yi put it, with Russia China has

> a comprehensive strategic partnership of coordination not because it's convenient; it's a strategic decision reached by both sides on the basis of our fundamental interests. The relationship has stood the test of

CONCLUSION: BEYOND STRATEGIC PARTNERSHIP?

international vicissitudes. It is as strong as it's ever been and our mutual trust has reached a historic high. The relationship will not be affected or weakened by any external factor.[29]

Russia's pivot to Asia – the result of Russia's actual interests as well as a reaction to the inimical attitude of the West – is largely irreversible. China extended support to Russia at a difficult time, and Moscow realizes that, despite a number of problems, China is a more reliable partner than the West. This is primarily because Beijing, like Moscow, long ago abandoned all ideological goals: China is not attempting to impose communism or Confucianism on Russia. For that reason, whatever challenge China might pose for Russia, it is not an existential threat, unlike that posed by the West prior to Trump. For this reason, Russia will never align itself with the US against China. In fact, Beijing would even look favorably at a certain warming of relations between Moscow and Washington. Both Russia and China believe that the "three countries should work with rather than against each other" and "should pursue win-win rather than zero-sum outcomes."[30] However, the Russian-Chinese understanding of the win–win cooperation and their vision of the future world is very different from that of the US.

From this standpoint, it would make more sense to search for new general principles and rules of world order that would suit everyone than for the US to continue attempting to use Russia and China against each other and taking the contradictory approach of exerting pressure on both countries, surrounding them with military bases and cobbling together inimical military alliances with their neighboring countries, while at the same time trying to reach separate agreements with each of them on specific issues.[31] Such principles of world order would also serve to contain emerging powers that increasingly act at their own discretion in the absence of such rules. However, that would require the US and its allies to relinquish the monopoly on interpreting international law to which they have become accustomed since the collapse of the Soviet Union – something their elite would find extremely objectionable. Nonetheless, the West must inevitably relinquish that dominant role because its influence in world politics is clearly decreasing, even as that of other players is growing.

The Russian-Chinese rapprochement is a natural result of broader changes taking place in world politics. After the collapse of the Soviet Union, many in the US and Europe were intent on achieving a system of world unity based on Western principles and values. However, the triumph of the West did not last long. Several new non-Western centers of power came to replace what had previously been a single Soviet center of power. Although not unilaterally inimical to the West as the Soviet Union had been, these new and weaker centers of power were nevertheless worried about Washington's use of pressure tactics in pursuing its selfish interests and therefore sought opportunities to coordinate efforts as a counterweight to Western influence in the world. They viewed a world unified on Western terms as a form of hegemony, a sort of restoration of the colonial system that would inevitably fail to give due consideration to their interests.

It was on this geopolitical basis that the concept of a multipolar world arose, as well as the ideas of pluralism and a more democratic system of international relations that would give due consideration to the interests of major non-Western states. Russia and China, along with other such states, want to found a new international order that places them on an equal footing with the US and its allies, and does not relegate them to the status of dependencies. What the West refers to as a desire by Russia and China to establish spheres of influence, Moscow and Beijing consider the minimum expression of their rights and interests as major world powers.

In an ideal multipolar world in which everyone recognizes the rights of each center of power, Russia and China would be equidistant, figuratively speaking, not only from each other, but also from all other such centers, including the United States. Russian-Chinese rapprochement would lead only to a normalization of relations, without the need to support each other in countering the West. However, the policy of the West aimed at preserving its monopolistic position in the world has had the effect of accelerating the rapprochement between Moscow and Beijing. We have shown how Western actions in Yugoslavia, Iraq, Syria, Ukraine, and the South China Sea – viewed by both Moscow and Beijing as aggressive – have consistently led to a deepening of Russian-Chinese strategic cooperation. This trend gained particular momentum following the outbreak of the conflict in Ukraine in 2014 and US attempts to counter Chinese influence in the South China Sea. The trend toward rapid Russian-Chinese rapprochement might slow if the West were to pursue less aggressive policies. However, their rapprochement will proceed regardless because, as the weaker centers of power in the emerging multipolar world, strategically they need each other more than the West needs either of them.

Thus, the short-term outlook for Russian-Chinese relations does not depend much on the international situation. Their partnership has developed steadily as a result of their common interests and the

CONCLUSION: BEYOND STRATEGIC PARTNERSHIP?

underlying global trend away from a bipolar and toward a multipolar world order. In fact, those relations have continued to progress for more than thirty years now, despite changes in leadership, national economic models, and even political systems.

On the other hand, the establishment of a formal Russian-Chinese alliance remains unlikely. Russia values its political and economic partnership with China but prefers not to tie up its channels of cooperation to one country exclusively. Therefore, Russia will try to maintain cooperation with the EU as far as it can, and as part of its pivot to Asia, it will develop multilateral cooperation with other Asian players, including those with whom China has uneasy relations: India, Japan, and ASEAN member states such as Vietnam, Indonesia, and others. China, for its part, values its relationship with the US and the EU states, with which it has close economic ties. China considers Russia, compared with the Western countries, as a friendlier but less economically significant partner. Russia also has strategic importance for China, but the US is far more important, despite tensions between the two countries, because so much depends on the United States. Therefore, even while it develops its strategic partnership with Russia, China will simultaneously strive to build mutually beneficial relations with other states, even if those states are hostile to Russia – its close partnership with Ukraine being one example.

Therefore, it would be an exaggeration to conclude that Russian-Chinese relations can be currently characterized as a de facto (although not a de jure) alliance, if by alliance we mean having certain clear obligations, whether formal or informal.[32] It is more reasonable to argue, as Timofey Bordachev does, that the creation of such an alliance "would have made the international system dangerously inflexible and, as a consequence, vulnerable to conflict."[33] This is not in the interests of either Russia or China.

For these reasons, a formal alliance between Russia and China would become a reality only if the US and its allies were to pursue an ideological course of "democratism" that brought them into serious confrontation with both Russia and China. However, Trump's electoral win and the rise of anti-establishment sentiment in Europe indicate that the ideology of "democratism" is experiencing a crisis and that its advocates will hardly be in a position to dictate future foreign policy. Forces in the West that favor greater pragmatism and realism are on the rise, and in this respect, they have more in common with the Russian and Chinese authorities who long ago abandoned any ideological underpinnings in their foreign policies.

In the longer term, much will depend on the domestic political situation and the fate of political regimes not only in Russia and China, but also in Western countries – especially the US. Major changes are possible in every country, but it is difficult to know when they might happen or to predict their consequences. For now, the Russian-Chinese partnership will remain one of the pillars of the emerging multipolar world order and a linchpin of global and regional stability.

NOTES

Preface

1. Elizabeth Wishnick, *Mending Fences: The Evolution of Moscow's China Policy from Brezhnev to Yeltsin* (Seattle: University of Washington Press, 2001); Jeanne L. Wilson, *Strategic Partners: Russian-Chinese Relations in the Post-Soviet Era* (Armonk, NY: M. E. Sharpe, 2004); Natasha Kuhrt, *Russian Policy towards China and Japan: The El'tsin and Putin Periods* (Abingdon: Routledge, 2007); Gilbert Rozman, *The Sino-Russian Challenge to World Order: National Identities, Bilateral Relations and East versus West in the 2010s* (Stanford: Stanford University Press, 2014); Marcin Kaczmarski, *Russia–China Relations in the Post-Crisis International Order* (New York: Routledge, 2015).
2. Bobo Lo, "Sino-Russian Relations," Europe China Research and Advice Network (ECRAN), Short Term Policy Brief 87, May 2014, p. 3. See also his earlier work, Bobo Lo, *Axis of Convenience: Moscow, Beijing and the New Geopolitics* (London: Royal Institute of International Affairs, 2008).
3. John Watts, Sofia Ledberg and Kjell Engelbrekt, "Brothers in Arms, Yet Again? Twenty-First Century Sino-Russian Strategic Collaboration in the Realm of Defence and Security," *Defence Studies*, 16(4) (2016): 444.
4. Bobo Lo, *A Wary Embrace: What the China-Russia Relationship Means for the World* (Melbourne: Penguin and Lowy Institute, 2017).
5. James Bellacqua, "Introduction: Contemporary Sino-Russian Relations: Thirteen Years of a 'Strategic Partnership'" and Charles E. Ziegler, "Russia and China in Central Asia," in James Bellacqua (ed.), *The Future of China-Russia Relations* (Lexington: University Press of Kentucky, 2010), pp. 8, 257–8; Kaczmarski, *Russia–China Relations*.
6. "Concept of the Foreign Policy of the Russian Federation: Approved by President of the Russian Federation V. Putin on 12 February 2013," February 18, 2013, http://www.mid.ru/en/foreign_policy/official_documents/-/asset_publisher/CptICkB6BZ29/content/id/122186.
7. The full text of Xi Jinping's first UN address is at http://qz.com/512886/read-the-full-text-of-xi-jinpings-first-un-address/.
8. Ezra F. Vogel, *Japan as Number One: Lessons for America* (Cambridge, MA: Harvard University Press, 1979).

9 Bobo Lo, "Sino-Russian Relations"; Bobo Lo, *A Wary Embrace*; Watts, Ledberg and Engelbrekt, "Brothers in Arms, Yet Again?"
10 Kuhrt, *Russian Policy*; Kaczmarski, *Russia–China Relations*; Geir Flikke, "Sino–Russian Relations: Status Exchange or Imbalanced Relationship?" *Problems of Post-Communism*, 63(3) (2016); Alexander Korolev, "Systemic Balancing and Regional Hedging: China–Russia Relations," *Chinese Journal of International Politics*, 9(4) (2016).
11 Geir Flikke, "Sino–Russian Relations"; Korolev, "Systemic Balancing."
12 Bobo Lo's writings are the most obvious example. See also Elizabeth Wishnick, "Why a 'Strategic Partnership'? The View from China," in Bellacqua, *The Future of China-Russia Relations*, pp. 56–80.
13 See, for example, Aleksandr Khramchikhin, "Pekin Moskve – partner, no ne drug: Kitayskiy vektor ne dolzhen preobladat' vo vneshney politike Kremlya" [Beijing is Moscow's partner, but not a friend: China vector should not dominate in Russia's foreign policy], *Nezavisimoe voennoe obozrenie*, November 7, 2014, http://nvo.ng.ru/realty/2014-05-16/1_china.html.
14 Viktor Martynyuk, "Politicheskiy soyuz Rossii i Kitaya neizbezhen, potomu chto vygoden obeim stranam" [Russian-Chinese political alliance is inevitable because it is in the interests of both countries], *Km.ru*, May 19, 2014, http://www.km.ru/world/2014/05/19/vladimir-putin/740321-politicheskii-soyuz-rossii-i-kitaya-neizbezhen-potomu-chto-vy.
15 Ian Bond, "Russia and China: Partners of Choice and Necessity?" Centre for European Reform Report, December 8, 2016, http://www.cer.org.uk/publications/archive/report/2016/russia-and-china-partners-choice-and-necessity.
16 Samuel Charap and Ely Ratner, "China: Neither Ally nor Enemy on Russia," *National Interest*, April 2, 2014, http://nationalinterest.org/commentary/china-neither-ally-nor-enemy-russia-10168.
17 Edward N. Luttwak, "5. Play Russia against China," *Politico*, January/February 2017, http://www.politico.com/magazine/story/2017/01/outside-the-box-ideas-policies-president-trump-administration-214661; Doug Bandow, "A Nixon Strategy to Break the Russia-China Axis," *National Interest*, January 4, 2017, http://nationalinterest.org/blog/the-skeptics/nixon-strategy-break-the-russia-china-axis-18946; James Nadeau, "Trump's Great Game: Courting Russia to Contain China," Foreign Policy Association, December 15, 2016, http://foreignpolicyblogs.com/2016/12/15/trump-courting-russia-contain-china/.
18 Bobo Lo, *A Wary Embrace*.
19 Constantine C. Menges, *China: The Gathering Threat* (Nashville: Nelson Current, 2005).
20 Rozman, *The Sino-Russian Challenge*.
21 Gilbert Rozman, "Asia for the Asians: Why Chinese-Russian Friendship Is Here to Stay," *Foreign Affairs*, October 24, 2014, https://www.foreignaffairs.com/articles/east-asia/2014-10-29/asia-asians.
22 Jacob Stokes, "Russia and China's Enduring Alliance: A Reverse 'Nixon Strategy' Won't Work for Trump," *Foreign Affairs*, February 22, 2017, https://www.foreignaffairs.com/articles/china/2017-02-22/russia-and-china-s-enduring-alliance?cid=int-lea&pgtype=hpg.
23 Michael Levin, *The Next Great Clash: China and Russia vs. the United States* (Westport, CT: Praeger, 2008).
24 John W. Garver, *China's Quest: A History of the Foreign Relations of*

the *People's Republic of China* (Oxford: Oxford University Press, 2016), p. 540.
25 Elizabeth Wishnick, "In Search of the 'Other' in Asia: Russia–China Relations Revisited," *Pacific Review*, July 7, 2016, p. 14.
26 Max Weber, "Objectivity of Social Science and Social Policy," originally in Max Weber, *The Methodology of the Social Sciences*, http://anthropos-lab.net/wp/wp-content/uploads/2011/12/Weber-objectivity-in-the-social-sciences.pdf.

1 RUSSIA, CHINA, AND THE CHANGING INTERNATIONAL SYSTEM

1 The West is understood in this book not geographically or culturally, but purely politically, as the United States and its allies. From that point of view, countries like Serbia, Belarus or Russia should not be seen as part of the West, while Australia, New Zealand and some Asian US allies, for example, Japan, can be understood as "Western" countries.
2 James Addison Baker, "Russia in NATO?" *Washington Quarterly*, 25(1) (Winter 2002): 95–103, https://muse.jhu.edu/login?auth=0&type=summary&url=/journals/washington_quarterly/v025/25.1baker.html.
3 Francis Fukuyama, *The End of History and the Last Man* (London: Hamish Hamilton, 1992).
4 Richard N. Haass, "The Unraveling: How to Respond to a Disordered World," *Foreign Affairs*, November/December 2014, https://www.foreignaffairs.com/articles/united-states/2014-10-20/unraveling?cid=nlc-foreign_affairs_this_week-111314-the_unraveling_5-111314&sp_mid=47406003&sp_rid=ZXNjaG51cmVyQHB1YmxpYy13b3Jrcy5vcmcS1.
5 Haass, "The Unraveling."
6 "Henry Kissinger on the Assembly of a New World Order," *Wall Street Journal*, August 29, 2014, http://www.wsj.com/articles/henry-kissinger-on-the-assembly-of-a-new-world-order-1409328075.
7 Ivan Krastev and Mark Leonard, "The New European Disorder," European Council on Foreign Relations, November 2014, p. 2, http://www.ecfr.eu/page/-/ECFR117_TheNewEuropeanDisorder_ESSAY.pdf.
8 US Department of State, "France: International Religious Freedom Report 2008," http://www.state.gov/j/drl/rls/irf/2008/108446.htm.
9 Bilahary Kausikan, "The Myth of Universality: The Geopolitics of Human Rights," in Bilahary Kausikan, *Dealing with an Ambiguous World* (Singapore: World Scientific, 2017), pp. 93–113.
10 Anwar Ibrahim, *The Asian Renaissance* (Kuala Lumpur: Times Books International, 1996), p. 51.
11 Alexander Pushkin/P. Ya. Chaadaevu, Letter, October 19, 1836, http://www.skeptik.net/skeptiks/push_rel.htm.
12 "National Security Concept of the Russian Federation: Approved by Presidential Decree No. 24 of January 10, 2000," http://www.mid.ru/en/foreign_policy/official_documents/-/asset_publisher/CptICkB6BZ29/content/id/589768.
13 "Putin's Prepared Remarks at 43rd Munich Conference on Security Policy," February 12, 2007, http://www.washingtonpost.com/wp-dyn/content/article/2007/02/12/AR2007021200555.html.

14 "Concept of the Foreign Policy of the Russian Federation," February 18, 2013.
15 "China's Independent Foreign Policy of Peace," September 19, 2003, http://www.fmprc.gov.cn/mfa_eng/wjb_663304/zzjg_663340/zcyjs_663346/xgxw_663348/t24942.shtml.
16 "Speech by Chinese President Hu Jintao at Yale University," New Haven, April 21, 2006, http://ph.china-embassy.org/eng/xwdt/t259486.htm.
17 See, for example, Deng Yuwen, "Hu-Wende zhengzhi guichan" [The political legacy of Hu and Wen], *Rujiagang*, September 2, 2012, http://www.rujiazg.com/article/id/2908/?from=singlemessage, and also the partial translation at https://www.thechinastory.org/2012/09/the-ten-grave-problems-facing-china/; "Guofang daxue jiaoshou: xiayi sou hangmu juebushi xianzai zheige shuiping" [Professor of the National Defense University: the next aircraft carrier will not be the same as the current level], December 17, 2012, http://mil.huanqiu.com/observation/2012-12/3387054.html.
18 Dai Xu, *C-xing baowei – neiyouwaihuanxiade Zhongguo tuwei* [The C-shape encirclement: China's breakthrough under domestic problems and foreign aggression] (Shanghai: Wenhui chubanshe, 2010), pp. 3–4.
19 Song Xiaojun, Wang Xiaodong, Huang Jisu, Song Qiang and Liu Yang, *Zhongguo bu gaoxing: dashidai, damubiao ji womende neiyouwaihuan* [Unhappy China: great epoch, great goals and our internal and external challenges] (Nanjing: Jiangsu renmin chubanshe, 2009), see pp. 80–1, 98–9, 106–8.
20 Wang Xiaodong, "Danddai Zhongguo minzuzhuyi lun" [Theory of contemporary Chinese nationalism], *Zhanlüe yu guanli*, 5 (2000): 69–82.
21 Liu Mingfu, *Zhongguo meng – houMeguo shidaide daguo siwei yu zhanlüe dingwei* [The China dream: great power thinking and the strategic position of China in the post-US world] (Beijing: Zhonguo youyi chubansh, 2010).
22 Liu Yuan, "Du Zhang Musheng" [Reading Zhang Musheng], Part 2, *Xinfajia*, August 28, 2011, http://www.xinfajia.net/9140.html.
23 As quoted in Chris Buckley, "China PLA Officer Urges Challenging US Dominance," March 1, 2010, http://uk.reuters.com/article/us-china-usa-military-exclusive-idUKTRE6200P620100301.
24 Luo Yuan, "Meiyou wujingshende minzu meiyou xiwang" [A nation with no military spirit has no hope], *Fenghuang wang*, October 21, 2012, http://news.ifeng.com/mainland/special/diaoyudaozhengduan/content-3/detail_2012_10/21/18411333_0.shtml#6467378-tieba-1-6092-c81271486ebd1591c28aa551fa3a2e54.
25 Willy Lam, "China's Hawks in Command," *Wall Street Journal*, July 1, 2012, http://www.wsj.com/articles/SB10001424052702304211804577500521756902802.
26 Jeremy Page, "China's Army Extends Sway," *Wall Street Journal*, October 4, 2010, http://www.wsj.com/articles/SB100014240527487034661045755298102348 51000.
27 Yoichi Kato, "Interview with Wang Jisi: China Deserves More Respect as a First-Class Power," *Asahi Simbun*, October 5, 2012, https://web.archive.org/web/20131018040918/http://ajw.asahi.com/article/views/opinion/AJ201210050003.
28 "Zhongguo waijiaobu qianfayanren Wu Jianmin yu 'Huanqiu shibao' zhubian Hu Xijin bao koushui zhan" [China's former foreign ministry

spokesman Wu Jianmin breaks out in a war of words against *Global Times* editor-in-chief Hu Xijin], Bowen Press, April 7, 2016, http://bowenpress.com/news/bowen_80971.html.
29 "Zhongguo waijiaobu qianfayanren Wu Jianmin."
30 "Zhongguo waijiaobu qianfayanren Wu Jianmin."
31 Pang Zhongying and Wang Ruiping, "Quanqiu zhili: Zhongguode zhanlüe yingdui" [Global governance: China's strategic response], *Guoji wenti yanjiu*, 4 (2013), http://www.ciis.org.cn/gyzz/2013-07/23/content_6145818.htm.
32 "Xi Calls for Reforms on Global Governance," *China Daily*, September 29, 2016, http://www.chinadaily.com.cn/china/2016-09/29/content_26931697.htm.
33 "Xi Calls for Reforms."
34 "The Central Conference on Work Relating to Foreign Affairs was Held in Beijing," Ministry of Foreign Affairs of the People's Republic of China, November 29, 2014, http://www.fmprc.gov.cn/mfa_eng/zxxx_662805/t1215680.shtml.
35 Zbigniew Brzezinski, "The Group of Two That Could Change the World," *Financial Times*, January 13, 2009, http://www.ft.com/cms/s/0/d99369b8-e178-11dd-afa0-0000779fd2ac.html.
36 See Yan Xuetong, "Gongping zhengyide jiazhiguan yu hezuo gongyingde waijiao yuanze" [The value approach of honesty and fairness and the diplomatic principle of mutually beneficial cooperation], *Guoji wenti yanjiu*, 1 (2013), http://www.360doc.com/content/13/0328/08/1281444_274386920.shtml; Yu Xintian, "Zhongguo jiazhiguade shijie yiyi" [The meaning of Chinese values to the world], *Guoji wenti yanjiu*, 4 (2013), http://www.360doc.com/content/14/0624/11/2186054_389302153.shtml.
37 David Shambaugh, "The Coming Chinese Crackup," *Wall Street Journal*, March 6, 2015, http://www.wsj.com/articles/the-coming-chinese-crackup-1425659198.
38 "PM Manmohan Singh's Speech at HT Leadership Summit," News 18.com, November 21, 2008, http://www.news18.com/news/india/pm-manmohan-singhs-speech-at-ht-leadership-summit-302246.html.
39 Narendra Modi, "Unity in Diversity Pride of India," *India*, October 25, 2015, http://www.india.com/news/india/narendra-modi-unity-in-diversity-pride-of-india-657153/.
40 As quoted in Tullo Vigevani and Gabriel Cepaluni, "Lula's Foreign Policy and the Quest for Autonomy through Diversification," *Third World Quarterly*, 28(7) (2007): 1311.

2 Russia in the Eyes of China

1 Liu Xiao, "Chushi Sulian" [Serving as ambassador to the Soviet Union], *Shijie zhishi*, 3 (1987): 15.
2 Liu Xiao, "Chushi Sulian."
3 See, for example, Qian Junrui, "Zhong-Su youyì wanji chang qing – qingzhu Zhong-Su youhao xiehui chengli shi zhōunian" [Sino-Soviet friendship – celebrating the 10th anniversary of the Sino-Soviet Friendship Association], *Renmin Ribao*, October 4, 1959; Li Suan, *Zhongguo de eluosi xingxi-*

ang (1949–2009) [The image of Russia in China (1949–2009)] (Harbin: Heilongjiang jiaoyu chubanshe, 2012), pp. 1–94.
4 Mao Zedong, "The Greatest Friendship," *Renmin Ribao*, March 9, 1953, https://www.marxists.org/reference/archive/mao/selected-works/volume-7/mswv7_299.htm.
5 Mao Zedong, "Speech at Moscow Celebration Meeting," November 6, 1957, https://www.marxists.org/reference/archive/mao/selected-works/volume-7/mswv7_479.htm.
6 Boris Kulik, *Sovetsko-kitayskiy raskol: prichiny i posledstviya* [The Soviet-Chinese split: causes and consequences] (Moscow: Institut Dal'nego Vostoka RAN, 2000), p. 14.
7 Li Fenglin, "Zhong-Su guanxide lishi yu Zhong-E guanxi weilai" [The history of Sino-Soviet relations and the future of Sino-Russian relations], in Shen Zhihua (ed.), *Zhong-Su guanxishi gang (1917–1991)* [Milestones in Chinese-Soviet relations, 1917–1991] (Beijing: Xinhua chubanshe, 2008), p. 2.
8 *Liening zhuyi wansui* [Long live Leninism] (Beijing: Renmin chubanshe, 1960).
9 Liu Danian, "Diguo zhuyi dui Zhongguo de qinlüe yu Zhongguo renmin fandui diguo zhuyi de douzheng" [The imperialist aggression in China and the struggle of the Chinese people against imperialism], *Lishi yanjiu*, 4 (1964): 103–20; Sergey Goncharov and Li Danhui, "O 'territorial'nykh pretenziyakh' i 'neravnopravnykh dogovorakh' v rossiysko-kitayskikh otnosheniyakh. Mify i real'nost" [On "territorial claims": and "unequal treaties" in Russian-Chinese relations: myths and reality], *Problemy Dal'nego Vostoka*, 4 (2004): 119.
10 Hu Sheng, *Zhongguo gongchandang de qishi nian* [Seventy years of the Chinese Communist Party] (Beijing: Zhonggong dangshi chubanshe, 1991), p. 402.
11 Chen Kaike, "Eluosi guanyu Taiping tianguo shiqi shaEde dui hua waijiao" [Russian Orthodox mission and the diplomacy of Tsarist Russia toward China during the Taiping Celestial State period], in Luan Jinghe and Guan Guihai (eds.), *Zhong-E guanxi de lishi yu xianshi* [History and the current state of sino-Russian relations] (Beijing: Shehui kexue wenxian chubanshe, 2009), vol. 2, pp. 185–207.
12 Zhang Li, "Weite yu yihetuan yundong shiqi eguo dui hua zhengce" [Witte and Russia's policy toward China during the period of the Boxer Movement], in Luan Jinghe and Guan Guihai, *Zhong-E guanxi de lishi yu xianshi*, vol. 2, pp. 230–44.
13 Wang Xiaoju, "Eluosi ren zai dongbei: Ban ge shiji de qiaomin lichen" [Russians in Northeastern China: émigrés' half-century long road], in Luan Jinghe and Guan Guihai, *Zhong-E guanxi de lishi yu xianshi*, vol. 2, pp. 208–17.
14 Qian Qichen, "Duli zizhu, nuli kaita" [All efforts on development of the basis of independence and self-governance], *Renmin Ribao*, December 16, 1991, p. 7.
15 Evgeny Bazhanov, "Ot druzhby cherez konfrontatsiyu k normalizatsii. Sovetsko-kitayskie otnosheniya s 1949 i do 1991 g" [From friendship through confrontation to normalization: Soviet-Chinese relations in 1949–1991], in Alexander Lukin (ed.), *Rossiya-Kitay: 400 let vzaimodeystviya* [Russia

and China: four hundred years of interaction] (Moscow: Ves' mir, 2013), p. 293.
16 Liu Dexi and Sun Yan, *Sulian jieti houde Zhong-E guanxi* [Sino-Russian relations after the disintegration of the Soviet Union] (Harbin: Heilongjiang jiaoyu chubanshe, 1996), pp. 64–5.
17 Deng Xiaoping, "Guoji xingshi he jingji wenti" [International situation and economic problems], in *Deng Xiaoping wenxuan* [Works of Deng Xiaoping] (Beijing: Renmin chubanshe, 1993), vol. 3, p. 53.
18 Qian Qichen, *Desyat' diplomaticheskih sobytiy* (Beijing, 2005), p. 189; trans. as *Ten Episodes in China's Diplomacy* (New York: HarperCollins, 2006).
19 Qian Qichen, *Desyat' diplomaticheskih sobytiy*.
20 Viktor Larin, *V teni prosnuvshegosya drakona* [In the shadow of an awakened dragon] (Vladivostok: Dal'nauka, 2006), p. 45.
21 Xi Laiwang, *Waijiao moulüe* [Foreign policy strategy] (Beijing: Hongqi chubanshe, 1996), p. 435.
22 "Zhong-E guanxi liudian yuanze zhuzhang" [Six principles of Chinese-Russian relations], CRI online, June 23, 2004, http://gb.cri.cn/3821/2004/06/23/107@206778.htm.
23 *Renmin Ribao*, December 19, 1996.
24 "Jiang Zemin: Khochu peredat' cherez 'Rossiyskuyu gazetu' narodu Rossii chuvstvo glubokoy druzhby i dobrye pozhelaniya. Otvety Predsedatelya Tsyan Tseminya na voprosy ITAR-TASS i 'Rossiyskoy gazety'" [Jiang Zemin: I would like to express through *Rossiyskaya Gazeta* my deep feeling of friendship and best wishes to the Russian People. Chairman Jiang Zemin replies to questions from ITAR-TASS and *Rossiyskaya Gazeta*], *Rossiyskaya Gazeta*, November 19, 1998, https://goths.ru/old_news.php?id=18963.
25 Li Jingjie, "Kitaysko-rossiyskie otnosheniya i amerikanskiy faktor" [Sino-Russian relations and the American factor], *Azyia i Afrika segodnya*, 3 (2002): 47–8.
26 Zhou Xiaopei, *Zhong-Su Zhong-E guanxi qinli ji* [Notes on personal experience in Sino-Soviet and Sino-Russian relations] (Beijing: Shijie zhishi chubanshe, 2010), pp. 100–1. Chinese diplomat Zhou Xiaopei describes the Chinese attitude toward the style of the Russian leader in an episode he recalled from that visit. "A reception at which no vodka was served was held in honor of the guests on the evening of April 24 in the Great Hall of the People. President Yeltsin hinted to Chairman Jiang Zemin, 'I remember that I drank some sort of vodka during the last visit to China.' President Chairman Jiang Zemin asked, 'Would you like to drink?' Yeltsin answered, 'Well, of course!' The waiter promptly served twenty-year-old Maotai. Yeltsin enthusiastically drank three shot glasses in a row. The president's wife tried to dissuade him and forbade him to drink more. Yeltsin said, 'Don't interfere in my affairs, or else next time I won't take you with me.'"
27 Liu Guchang, "'Dogovor veka' i sozdanie novoy real'nosti kitaysko-rossiyskikh otnosheniy" ["Agreement of the Century" and the creation of a new reality in Sino-Russian relations], *Rossiya-Kitay: 21 vek*, May–July 2006, p. 5.
28 Liu Guchang, "'Dogovor veka.'"
29 See Wilson, *Strategic Partners*, pp. 167–70.
30 Wan Chengcai, "Xin Eluosi guancha" [Watching New Russia] (Beijing: Xinhua chubanshe, 2010), p. 263.

NOTES TO PP. 48–56

31 "Hu Jintao zai Mosike guoji guanxi xueyuan yanjiang" [Speech by Hu Jintao at Moscow State Institute of International Relations], May 29, 2003, http://news.sohu.com/20060308/n242188760.shtml.
32 Alexander Lukin, "Hu Jintao – zagadochnyy lider?" [Hu Jintao – a mysterious leader?], *Rossiya-Kitay: 21 vek*, June 2005, p. 17.
33 Yang Jiechi, "Kitayskie i rossiyskie SMI sodeystvuyut razvitiyu dvustoronnikh otnosheniy" [The Chinese and Russian media contribute to the development of bilateral relations], *Rossiya-Kitay: 21 vek*, June 2007, p. 15.
34 Yang Jiechi, "Kitayskie i rossiyskie SMI."
35 Li Jingjie, "Kitaysko-rossiyskie otnosheniya v novom veke" [Sino-Russian relations in the new century], *Rossiya-Kitay: 21 vek*, October 2006, pp. 20–1.
36 Guan Guihai, "Kul'turnye factory v kitaysko-rossiyskom strategicheskom vzaimodeystvii" [Cultural factors in Sino-Russian strategic interaction], *Rossiya-Kitay: 21 vek*, February 2006, p. 39.
37 Liu Guchang, "Izdanie zhurnala 'Rossiya-Kitay: 21 vek' – innovatsionnyy proryv v rossiyskoy zhurnalistike" [Publication of *Rossiya-Kitay: 21 vek* magazine is an innovative breakthrough in Russian journalism], *Rossiya-Kitay: 21 vek*, March 2007, p. 1.
38 Li Jingjie, "Kitaysko-rossiyskie otnosheniya v novom veke," p. 23.
39 Li Jingjie, "Kitaysko-rossiyskie otnosheniya v novom veke."
40 Dong Xiaoyang, "Perspektivy rossiysko-kitayskikh otnosheniy na blizhayshie desyat' let" [Prospects for Russian-Chinese relations in the next decade], *Rossiya-Kitay: 21 vek*, June 2007, p. 25.
41 Ming Jinwei, "Commentary: The West's Fiasco in Ukraine," *Renminwang*, March 7, 2014, http://en.people.cn/90777/8558083.html.
42 Ming Jinwei, "Commentary."
43 Feng Shaolei, "Otnosheniya mezhdu Rossiey, Kitaem i SSHA na fone krizisa na Ukraine" [Relations between Russia, China and the United States against the backdrop of the crisis in Ukraine], *Ezhegodnik IMI*, 4(14) (2015): 66.
44 Fu Ying, "How China Sees Russia: Beijing and Moscow Are Close, but Not Allies," *Foreign Affairs*, January/February 2016, https://www.foreignaffairs.com/articles/china/2015-12-14/how-china-sees-russia.
45 "Fu Ying tan Zhong-E guanxi: shi huoban haishi mengyou" [Fu Ying on Sino-Russian relations: partners or allies], *Guangming Ribao*, December 23, 2015.
46 Fu Ying, "How China Sees Russia."
47 Fu Ying, "How China Sees Russia."
48 Zhao Huasheng, "Zhong-E guanxi zhibianle ma?" [Have Sino-Russian relations changed qualitatively?] *Zhongguo xuanju yu zhili*, June 6, 2016, http://www.chinaelections.com/article/778/242900.html.
49 Zhao Huasheng, "Ping Eluosi zhuanxiang Dongfang" [On Russia's pivot to the East], *Eluosi Dongou Zhongya yanjiu*, 4 (2016): 15.
50 Zhao Huasheng, "Novaya situatsiya v Tsentral'noy Azii i Shanhaiskaya Organizatsiya Sotrudnichestva" [The new situation in Central Asia and the Shanghai Cooperation Organization], in *Situatsiya v Tsentral'noy Azii i Shanhaiskaya Organizatsiya Sotrudnichestva* [The situation in Central Asia and the Shanghai Cooperation Organization], Conference proceedings (Shanghai: Shanghai Institute for International Studies, 2003), p. 250.
51 Dong Xiaoyang, "Perspektivy rossiysko-kitayskikh otnosheniy na blizhayshie desyat' let," p. 24.

NOTES TO PP. 56-64

52 Qiu Huafei, "International System and China's Asia-Pacific Strategy," *Contemporary International Relations*, 20(1) (2010): 66.
53 "Seminar 'Rossiya i Kitay v novoy mezhdunarodnoy srede' (SHoS)" [Seminar "Russia and China in a New International Environment" (SCO)], March 22, 2009, http://www.rodon.org/polit-091009104944.
54 Zhao Huasheng, *Zhongguode Zhonya waijiao* [China's diplomacy in Central Asia] (Beijing: Shishi chubanshe, 2008), p. 85.
55 Zhao Huasheng, *Zhongguode Zhonya waijiao*.
56 "Seminar 'Rossiya i Kitay v novoy mezhdunarodnoy srede' (SHoS)."
57 Zhao Huasheng, *Zhongguode Zhonya waijiao*, pp. 308-10.
58 Qiu Huafei, "International System," p. 66.
59 Feng Shaolei, "Otnosheniya mezhdu Rossiey, Kitaem i SSHA," p. 69.
60 Li Xin, Liu Zongyi, Qian Zongqi and Wang Yuzhu, "Sichouzhilu jingjidai duijie Ouya jingji lianmeng gongjian Ouya gongtong jingji kongjian" [The SREB docking to the EAEU: co-creating a common Eurasian Economic Area], Shanghai Institute for International Studies, March 2016.
61 Feng Yujun, "My View on Contemporary China-Russia Relations," *Asan Forum*, July 25, 2014, http://www.theasanforum.org/chinese-view/.
62 Xing Guangcheng, "The Ukraine Crisis and Russia's Choices in 2015," *Russian Analytical Digest*, 168, June 11, 2015, p. 7. See also Deng Yujun, "Dui Zhongguo waijiao jiuge fausi" [A nine-point reassessment of China's diplomacy] *FT zhongwen wang*, July 7, 2017 http://www.ftchinese.com/story/001073219?full=y&ccode=2G172001.
63 Han Kedi, "Russian Suspicions of China Hold Back Ties," *Global Times*, July 24, 2016, http://www.globaltimes.cn/content/996163.shtml.
64 Yan Xuetong, "Eluosi kekao ma?" [Is Russia reliable?], *Guoji jingji pinglun*, 3 (2012), http://www.faobserver.com/NewsInfo.aspx?id=6627.
65 Dai Xü, "ZhongE ying goujian lianmeng zuzhi Meiguo tulu ruoguo" [China and Russia should form an alliance to prevent US from brutally killing people in weak countries], 360doc, January 21, 2012, http://www.360doc.com/content/12/0129/11/774009_182458975.shtml.
66 Zhang Wenmu, "Wukelan shijiande shijie yiyi ji qi dui Zhongguode jingshi" [The international significance of the Ukrainian incident and its meaning as a warning to China], *Guanchazhe*, December 28, 2014, http://www.guancha.cn/ZhangWenMu/2014_12_28_304621.shtml; Zhang Wenmu, "ZhongE jiemengde xiandu mubiao he yiyi" [The limits, aims and meaning of forming a Sino-Russian alliance], *Guanchazhe*, March 5, 2012, http://www.guancha.cn/ZhangWenMu/2012_03_05_66973.shtml.
67 "Full Text of Chinese President Xi's Written Interview with Russian Media," *Xinhua*, July 4, 2017, http://news.xinhuanet.com/english/2017-07/04/c_136414457.htm.
68 Feng Shaolei, "Otnosheniya mezhdu Rossiey, Kitaem i SSHA," pp. 59-60.
69 Xü Zhixin, "ZhongE guojia liyide jianhe" [The harmonization of Sino-Russian national interests], in Jiang Yi (ed.), *Xin shijide ZhongE guanxi* [Sino-Russian relations in the new century] (Beijing: Shijie zhishi chubanshe, 2007), pp. 30-3.
70 Gao Fei, *Zhengzhi wenhua bianqian yu ZhongE guanxide yanbian (1949-2008)* [Changes in political culture and the evolution of Sino-Russian relations in 1949-2008] (Beijing: Shijie zhishi chubanshe, 2008).

NOTES TO PP. 67–76

3 RUSSIA'S PIVOT TO ASIA OR JUST CHINA?

1 *Yeya Impertorskogo Velichestva Nakaz komissii o sochinenii proekta novogo ulozheniya* [Her Imperial Majesty's instruction to the commission for composing a project of a new code of laws] (Moscow, 1767), pp. 4–5.
2 See Natasha Kuhrt, "The Russian Far East in Russia's Asia Policy: Dual Integration or Double Periphery?" *Europe-Asia Studies*, 64(3) (2012): 471–93.
3 Andrey Kozyrev, *Preobrazhenie* [Transformation] (Moscow: Mezhdunarodnyye otnosheniya, 1995), p. 211.
4 "Preobrazhennaya Rossiya v novom mire" [A transformed Russia in the new world], Conference proceedings, *Mezhdunarodnaya zhizn'*, 3–4 (1992): 92.
5 Evgeny Bazhanov, "Evolyutsiya vneshney politiki Rossii" [The evolution of Russian foreign policy], in Anatoly Torkunov (ed.), *Sovremennyye mezhdunarodnyye otnosheniya* [Contemporary international relations] (Moscow: ROSSPEN, 1999), section 3, ch. 2, pp. 485–6.
6 See Alexander Lukin, *The Political Culture of the Russian 'Democrats'* (Oxford: Oxford University Press, 2000), ch. 7.
7 Bazhanov, "Evolyutsiya vneshney politiki Rossii," p. 486.
8 Text of Boris Yeltsin's speech to the UN Security Council, in Richard Weitz, *Global Security Watch: Russia* (Santa Barbara: Praeger Security International, 2009), p. 200.
9 Aleksey Borodavkin, "Rossiya i Kitay: po puti dobrososedstva i sotrudnichestva," [Russia and China: towards good neighbourliness and cooperation], *Problemy Del'nego Vostoka*, 5 (2009), http://www.ifes-ras.ru/publications/pdv/120-aaieiaeaaeei-einney-e-eeoae-ii-iooe-aeiaeininaaenoaa-e-nioeoaeied anoaa.
10 *Rossiiskaya gazeta*, February 2, 1992, p. 1.
11 *Rossiiskaya gazeta*, February 2, 1992, p. 1.
12 "Pyataya sessiya Verkhovnogo Soveta Rossiyskoy Federatsii. Voprosy neprostyye. Obstanovka delovaya" [The Fifth Session of the Supreme Council of the Russian Federation: difficult questions – atmosphere business-like], *Rossiiskaya gazeta*, October 23, 1992, p. 1.
13 "Pyataya sessiya Verkhovnogo Soveta Rossiyskoy Federatsii."
14 *Nezavisimaya gazeta*, December 18, 1992, p. 2.
15 Yegor Gaydar, "Rossiya XXI veka: ne mirovoy zhandarm, a forpost demokratii v Yevrazii" [21st century Russia: not a global gendarme, but an outpost of democracy in Eurasia], *Izvestia*, May 18, 1995, p. 4.
16 Yuri Savenkov, "Kitay i Rossiya sozdayut novyy mekhanizm torgovykh otnosheniy" [China and Russia create a new mechanism for trade relations], *Izvestia*, March 7, 1992, p. 4.
17 Grigory Karasin, "Rossiya i Kitay na poroge tysyacheletiya" [Russia and China on the threshold of the millenium], *Mezhdunarodnaya zhizn'*, 6 (1997): 16.
18 "Aktual'nyye problemy rossiysko-kiatyskikh otnosheniy i puti ikh resheniya" [Current problems in Russian-Chinese Relations and the path to resolving them], *Analytical Reports of the NKSMI MGIMO*, 1(16) (March 2006): 25–6.
19 Igor Rogachev, *Rossiysko-kitayskiye otnosheniya v kontse XX–nachale XXI*

veka [Russian-Chinese relations in the late 20th and early 21st centuries] (Moscow: Izvestia, 2005), p. 48.
20 As quoted in Evgeny Bazhanov, *Aktual'nye problemy mezhdunarodnykh otnosheniy* [Current problems of international relations] (Moscow: Nauchnaya kniga, 2002), vol. 2, p. 419.
21 Rogachev, *Rossiysko-kitayskiye otnosheniya*, pp. 31–2, 130.
22 Grigory Karasin, "Vzgliad dvuglavnogo orlai na Zapad, i na Vostok" [The double headed eagle looks both West and East], *Rossiiskie vesti*, December 19, 1996, p. 7; Sergey Tsekhmisterenko, "Dvuglavyy orel otkvyl glaza na Vostok" [The double headed eagle opened its eyes to the East], *Delovye liudi*, 73 (January 1997): 17 (interview with Grigory Karasin).
23 Evgeny Afanas'ev and Grigory Logvinov, "Rossiia i Kitai: na poroge tret'ego tysyacheletiya" [Russia and China on the threshold of the third millenium], *Mezhdunarodnaia zhizn'*, 11–12 (1995): 53.
24 Tsekhmisterenko, "Dvuglavyy orel otkvyl glaza na Vostok," p. 17.
25 Tsekhmisterenko, "Dvuglavyy orel otkvyl glaza na Vostok," p. 17.
26 "Rossii nuzhen sil'nyy Kitay" [Russia needs a strong China], interview with Grigory Karasin, *Rossiya*, 3 (1997): 13.
27 "Partnerstvo v obshchikh interesakh" [Partnership in the interests of all], interview with Igor Rogachev, *Nezavisimaya gazeta*, April 19, 1997, p. 1.
28 Karasin, "Rossiya i Kitay na poroge tysyacheletiya," p. 14.
29 Vadim Sukhoverkhov, "Druzhili dva tovarishcha ..." [There were two friends ...], *Moskovskiy komsomolets*, December 10, 1999, p. 1.
30 Sukhoverkhov, "Druzhili dva tovarishcha..."
31 See Gennady Chufrin, "Kak perelezt' cherez Velikuyu kitayskuyu stenu?" [How to climb over the Great Chinese Wall?], *Moskovskie novosti*, 36, May 21–8, 1995, p. 5.
32 As quoted in Galina Vitkovskaya, Zhanna Zayonchkovskaya and Kathleen Newland, "Chinese Migration into Russia," in Sherman W. Garnett (ed.), *Rapprochement or Rivalry? Russia-China Relations in a Changing Asia* (Washington, DC: Carnegie Endowment for International Peace, 2000), pp. 348–9.
33 See Igor Korotchenko, "Igor Rodionov vystupil za sozdanie oboronnogo soyuza v SNG" [Igor Rodionov called for creation of a defence alliance within the CIS], *Nezavisimaya gazeta*, December 26, 1996, p. 1; A. Platkovsky, "Generaly v Pekine raskusili igru Moskvy" [Generals in Beijing caught on to Moscow's game], *Izvestia*, May 25, 1997, p. 3; I. Shomov, "Partnerstvo s prishchurom na Zapad" [A partnership squinting at the West], *Segodnya*, April 25, 1997, p. 4.
34 *Izvestia*, September 17, 1992, p. 6.
35 For a detailed analysis, see Alexander Lukin, *The Bear Watches the Dragon* (Armonk, NY: M. E. Sharpe, 2003); Andrew Kuchins, "Russian Perspectives on China: Strategic Ambivalence," in Bellacqua, *The Future of China-Russia Relations*, pp. 33–55.
36 Chufrin, "Kak perelezt' cherez Velikuyu kitayskuyu stenu?"
37 Article by Russian President Vladimir Putin, "Russia: New Eastern Perspectives," November 9, 2000, http://en.kremlin.ru/events/president/transcripts/21132.
38 Vladimir Putin, "Interview with the Chinese Newspaper *Renmin Ribao*, the

NOTES TO PP. 81–90

Chinese News Agency Xinhua and the RTR TV Company," July 16, 2000, http://en.special.kremlin.ru/events/president/transcripts/24168.
39 Vladimir Putin, "Remarks at a Meeting of Top Members of the Russian Diplomatic Service," January 26, 2001, http://en.kremlin.ru/events/president/transcripts/21169.
40 Vladimir Putin, "Answers to Russian Journalists' Questions before a Meeting with Tajik President Emomali Rakhmonov," July 5, 2000, http://en.kremlin.ru/events/president/transcripts/24175.
41 Igor Ivanov, "Nashi otnosheniya svobodny ot emotsiy" [Our relations are free of emotions], *Rossiyskaya Federatsiya*, 10(155) (July 2000): 3.
42 Ivanov, "Nashi otnosheniya svobodny ot emotsiy."
43 Putin, "Interview," July 16, 2000.
44 Rogachev, *Rossiysko-kitayskiye otnosheniya*, pp. 117–18.
45 "Article by Russian Foreign Minister Sergey Lavrov in the Newspaper *Renmin Ribao*, July 15, 2011," http://www.mid.ru/en/web/guest/press_service/minister_speeches/-/asset_publisher/7OvQR5KJWVmR/content/id/199886.
46 Vladimir Putin, "Speech at a Ceremony Marking the 15th Anniversary of Signing of the Treaty on Good-Neighbourliness, Friendship and Cooperation between the Russian Federation and the People's Republic of China," June 25, 2016, http://en.kremlin.ru/events/president/transcripts/52274/print.
47 "Rech ne o tom, kogo Rossiya predpochtet: Yaponiyu ili Kitay" [The question is not whether Russia chooses Japan or China], interview with A. P. Losyukov, *Vremya novostey*, July 24, 2003, http://www.mid.ru/press_service/deputy_ministers_speeches/-/asset_publisher/O3publba0Cjv/content/id/512562.
48 "Joint Declaration between the Russian Federation and the Republic of India on Deepening the Strategic Partnership to Meet Global Challenges," December 7, 2009, http://en.kremlin.ru/supplement/408.
49 "Foreign Minister Sergey Lavrov's News Conference on the Sidelines of the BRICS and SCO Summits in Ufa, July 9, 2015," http://www.mid.ru/en/web/guest/sanhajskaa-organizacia-sotrudnicestva-sos-/-/asset_publisher/0vP3hQoCPRg5/content/id/1551620.
50 Vladimir Putin, "Interview to the Xinhua News Agency of China," St. Petersburg, June 23, 2016, http://en.kremlin.ru/events/president/news/52204.
51 "Foreign Minister Sergey Lavrov's Remarks and an Answer to a Media Question at a News Conference Following a Meeting of the SCO Council of Foreign Ministers, Astana, April 21, 2017," http://www.mid.ru/ru/sanhajskaa-organizacia-sotrudnicestva-sos-/-/asset_publisher/0vP3hQoCPRg5/content/id/2734712?p_p_id=101_INSTANCE_0vP3hQoCPRg5&_101_INSTANCE_0vP3hQoCPRg5_languageId=en_GB.
52 Putin, "Interview to the Xinhua News Agency."
53 "President Vladimir Putin Sent a Message to Shanghai Cooperation Organization (SCO) Secretary-General Zhang Deguang Following the Start of the SCO Secretariat's Work," January 15, 2004, http://en.kremlin.ru/events/president/news/30147.
54 Alexander Gabuev, "Kitayskie sovety. Na kakoy intellektual'nyy resurs opiraetsya Pekin pri vyrabotke politiki v otnoshenii Moskvy" [Chinese advice: the intellectual resource underpinning Beijing's Moscow policy], *Kommersant-Vlast*, October 13, 2014, http://www.kommersant.ru/doc/

2584423; Alexander Gabuev, "Gosudarstvo ushlo iz kitaistiki. Chto ostalos' ot rossiyskoy shkoly kitaevedeniya" [The government leaves Sinology: what remains of the Russian School of China Studies], *Kommersant-Vlast*, October 20, 2014, http://www.kommersant.ru/doc/2593673.
55 Mikhail Titarenko, Artem Kobzev, Anatoly Lukyanov (eds.), *Dukhovnaya kul'tura Kitaya* [The Spiritual Culture of China], vols 1–6 (Moscow: Vostochnaya literatura, 2006–10).
56 Alexander Gabuev, "Kitayskaia negramota" [Chinese illiteracy], *Kommersant-Vlast*, November 22, 2012, http://www.kommersant.ru/doc/2073821.
57 "Pryamaya liniya s Vladimirom Putinym" [Direct line with Vladimir Putin], transcript, April 17, 2014, http://2014.moskva-putinu.ru/#page/question.
58 Putin, "Interview to the Xinhua News Agency."
59 Vladimir Putin, "Russia and the Changing World," *RT*, February 27, 2012, https://www.rt.com/politics/official-word/putin-russia-changing-world-263/.

4 From Normalization to Strategic Partnership

1 Grigory Karasin (ed.), *Sbornik Rossiisko-kitaiskikh dogovorov 1949–1999* [Collection of Russian-Chinese agreements, 1949–1999] (Moscow: Terra-Sport, 1999), pp. 134–5.
2 Konstantin Makienko, *Voenno-tekhnicheskoe sotrudnichestvo Rossii i KNR v 1992–2002: dostizheniya, tendentsii, perspektivy* [Cooperation between Russia and the PRC in military technology in 1992–2002: achievments, tendencies and prospects], Report 2, Russian Office of the Center for Defense Information (Moscow: Gendalf, October 2002), p. 10.
3 "Sovmestnaya deklaratsiya ob osnovakh vzaimootnosheniy mezhdu Rossiyskoy Federatsiey i Kitayskoy Narodnoy Respublikoy" [Joint declaration on the basis of relations between the Russian Federation and the People's Republic of China], in Karasin, *Sbornik Rossiisko-kitaiskikh dogovorov 1949–1999*, p. 150.
4 "Sovmestnaya deklaratsiya ob osnovakh vzaimootnosheniy."
5 "Sovmestnaya deklaratsiya ob osnovakh vzaimootnosheniy," pp. 151–2.
6 Georgy Zinoviev, *Kitay i sverkhderzhavy. Istoriya vneshney politiki Kitaya (1949–1991)* [China and the superpowers: history of China's foreign policy (1949–1991)] (St. Petersburg: Izdatel'stvo Sankt-Peterburgskogo universiteta, 2010), p. 312.
7 Rogachev, *Rossiysko-kitayskiye otnosheniya*, p. 47.
8 "Sovmestnaya rossiysko-kitayskaya deklaratsiya," in Karasin, *Sbornik Rossiisko-kitaiskikh dogovorov 1949–1999*, p. 271.
9 *Diplomaticheskiy vestnik*, special issue, January 1993, pp. 15–16.
10 Alexander A. Sergounin and Sergey V. Subbotin, "Sino-Russian Military Co-operation: Russian Perspective," *Regional Studies*, 15(4) (1997): 26.
11 Vladimir Mikheev, "Boris Yeltsin vypolnit v Pekine osoboe zadanie 'semerki'" [In Beijing, Boris Yeltsin will carry out a special assignment of the G7], *Izvestia*, April 26, 1996, p. 1.
12 Zhou Xiaopei, *Zhong-Su Zhong-E guanxi qinli ji* , pp. 100–1.
13 "Sovmestnaya rossiysko-kitayskaya deklaratsiya," pp. 333, 335.
14 Afanas'ev and Logvinov, "Rossiia i Kitai," p. 60.

15 "Rossiysko-kitayskie otnosheniya na poroge XXI veka. Sovmestnoe zayavlenie po itogam vsrechi na vysshem urovne" [Russian-Chinese Relations on the threshold of the 21st century. Joint statement of the summit meeting], *Nezavisimaya gazeta*, December 5, 1998, p. 6.
16 Rogachev, *Rossiysko-kitayskiye otnosheniya*, pp. 56–7.
17 Rogachev, *Rossiysko-kitayskiye otnosheniya*, p. 144.
18 "Treaty of Good-Neighborliness and Friendly Cooperation between the People's Republic of China and the Russian Federation," Ministry of Foreign Affairs of the People's Republic of China, July 24, 2001, http://www.fmprc.gov.cn/mfa_eng/wjdt_665385/2649_665393/t15771.shtml.
19 "Sostoyalsya telefonnyy razgovor Vladimira Putina s Predsedatelem KNR Tzyan Tzeminem" [A telephone conversation took place between Vladimir Putin and Chairman of the PRC Jiang Zemin], September 18, 2001, http://kremlin.ru/events/president/news/40113.
20 "Kitay-Rossiya, god 2001: khronika dvustoronnikh otnosheniy" [China-Russia 2001: a chronicle of bilateral relations], http://russian.china.org.cn/archive2006/txt/2002-07/15/content_2036391.htm.
21 "Kitay-Rossiya, god 2001."
22 "Sovmestnoe zayavlenie ministrov inostrannykh del gosudarstv-uchastnikov Shanhayskoy organizatsii sotrudnichestva" [Joint statement of the ministers of foreign affairs of the Shanghai Cooperation Organization], Beijing, January 7, 2002, http://www.mid.ru/sanhajskaa-organizacia-sotrudnicestva-sos-/-/asset_publisher/0vP3hQoCPRg5/content/id/569928.
23 See, for example, Catharin Dalpino and David Steinberg, "Let the Locals Combat Terrorism," *International Herald Tribune*, March 28, 2002.
24 "Sostoyalsya telefonnyy razgovor Vladimira Putina s Predsedatelem KNR Tzyan Tzeminem" [A telephone conversation took place between Vladimir Putin and Chairman of the PRC Jiang Zemin], February 19, 2003, http://kremlin.ru/events/president/news/28192.
25 "Sovmestnoe kommyunike ministrov inostrannykh del RF i KNR po irakskomu voprosu" [Joint communiqué of the ministers of foreign affairs of the RF and the PRC on the Iraqi question," February 27, 2003, http://www.mid.ru/ru/maps/cn/-/asset_publisher/WhKWb5DVBqKA/content/id/530846.
26 "Russian Minister of Foreign Affairs Igor Ivanov Speaks to Minister for Foreign Affairs of the PRC Li Zhaoxing," press release, unofficial translation from Russian, March 23, 2003, http://www.mid.ru/foreign_policy/news/-/asset_publisher/cKNonkJE02Bw/content/id/527950?p_p_id=101_INSTANCE_cKNonkJE02Bw&_101_INSTANCE_cKNonkJE02Bw_languageId=en_GB.
27 "Sovmestnoe kommyunike ministrov inostrannykh del RF i KNR o situatsii na Koreyskom poluostrove" [Joint communiqué of the ministers of foreign affairs of the RF and the PRC on the situation on the Korean peninsular], February 27, 2003, http://www.mid.ru/ru/maps/cn/-/asset_publisher/WhKWb5DVBqKA/content/id/530622.
28 "Otvety ofitsial'nogo predstavitelya MID Rossii A. V. Yakovenko na voprosy rossiyskikh SMI po rossiysko-kitayskim otnosheniyam" [Answers of the official representative of the MFA of Russia A. V. Yakovenko to the questions of the Russian media on Russian-Chinese relations], May 23, 2003, http://www.mid.ru/ru/maps/cn/-/asset_publisher/WhKWb5DVBqKA/content/id/519550.

29 "Sovmestnaya deklaratsiya Rossiyskoy Federatsii i Kitayskoy Narodnoy Respubliki" [Joint declaration of the Russian Federation and the People's Republic of China], May 27, 2003, http://kremlin.ru/supplement/1669.
30 "Intervyu zamestitelya Ministra inostrannykh del Rossii A. P. Losyukova agentstvu 'Interfax' po voprosam rossiysko-kitayskikh otnosheniy" [Interview of the deputy minister of foreign affairs of Russia A. P. Losyukov to Interfax news agency on the questions of Russian-Chinese relations], September 12, 2003, http://www.mid.ru/press_service/deputy_ministers_speeches/-/asset_publisher/O3publba0Cjv/content/id/507314.
31 "Vystuplenie zamestitelya ministra inostrannykh del Rossii A. Yu. Alekseva na torzhestvennom zasedanii, posvyashchennom 5-y godovshchine podpisaniya Dogovora odobrososedstve, druzhbe i sotrudnichestve mezhdu RF i KNR" [Speech of deputy minister of foreign affairs of Russia A. Yu. Alekssev at a ceremonial meeting on the occasion of the 5th anniversary of the signing of the Treaty of Good-Neighborliness and Friendly Cooperation between the RF and the PRC], June 30, 2006, *Rossiya-Kitay: 21 vek*, May–July 2006, p. 1.
32 "Zayavleniya dlya pressy posle podpisaniya rossiysko-kitayskikh dokumentov" [Statements to the press after signing the Russian-Chinese documents], October 14, 2004, http://www.kremlin.ru/events/president/transcripts/22636.
33 "Zayavleniya dlya pressy."
34 "Putin utverdil ratifikatsiyu Dopsoglasheniya o granitse Rossii i Kitaya" [Putin confirmed ratification of the additional agreement on the border between Russia and China], *Izvestia*, June 1, 2005, http://iz.ru/news/302954.
35 "Rossiya i Kitay podelyat spornye ostrova" [Russia and China will divide the disputed islands], BBC Russian.com, October 21, 2004, http://news.bbc.co.uk/hi/russian/russia/newsid_3762000/3762766.stm.
36 "Mikhail Kamynin, the Spokesman of Russia's Ministry of Foreign Affairs, Answers Questions from ITAR-TASS News Agency Regarding Russian-Chinese Cooperation in Overcoming the Consequences of the Accident at the Chemical Plant in Jilin," November 29, 2005, http://www.mid.ru/ru/maps/cn/-/asset_publisher/WhKWb5DVBqKA/content/id/419116?p_p_id=101_INSTANCE_WhKWb5DVBqKA&_101_INSTANCE_WhKWb5DVBqKA_languageId=en_GB.
37 M. Vorobyov, "U benzol'nykh beregov Amura" [On the benzene banks of the Amur], *Rossiya-Kitay: 21 vek*, February 2006, p. 19.
38 As the official closing ceremony was conducted in November, the real number of events exceeded three hundred.
39 "Rech Predsedatelya Pravitel'stva Rossiyskoy Federatsii M. E. Fradkova na tseremonii ofitsial'nogo zakrytiya Goda Rossii v Kitae" [Speech of the Chairman of the Government of the Russian Federation M. E. Fradkov at the official closing ceremony of the Year of Russia in China], *Rossiya-Kitay: 21 vek*, January 2007, p. 5.
40 "Vystupleniye Prem'era Gossoveta KNR Wen Jiabao" [Speech of the Premier of the State Council of the PRC Wen Jiabao], November 6, 2007, *Rossiya-Kitay: 21 vek*, November 2007, p. 12.
41 "Vzaimnoe provedeniye natsional'nikh godov Kitaem i Rossiey dalo plodotvornye resul'taty" [Mutual holding of National Years of China and Russia brought fruitful results], *Renminwang*, November 7, 2007, http://russian.people.com.cn/31519/6298187.html.

NOTES TO PP. 113–121

42 "Russian MFA Information and Press Department Commentary Regarding Developments in Tibet Autonomous Region of PRC," March 17, 2008, http://www.mid.ru/ru/maps/cn/-/asset_publisher/WhKWb5DVBqKA/content/id/345510?p_p_id=101_INSTANCE_WhKWb5DVBqKA&_101_INSTANCE_WhKWb5DVBqKA_languageId=en_GB.

43 "Zayavleniya dlya pressy po itogam rossiysko-kitayskikh peregovorov" [Statements to the press after Russian-Chinese talks], May 23, 2008, http://www.kremlin.ru/events/president/transcripts/191.

44 "Comments by the Russian MFA Information and Press Department Regarding the Situation in Xinjiang," July 8, 2009, http://www.mid.ru/ru/maps/cn/-/asset_publisher/WhKWb5DVBqKA/content/id/286358?p_p_id=101_INSTANCE_WhKWb5DVBqKA&_101_INSTANCE_WhKWb5DVBqKA_languageId=en_GB.

45 "Rossiya i Kitay nalozhili veto na proekt rezolutsii SB OON o vvedenii sanktsiy protiv Zimbabve" [Russia and China vetoed the UN Security Council draft resolution on sanctions against Zimbabwe], *Renminwang*, July 12, 2008, http://russian.people.com.cn/31520/6448959.html.

46 "Foreign Ministry Spokesperson Qin Gang's Remarks on Russia's Recognition of the Independence of South Ossetia and Abkhazia," Permanent Mission of the PRC to the UN, August 27, 2008, http://www.china-un.org/eng/fyrth/t509344.htm.

47 "Transcript of Remarks by Russian Foreign Minister Sergey Lavrov and Response to Media Question at Joint Press Conference Following Meeting with Chinese Foreign Minister Yang Jiechi, Moscow, May 6, 2011," http://www.mid.ru/en/maps/cn/-/asset_publisher/WhKWb5DVBqKA/content/id/208126.

48 "Article by Russian Foreign Minister Sergey Lavrov in the Newspaper *Renmin Ribao*, July 15, 2011," http://www.mid.ru/foreign_policy/news/-/asset_publisher/cKNonkJE02Bw/content/id/199886.

49 "O besede zamestitelya Ministra inostrannykh del Rossii M. L. Bogdanova s Poslom Kitaya v Moskve Li Hueem" [On the conversation of deputy foreign minister of Russia M. L. Bogdanov with China's ambassador to Moscow Li Hui], July 29, 2011, http://www.mid.ru/ru/maps/cn/-/asset_publisher/WhKWb5DVBqKA/content/id/198714.

50 Karasin, *Sbornik Rossiisko-kitaiskikh dogovorov 1949–1999*, pp. 365–72, 385–92.

51 Charter of the Shanghai Cooperation Organization, en.sco-russia.ru/load/1013181846.

52 Zhou Gang, "Sotrudnichestvo v oblasti bor'by s terrorizmom mezhdu Kitaem, Indiey i Rossiey" [Cooperation between China, India and Russia in fighting terrorism], in *Vzaimodeystvie Rossii, Indii i Kitaya v XXI veke* [Interaction between Russia, India and China in the 21st century] (Moscow: IDV RAN, 2004), vol. 2, p. 156.

53 "Sovmestnoe zayavlenie ministro inostrannykh del gosudarstv-uchastnikov Shanhayskoy organizatsii sotrudnichestva."

5 The Strategic Partnership Matures

1 Mao Weizhun, "Strategic Partnerships Need Common Values, Not Temporary Interests," *Global Times*, December 12, 2012, http://www.globaltimes.cn/content/749818.shtml.
2 "Joint Statement by the Government of the Russian Federation and the Government of the People's Republic of China Following the First Joint Inspection of the Russia-China Border, St. Petersburg, November 7, 2016," http://www.mid.ru/en/foreign_policy/news/-/asset_publisher/cKNonkJE02Bw/content/id/2515347.
3 "SSHa i Kitay dogovorilis' o novikh sanktsiyakh v otnoshenii Severnoy Korei" [The US and China agreed on new sanctions against North Korea], *Regnum*, November 23, 2016, https://regnum.ru/news/polit/2209060.html.
4 During the author's discussion with China's former state councillor Dai Bingguo and officers of the Chinese embassy in Russia of the North Korea sanctions case during Dai's visit to Moscow on June 1, 2016 he admitted a "communication failure" and blamed the embassy staff for it.
5 "SCO Supports Peace and Stability in South China Sea," Xinhua, June 25, 2016, http://news.xinhuanet.com/english/2016-05/25/c_135385276.htm.
6 "Comment by the Ministry on SCO Secretary-General Rashid Alimov's Statement on South China Sea Issue," May 26, 2016, http://www.mid.ru/foreign_policy/news/-/asset_publisher/cKNonkJE02Bw/content/id/2292783.
7 Vladimir Putin, "Answers to Journalists' Questions," Hangzhou, September 5, 2016, http://en.special.kremlin.ru/events/president/news/52834.
8 Russia has eighty-five federal-level regions in total, which means that some of them have cooperation agreements with more than one Chinese province.
9 "EGE po kitayskomu proydet v rossiyskikh sholakh v 2017 godu" [A unified state examination in Chinese will be held in Russian schools in 2017], EGE, October 11, 2016, http://ege.edu.ru/ru/news/News/?id_4=22923.
10 A. V. Novikov, "Sostoyanie i perspektivy razvitiya rossiysko-kitayskoy torgovli i investitsiy v 2006–2010 gody" [The current state and prospects of Russian-Chinese trade and investments in 2006–2010], in Alexander Lukin (ed.), *Rossiyasko-kitayskoe sotrudnichesvo: problemy i resheniya* [Russian-Chinese cooperation: problems and solutions] (Moscow: MGIMO-University, 2007), pp. 51–2.
11 Novikov, "Sostoyanie i perspektivy."
12 "Tovarooborot mezhdu Rossiey i Kitaem v 2010 godu vyshel na dokrizisnyy uroven" [Trade turnover between Russia and China in 2010 reached the pre-crisis level], *Golos Rossii*, January 17, 2011, https://news.rambler.ru/economics/8726188-tovarooborot-mezhdu-rossiey-i-kitaem-v-2010-godu-vyshel-na-dokrizisnyy-uroven/.
13 Chen Aizhu and Meng Meng, "Russia Beats Saudi Arabia as China's Top Crude Oil Supplier in 2016," Reuters, January 23, 2017, http://www.reuters.com/article/us-china-economy-trade-crude-idUSKBN1570VJ.
14 Vasily Kashin, "Bol'she, chem partnerstvo" [More than a partnership], *Vedomosti*, 4141, August 18, 2016, http://www.vedomosti.ru/opinion/articles/2016/08/17/653493-bolshe-chem-partnerstvo; Vasily Kashin, "Is China Investing Much in Russia," Valdai Discussion Club, June 9, 2017, http://valdaiclub.com/a/highlights/chinese-investments-in-russia/.
15 Alexander Ivlev and Albert Ng, "Perspectives from China: How Concerns

about the Russian Market Influence Chinese Investment Strategies," EY, 2015, http://www.ey.com/Publication/vwLUAssets/EY-perspectives-from-china-survey/$FILE/EY-perspectives-from-china-survey-eng.pdf.

16 Catherine Locatelli, Mehdi Abbas and Sylvain Rossiaud, "The Emerging Hydrocarbon Interdependence between Russia and China: Institutional and Systemic Implications," *Europe-Asia Studies*, 69(1) (2017): 168.

17 "'Rosneft' i kitayskaya CNPC utverdili tekhnologicheskuyu konfiguratsiyu Tyan'tzin'skogo NPZ" [Rosneft and China's CNPC certified technology configuration of the Tianjin oil refinery], *NefteRynok*, January 10, 2017, http://www.nefterynok.info/news.phtml?news_id=21392.

18 "Kitayskaya korportya kupila dolyu v neftegazovoy rossiyskoy kompanii" [Chinese corporation bought a share in a Russian oil and gas company], *ChinaPro*, October 19, 2009, http://www.chinapro.ru/rubrics/1/2867/.

19 Sergey Filatov, "Istoricheskiy visit Putina v Kitay koronovan 51 soglasheniem" [Putin's historic visit to China crowned with 51 agreements], *Mezhdunarodnaya zhizn'*, May 22, 2015, https://interaffairs.ru/news/show/11178.

20 "Sila Sibiru" [Power of Siberia], Gazprom, http://www.gazprom.ru/about/production/projects/pipelines/built/ykv/.

21 Vladislav Gordeev, "Dvorkovich dopustil uchastie Kitaya v osvoenii strategicheskikh mestorozhdeniy" [Dvorkovich allowed for China's participation in the development of strategic oilfields], *RBK*, February 27, 2015, http://www.rbc.ru/economics/27/02/2015/54f002189a7947255e32ef80.

22 "'Novatek' prodal Fondu shelkovogo puti 9,9% 'Yamal SPG'" [Novatek sold 9.9% of Yamar LNG to the Silk Road Fund], Forbes, December 17, 2015, http://www.forbes.ru/news/308637-novatek-prodal-fondu-shelkovogo-puti-99-yamal-spg.

23 "'Yamal SPG' privlek €10,6 u kitayskikh bankov" [Yamal LNG acquired €10,6 from Chinese banks], *RBK*, April 29, 2016, http://www.rbc.ru/business/29/04/2016/57232d639a7947987f649167.

24 "Vstrecha s predstavitelyami obshchestvennosti, delovykh krugov i mediasoobshchestv Rossii i Kitaya" [Meeting with representatives of public organizations, business circles and media communities of Russia and China], July 4, 2017, http://kremlin.ru/events/president/news/54978.

25 "Full text of Chinese President Xi's written interview with Russian media," July 4, 2017.

26 Dmitry Kudryashov, "V Kitay bez konkursa" [To China without a competition], *RBK-Daily*, September 28, 2007, http://www.rbcdaily.ru/2007/09/28/industry/295531.

27 "Rossiya i Kitay dogovorilis' o strategicheskom sotrudnichestve v oblasti yadernoy energetiki" [Russia and China agreed on strategic cooperation in nuclear energy], RT, November 7, 2016, https://russian.rt.com/world/news/331106-rossiya-i-kitai-dogovorilis-o-sotrudnichestve.

28 "RF i Kitay do kontsa goda podpishut dokumenty po chetyrem proektam Rosatoma" [Russian Federation and China will sign documents on four Rosatom projects with China by the end of the year], *Rossiyskoe atomnoe obshchestvo*, July 5, 2017, http://www.atomic-energy.ru/news/2017/07/05/77452.

29 "Na chetvertoy ocheredi gazotsentrifuzhnogo zavoda v Kitae poluchena pervaya produktsiya" [The fourth stage of the gas centrifuge enrichment

plant in China achieved its first products], SKTs Rosatoma, http://www.skc.ru/press/news/item/4173757/; "OAO 'Tekhsnabeksport' vypolnilo vse obyazatel'stva po kontraktu s CNEIC (Kitay)" [Tekhsnabeksport OJSC has fulfilled all obligations under the contract with CNEIC (China)], *Rossiyskoe Atomnoe Soobshchestvo*, August 5, 2014, http://www.atomic-energy.ru/news/2014/08/05/50735.

30 Andrey Kolesnikov, "Vladimir Putin porabotal na nauku" [Vladimir Putin worked for science], *Kommersant*, January 12, 2005, https://www.kommersant.ru/doc/537896.

31 Vasily Kashin, "Sputniki velikogo pohoda. U Kitaya i Rossii est' obshchie interesy za predelami zemli" [Satellites in the Long March: China and Russia have commun interests outside the Earth], *VPK*, April 6, 2016, http://vpk-news.ru/articles/30083.

32 Pavel Felgengauer, "Oruzhie dlya Kitaya i natsional'naya bezopasnost' Rossii" [Arms for China and Russia's national security], in *Rossiya v mirovoy torgovle oruzhiem: strategiya, politika, ekonomika* [Russia in the world arms trade: strategy, politics, economy] (Moscow: Moscow Carnegie Center, 1996), p. 128.

33 Sergounin and Subbotin, "Sino-Russian Military Co-operation," p. 24.

34 Felgengauer, "Oruzhie dlya Kitaya i natsional'naya bezopasnost' Rossii," p. 135.

35 Alexander A. Sergounin and Sergey V. Subbotin, *Russian Arms Transfers to East Asia in the 1990s* (Oxford: Oxford University Press, 1999), pp. 44–70.

36 "Rossii nuzhen sil'nyy Kitay," p. 14.

37 Felgengauer, "Oruzhie dlya Kitaya i natsional'naya bezopasnost' Rossii," p. 136.

38 Sergey Safronov, "Glavnye partner RF po VTS – Indiya, Kitay, Alzhir, Venesuela i Vietnam" [Russia's main arms trade partners are India, China, Algeria, Venezuela, and Vietnam], RIA Novosti, March 2, 2010, https://ria.ru/defense_safety/20100302/211809823.html.

39 Konstantin Makienko, "Za 15 let Kitay potrebil do poloviny vsekh rossiyskikh voennykh postavok za rubezh" [Over fifteen years China purchased up to one half of all Russia's arm exports], *Novosty VPK*, February 6, 2007, http://vpk.name/news/2890_konstantin_makienko_za_15_let_kitai_potrebil_do_polovinyi_vseh_rossiiskih_voennyih_postavok_za_rubezh.html.

40 Makienko, *Voenno-tekhnicheskoe sotrudnichestv*, p. 38.

41 "Ministr oborony Kitaya o perspektivakh v oblasti voennogo i voenno-tekhnicheskogo sotrudnichestva Rossii i Kitaya" [China's defence minister on the prospects of Russian-Chinese military and military technological cooperation], *Rodon*, May 28, 2009, http://www.rodon.org/polit-090528100842.

42 "Interv'yu zamestitelya Ministra inostrannykh del Rossii A. P. Losyukova agentstvu 'Kyodo Tsusin' June 28, 2001" [Interview of deputy foreign minister of Russia A. P. Losyukov to Kyodo News Agency, June 28, 2001], http://www.mid.ru/foreign_policy/rso/-/asset_publisher/0vP3hQoCPRg5/content/id/577926.

43 "Proshchay, kitayskoe oruzhie!" [Farewell to Chinese arms!], *Argumenty Nedeli*, 19(156), May 14, 2009, http://argumenti.ru/politics/n183/40333.

44 "Za tri goda Rossiya postavit v Kitay oruzhiya na $1,3mlrd" [Russia will sell China $1.3 billion worth of arms in three years], *Izvestia*, November 23, 2010, http://www.newsland.ru/news/detail/id/590445/.

45 "Voennoe i voenno-technicheskoe sotrudnichestvo Rossii i Kitaya" [Military and military technological cooperation between Russia and China], RIA Novosti, May 20, 2014, https://ria.ru/spravka/20140520/1008416110.html.
46 Vassily Kashin, "Why Is China Buying Russian Fighter Jets?" Carnegie Moscow Center, February 9, 2016, http://carnegie.ru/commentary/?fa=62701.
47 Kashin, "Why Is China Buying Russian Fighter Jets?"
48 "Shoygu: Rossiya i Kitay za god realizovali kontrakty v sfere VTS na 3 mlrd dollarov" [Shoygu: Russia and China carried out $3 billion worth of arms trade contracts in one year], *Vzglyad*, November 23, 2016, http://www.vz.ru/news/2016/11/23/845346.html.
49 "Rossiya i Kitay rasshiryayut voennoe sotrudnichestvo protiv obshchikh ugroz" [Russia and China broaden military cooperation against common threats], TRK "Zvezda," May 11, 2015, http://tvzvezda.ru/news/forces/content/201505111109-4uqh.htm.
50 D. D. Wu, "China and Russia Sign Military Cooperation Roadmap," *The Diplomat*, June 30, 2017, http://thediplomat.com/2017/06/china-and-russia-sign-military-cooperation-roadmap/?utm_content=buffera10d0&utm_medium=social&utm_source=facebook.com&utm_campaign=buffer.
51 "N. Korean Nuclear Issue Should Not Be Pretext for America to Deploy Air Defenses in Region – Lavrov," RT, March 11, 2016, https://www.rt.com/news/335211-north-korea-nuclear-russia-china/.
52 "Kitay i Rossiya opublikovali Sovmestnoe zayavlenie o tekushchey situatsii v mire i vazhnykh mezhdunarodnykh porblemakh" [China and Russia published a joint statement on the current world situation and important international problems], CCTV.com, July 6, 2017, http://russian.cctv.com/2017/07/06/ARTIOxsELLcMQ0ilZYwSP2DX170706.shtml.
53 Adam Taylor, "Why China Is So Mad about THAAD, a Missile Defense System Aimed at Deterring North Korea," *Washington Post*, March 7, 2016, https://www.washingtonpost.com/news/worldviews/wp/2017/03/07/why-china-is-so-mad-about-thaad-a-missile-defense-system-aimed-at-deterring-north-korea/?utm_term=.d5c410707fba.
54 Zhang Yunbi, "China, Russia to Hold First Joint Anti-Missile Drill," *China Daily*, May 5, 2016, http://www.chinadaily.com.cn/world/cn_eu/2016-05/05/content_25067674.htm.
55 Thomas Colson, "The Top Ten Countries Where Chinese Students Study Abroad," September 16, 2016, http://www.businessinsider.com/knight-frank-ranking-countries-where-chinese-students-study-abroad-2016-9/#9-germany-19441-students-2.
56 "2015 nian quanguo laihua liuxuesheng shuju fabu" [National figures on foreign students in China for 2015 released], Ministry of Education of the PRC, April 14, 2016, http://www.moe.edu.cn/jyb_xwfb/gzdt_gzdt/s5987/201604/t20160414_238263.html.
57 "Vyborochnaya statisticheskaya informatsiya, rasschitannaya v sootvetstvii s ofitsial'noy statisticheskoy metodologiey otsenki chisla v'ezdnykh i vyezdnykh turisticheskikh poezdok" [Selected statistical information calculated according to the official statistical methodology of estimating incoming and outgoing tourist trips], Federal Agency for Tourism, http://www.russiatourism.ru/contents/statistika/statisticheskie-pokazateli-vzaimnykh-poezdok-grazhdan-rossiyskoy-federatsii-i-grazhdan-inostrannykh-gosudarstv/vy

NOTES TO PP. 162–72

borochnaya-statisticheskaya-informatsiya-rasschitannaya-v-sootvetstvii-s-of
itsialnoy-statisticheskoy-metodologiey-otsenki-chisla-vezdnykh-i-vyezdnykh
-turistskikh-poezdok/.
58 "Vstrecha s predstavitelyami obshchestvennosti, delovykh krugov i mediasoobshchestv Rossii i Kitaya."
59 "Kitay v XXI veke: strategicheskiy partner ili strategicheskaya ugroza?" [China in the 21st century: a strategic partner or strategic threat?], transcript of the 17th meeting of the discussion club "Modernization of Russia: New Vector," October 17, 2006, http://www.viperson.ru/wind.php?ID=263119&soch=1.
60 "Natsional'nyy sostav naseleniya Rossii v 2010 godu" [Ethnic composition of the population of Russia in 2010], Wikipedia, https://ru.wikipedia.org/wiki/_состав_населения_России_в_2010_году#.D0.9A.
61 "Meeting on Customs and Migration Issues in Border Regions," Blagoveshchensk, July 3, 2010, http://en.kremlin.ru/events/president/news/8255.
62 "Glava FMS zayavil, chto v Rossii net kitayskoy ekspansii" [The head of the Federal Migration Service claimed that there was no Chinese expansion in Russia], RIA Novosti, June 20, 2015, https://ria.ru/society/20150620/1080051756.html.
63 Yuri Galenovich, *Moskva–Pekin, Moskva–Taibei* [Moscow–Beijing, Moscow–Taipei] (Moscow: Izografus, 2002), pp. 130, 134, 141.
64 Vilya Gelbras, *Rossiya v usloviyakh global'noy migratsii* [Russia in the situation of global migration] (Moscow: Muravei, 2004), pp. 24–5.
65 Vasily Mikheev, *Kitay-Yaponiya: Sttrategicheskoe sopernichestvo i partnerstvo v globalizuyushchemsya mire* [China–Japan: strategic rivalry and partnership in a globalizing world] (Moscow: IMEMO RAN, 2009), pp. 182, 202.
66 Alexander Gabuev, "Bigger, Not Better: Russia Makes the SCO a Useless Club," Moscow Carnegie Center, June 23, 2017, http://carnegie.ru/commentary/71350.
67 Wilson, *Strategic Partners*, p. 201; Kuhrt, *Russian Policy*, p. 161; Alexander Cooley, *Great Games, Local Rules: The New Great Power Contest in Central Asia* (Oxford: Oxford University Press, 2012); Kaczmarski, *Russia–China Relations*, pp. 165–9.
68 "Shuvalov: Kitay i EAES gotovy k sozdaniyu Zony svobodnoy torgovli" [Shuvalov: China and EAEU are ready to create a free trade zone], *Vesti*, May 31, 2016, http://www.vestifinance.ru/videos/27650.
69 "Rossiya i Kitay zaklyuchat soglashenie o Zony svobodnoy torgovli" [Russia and China to enter an agreement on a free trade zone], *AIS*, October 5, 2016, http://vg-news.ru/n/123926.

CONCLUSION: BEYOND STRATEGIC PARTNERSHIP?

1 See, for example, Mikhail Korostikov, "Nedovorot na Vostok. Itogi Rossiyskoy politiki povorota v Aziyu protivorechivy" [A half-turn to the East: the results of Russia's policy of pivot to Asia are contradictory], *Kommersant*, December 25, 2015, http://kommersant.ru/doc/2884691; Alexander Gabuev, "Povorot v nikuda: itogi aziatskoy politiki Rossii v 2015

godu" [A turn to nowhere: the results of Russia's Asian policy in 2015," Moscow Carnegie Center, December 29, 2015, http://carnegie.ru/commentary/2015/12/29/ru-62369/ioe2.
2 Yegor Gaydar, "Russiya XXI veka: ne mirovoy zhandarm, a forpost demokratii v Evrazii" [Russsia in the 21st century: not a world policeman, but an outpost of democracy in Eurasia," *Izvestia*, May 18, 1995, p. 4.
3 Sergounin and Subbotin, "Sino-Russian Military Cooperation," p. 26.
4 Stokes, "Russia and China's Enduring Alliance."
5 Sergey Karaganov, "Prazdnovat' eshche rano" [It's too early to celebrate], *Rossiyskaya gazeta*, January 11, 2016, http://www.rg.ru/2016/01/12/karaganov.html.
6 "Ekonomika Kitaya: vozmozhnye stsenarii razvitiya" [China's economy: possible future scenarios], video recording of the 7th Gaydar Forum plenary session, https://www.youtube.com/watch?v=M_FC2swBKhY.
7 "Ekonomika Kitaya."
8 "Kommentariy: otnosheniya kitaysko-rossiyskogo partnerstva ustoyat pered vyzovami" [Commentary: Sino-Russian partnership relations will withstand challenges], Xinhua, January 28, 2016, http://russian.people.com.cn/n3/2016/0128/c95181-9010535.html.
9 I. Starodubtseva, "Analiz izmeneniy, vnesennykh soglashenie mezhdu pravitel'stvon RF and pravitel'stvom Kitaya ob izbezhanii dvoynogo nalogoooblazheniya" [An analysis of the changes to the agreement between the governments of the Russian Federation and China on the avoidance of double taxation], RosCo, June 7, 2015, http://rosco.su/press/analiz_izmeneniy_vnesennykh_v_soglashenie_mezhdu_pravitelstvom_rf_i_pravitelstvom_knr_ob_izbezhanii_/.
10 "Yearender: China, Russia Set Example of Int'l Relations with Overall Promotion of Bilateral Ties," CCTV.com, December 24, 2015, http://english.cntv.cn/2015/12/24/ARTI1450937711581948.shtml.
11 Mikhail Korostikov, "Beri bol'she, Kitay dal'she" [Take more, China is further], *Kommersant*, July 9, 2017, https://www.kommersant.ru/doc/3343375; Alexander Gabuev, "Kak sokhranit' vnimanie na Kitae?" [How to keep attention on China?], *Vedomosti*, July, 5, 2017, https://www.vedomosti.ru/newspaper/articles/2017/07/05/709434-kak-sohranit-vnimanie-na-kitae.
12 Kaczmarski, *Russia–China Relations*, pp. 69–73.
13 "Russia-Japan Trade Drops Almost 25% in 2016," TASS, March 24, 2017, http://tass.com/economy/937256.
14 Andrey Vinokurov, "Rossiya dovedet Yapontsev do kuril'skikh mogil" [Russia will lead the Japanese to the Kuril graves], Gazeta.ru, April 27, 2017, https://www.gazeta.ru/politics/2017/04/27_a_10647191.shtml.
15 Shinji Hyodo, "Putin's Visit to Japan and the Russia-Japan Summit," *The Diplomat*, December 31, 2016, http://thediplomat.com/2016/12/putins-visit-to-japan-and-the-russia-japan-summit/.
16 "Statement for the Press Following Russian-Indian Talks," December 24, 2015, http://en.kremlin.ru/catalog/persons/423/events/51011.
17 "India-Russia Relations," Ministry of External Affairs, Government of India, December 2016, https://www.mea.gov.in/Portal/ForeignRelation/India_Russia_Relation_DEC2016.pdf.
18 Dmitri Trenin, "From Greater Europe to Greater Asia? The Sino-Russian

Entente," Carnegie Moscow Center, April 9, 2015, http://carnegie.ru/2015/04/09/from-greater-europe-to-greater-asia-sino-russian-entente-pub-59728.
19 Alexander Lukin, "Russia, China and the Emerging Greater Eurasia," *Asan Forum*, http://www.theasanforum.org/russia-china-and-the-emerging-greater-eurasia/.
20 "Plenary Session of St. Petersburg International Economic Forum," June 17, 2016, http://en.kremlin.ru/events/president/news/52178.
21 "Sovmestnoe zayavlenie Rossiyskoy Federatsii i Kitayskoy Narodnoy Respubliki [Joint statement of the Russian Federation and the People's Republic of China], June 25, 2016, http://www.kremlin.ru/supplement/5100.
22 "Medvedev: Rossiya formiruet evraziyskoe partnerstvo s Kitaem [Medvedev: Russia forms a Eurasian partnership with China], RIA Novosti, November 16, 2016, https://ria.ru/east/20161116/1481497327.html.
23 "Meeting with Chinese Foreign Minister Wang Yi," May 25, 2017, http://en.kremlin.ru/events/president/news/54576.
24 "China and Russia Sign the Joint Declaration of Feasible Study on Eurasian Economic Partnership Agreement," Ministry of Commerce, People's Republic of China, July 6, 2017, http://english.mofcom.gov.cn/article/newsrelease/significantnews/201707/20170702605903.shtml.
25 Sergey Karaganov, "Ot povorota na-Vostok-k-Bolshoi-Evrazii" [From pivot to the East to Greater Eurasia], *Rossiaya v global'noy politike*, May 30, 2017, http://www.globalaffairs.ru/pubcol/Ot-povorota-na-Vostok-k-Bolshoi-Evrazii-18739.
26 Sergey Karaganov, "From East to West, or Greater Eurasia," *Russia in Global Affairs*, October 25, 2016, http://eng.globalaffairs.ru/pubcol/From-East-to-West-or-Greater-Eurasia-18440.
27 "Xi Jinping yu Eluosi zongtong Pujing juxing huitan dazao Daouya huobanguanxi" [Xi Jinping conducted talks with the Russian President Putin on establishing relations of Greater Eurasian partnership], Ifeng, June 27, 2016, http://news.ifeng.com/a/20160627/49247845_0.shtml.
28 "The Declaration of the Russian Federation and the People's Republic of China on the Promotion of International Law," June 25, 2016, http://www.mid.ru/en/foreign_policy/position_word_order/-/asset_publisher/6S4RuXfeYlKr/content/id/2331698; "Kitay i Rossiya opublikovali Sovmestnoe zayavlenie o tekushchey situatsii v mire i vazhnykh mezhdunarodnykh porblemakh."
29 "Foreign Minister Wang Yi Meets the Press," Ministry of Foreign Affairs of the PRC, March 8, 2017, http://www.fmprc.gov.cn/mfa_eng/zxxx_662805/t1444204.shtml.
30 "Foreign Minister Wang Yi Meets the Press."
31 Stokes, "Russia and China's Enduring Alliance."
32 Karaganov, "Ot povorota na-Vostok-k-Bolshoi-Evrazii."
33 Timofey Bordachev, "Russia-China: An Alliance for Peace or War?" *Russia in Global Affairs*, June 20, 2017, http://eng.globalaffairs.ru/book/Russia-China-An-Alliance-for-Peace-or-War-18783.

INDEX

Amur river, 69, 76, 110–11, 164
antiterrorism, 105–7
APEC. *See* Asia–Pacific Economic Cooperation
ASEAN. *See* Association of Southeast Asian Nations
Asian Infrastructure Investment Bank, 19, 187
Asia–Pacific Economic Cooperation (APEC), 63, 90, 106, 128, 170, 173–4
Association of Southeast Asian Nations (ASEAN), 32, 70, 92, 182–4, 186–7, 192
authoritarianism, 10, 71

Beijing consensus, 6
Beijing Olympic Games, 113–14
bilateral trade, 65, 99, 113, 139, 140–2, 144, 170
bipolar system, 1–2, 31
Brezhnev, Leonid, 40, 174
BRICS, 32, 63, 94–5, 127–8, 176, 183, 186

China National Petroleum Corporation (CNPC), 148–149, 150
Chinese threat, 19, 46, 51–2, 54
CNPC. *See* China National Petroleum Corporation
Cold War, 9–10, 13, 31–2, 42, 49, 53–4, 78, 104, 169, 188

collapse of the Soviet Union, 8–9, 11, 31, 40–2, 44, 51, 68, 69, 71, 78, 84, 190, see also Soviet Union's breakup
Collective Security Treaty Organization (CSTO), 84, 121, 167
Communist Party of China (CPC), 16–17, 24–5, 41, 43, 48
confidence–building measures, 84, 117–18, 166–8
Confucianism, 7, 190
Confucius Institute, 161
Convention on Combating Terrorism, Separatism and Extremism (2001), 120
counterterrorism, 106, 122. *See also* antiterrorism
CPC. *See* Communist Party of China
Crimea, 12–13, 91, 158, 170
crisis in Ukraine, 8–9, 15, 55
CSTO. *See* Collective Security Treaty Organization
Cultural Revolution, 16, 37, 45, 52

democratism, 3, 5–8, 13, 18–19, 28–29, 30, 192
demographic expansion, 76, 162, 165
Deng Xiaoping, 16–17, 19, 21–3, 25, 37, 42–3, 74, 83

EAEU. *See* Eurasian Economic Union
East Asia Summit, 26, 173

217

INDEX

Eastern Economic Forum, 136–7
Eastern Siberia–Pacific Ocean (ESPO) pipeline, 149
encirclement, 12, 17, 159
energy cooperation, 116, 129, 132, 148, 151
ESPO. *See* Eastern Siberia–Pacific Ocean pipeline
Eurasian Economic Union (EAEU), 58, 66, 170, 179, 183–44, 186–7
Eurasian integration, 10, 58, 66, 70, 92
European Union (EU), 5, 10–11, 52

Far East, 69, 71, 76, 79, 95, 105, 110, 129, 133, 135, 138, 153, 166, 170, 174
financial crisis, 4, 22
former Soviet republics, 7, 9, 13, 42, 65, 84, 92, 101, 118
Fukuyama, Francis, 4, 9, 31

G20. *See* Group of 20.
Gazprom, 150
global governance, 25–6, 30, 33, 95, 127, 178
globalization, 7, 26, 57
Gorbachev, Mikhail, 40, 68, 71–2, 96, 174
Greater Eurasia, 93, 167, 179, 183, 185–7
Group of 20 (G20), 63, 94, 128
Group of Two, 24, 27

harmonious world, 17–18, 23
Hu Jintao, 18, 24, 48, 83, 106, 109, 113, 114, 129, 142
human rights, 3, 7, 11, 12, 41, 73, 77, 104, 114

IAEA. *See* International Atomic Energy Agency
International Atomic Energy Agency (IAEA), 107
international law, 11, 44, 49, 64, 82–3, 94, 97, 104, 110, 134, 176, 186, 190
international peace, 14, 29, 46, 105, 107
Islamic extremism, 33, 85, 120

Jiang Zemin, 43, 75, 80, 83, 98–9, 100–1, 105, 148
Joint Sea exercise in the Mediterranean Sea, 158

Kausikan, Bilahary, 7
Kissinger, Henry, 5
Korean Peninsula, 59, 66, 70, 107–8, 159, 181
Korean War, 34, 59
Kuomintang, 34, 37, 39, 48

Lavrov, Sergey, 83, 88, 115–117, 159
Li Keqiang, 151, 170, 184

Mao Zedong, 16, 35–8, 62
Maritime Silk Road, 18, 187
Medvedev, Dmitry, 112–15, 129, 151, 163, 170, 184
military–industrial complex, 45, 98, 155, 175
Modi, Narendra, 30, 181
multipolar world, 10, 15, 23, 31–3, 48–9, 64, 78, 89, 94, 100, 104, 124–26, 155, 175–6, 180, 191–3
Munich security conference, 14

NATO. *See* North Atlantic Treaty Organization
nonproliferation, 33, 108
Non–Western centers, 2, 4, 8, 29, 30–32
North Atlantic Treaty Organization (NATO), 3, 9–10, 13–15, 45–7, 58, 72, 82, 103, 106, 115, 117, 121, 125, 158, 168
Northern Sea Route, 151
nuclear problem, 49, 108–9

oil pipeline, 116, 148–9
One Belt, One Road, 167, 185

peaceful coexistence, 33, 37, 42, 44, 73, 97–8, 182, 186
peaceful rise, 17, 23
pivot to Asia, 55–6, 60, 67, 89, 172–7, 180–3, 185, 190, 192
post–Soviet consensus, 9–10
power of Siberia gas pipeline, 150

INDEX

Putin, Vladimir, 9, 12, 45, 48, 53, 55, 81, 83, 102, 105, 109, 114,130, 139, 152, 173–4, 181, 184

radical Islamists, 33, 169, 188
RATS. *See* Regional Anti–Terrorist Structure
raw materials, 17, 66, 89, 131, 141–2, 144–5, 170, 173, 179
realism, 4, 192
Regional Anti–Terrorist Structure (RATS), 120, 122, 168
regional security, 49, 70, 157
Rousseff, Dilma, 30–1
Russia's foreign policy concept, 14
Russian Federation's National Security Concept, 14
Russian–Chinese cooperation, 33, 56, 76, 82, 103, 112, 126, 153, 160, 183
Russian–Chinese Economic Forum, 113
Russian–Chinese Joint Declaration on a Multipolar World and the Establishment of a New International Order (1997), 100
Russian–Chinese rapprochement, 1, 63, 180, 183, 186–7, 190–1

sanctions, 53, 55, 77, 88, 91, 93, 114, 117, 122, 126, 133, 150, 154, 171, 173, 177, 181, 188; Western sanctions, 87, 95, 98, 180
security cooperation, 105, 122
Shanghai Cooperation Organization, 21, 26, 32, 56, 70, 84, 89, 95, 106, 117–18, 161, 166–7
Silk Road Economic Belt (SREB), 18, 58, 66, 179, 183–4, 186–7
Silva, Lula da, 30–1
Singh, Manmohan, 29, 86
Sino–Russian cultural cooperation, 50
six–party talks on North Korean nuclear program, 108–9
Skovorodino–Daqing pipeline, 116, 149
soft power, 6, 18, 33
South China Sea, 19, 26, 134, 158, 172, 189, 191
Soviet intervention in Afghanistan, 40

Soviet Union's breakup, 3, 158, *see also* collapse of the Soviet Union
SREB. *See* Silk Road Economic Belt
strategic partnership, 34, 40, 51, 54, 78–9, 82, 86, 96, 100, 128–9, 137, 155, 157, 172, 174, 181, 192

Taiwan, 17, 19, 21, 26, 28, 39, 79, 97, 142, 155, 157, 170, 189
Terminal High Altitude Area Defence (THAAD) missile system, 159
territorial integrity, 12, 17, 48, 52–3, 55, 65, 97, 104, 115, 170
terrorism, 33, 46–8, 55–8, 82, 87, 95, 105–7, 115–16, 120–2, 181, 187–8
THAAD. *See* Terminal High Altitude Area Defence
Third World, 2, 16
Three Worlds Theory, 16
Tiananmen Square crisis, 52
Tibet, 17, 19, 26, 46, 77, 104, 113–14, 116, 170
TPP. *See* Trans–Pacific Partnership
Trans–Pacific Partnership (TPP), 170
Treaty of Friendship (1950), 35, 38, 103
Treaty of Good–Neighborliness and Friendly Cooperation (2001), 45, 82, 101–2, 109, 168
Trump, Donald, 7, 187

Ukrainian crisis, 14–15, 53, 55, 89, 90, 153, 157–8, 172, 174, 176, 183. *See also* crisis in Ukraine
unipolar world, 11, 43, 49, 63, 175, 186
United Nations (UN) Security Council, 11, 33, 48, 63–4, 73, 82, 88, 94, 101, 103, 106–7, 114, 117, 121, 124, 133, 168, 186
universal values, 4, 7, 176

Volga–Yangtze interregional cooperation, 135

weapons of mass destruction, 2, 14, 33
Western expansion, 13, 15, 53

219

INDEX

Western system, 3, 6, 9, 12
Westernization, 8, 28
World War II, 1, 6, 42, 63, 83, 99, 100, 136, 176, 180, 186

Xinjiang, 19, 36, 39, 46, 77, 104, 114, 116, 120, 122, 137, 170

Yeltsin, Boris, 9, 12, 44–5, 65, 71–6, 78–9, 96, 99, 100–2, 138, 154

Zinoviev, Georgy, 97